"The Not Quite English Teacher"

Eliza Jane Goés

Eliza Jane Goés

May 26th 2012

Author's Note

Just as in *Fusion,* where Ella grows upwards and outwards from remote Caithness to the bustling cosmopolitan world of the late sixties, and *The Cosmopolites,* in which Rick and Ella, a mixed race couple, take on the global village in all its diversity, I hope to tantalise you with who might or might not be real in *The Not Quite English Teacher.* Is this book a *roman à clef?* I'm not sure. But it *is* fictionalised memoir.

Published in March 2012 by emp3books,
Kiln Workshops, Pilcot Road, Crookham Village,
Fleet, Hampshire, GU51 5RY, England

©Eliza Jane Goés

The author asserts the moral right to be identified as the author of this work

ISBN-13: 978-1-907140-58-7

Thank you to Head Teacher Kevin McKellar for the permission to use the front cover image which is from the Hendon School Prospectus.

www.emp3books.com

Contents

To those pupils who are all equal, all
different and all special

I Can Do This

July 2006

Ella Fonseca wakes up basking in happy memories of her last day at Brentgold Comprehensive. The throbbing, cheap plonk head can be explained but the spreading bruise on her toe is just coming into focus as she kicks off the duvet and circles her ankle in the air.

'How on earth did you do that?' Rick, her usually doting husband asks.

'I 'think' it was when the teachers played inter-faculty rounders after the kids went home; I didn't know I could still run.'

'Huh. I 'think', old girl, you can give all that a miss now. Leave it to the youngsters.' In seconds he's snoring again.

Ella ruffles Rick's hair and reminds herself to check the roots of her ginger curls to see if she needs to hit the bottle again. Was it burnished copper last time? His thick silver waves look distinguished against his Asian skin but she's not ready to add white locks to her own freckles and laughter crinkles.

Ah well, there's no rush. The retirement party is over.

No more deadlines and restrictions, development plans, action plans, targets and reviews, registers, incident reports or - fitted in somehow - lesson plans, teaching and marking. And no more rowdy 10D. Bliss.

Now, there is nothing to stop her from fulfilling her lifelong dream - except a nagging awareness that she would be joining a growing army of would-be writers who are marching hopelessly along the path to fame and acclaim.

Her farewell speech, Ella smugly reflects, was innocuous – with none of her usual sharp innuendos reserved for her least favourite people. She'd abandoned the longer version but retained the praise for the worn out bunch of staff who couldn't wait to begin their summer break. After a cheesy tear jerker about 'friends for a reason, friends for a season and friends for life' she'd thrown her last black marker at some poor unfortunate who still didn't have an interactive whiteboard

– in case the heat-wave conditions brought on some embarrassing snores. She'd have thrown her red pen up in the air but, as she told everyone, it had already been nicked.

Ella hobbles downstairs to fill the kettle. The dining table looks like a flower shop and Rick has arranged her cards and presents. There is even a helium balloon, next to some pink champagne. Her eyes are drawn to a bright, laminated A4 document which she knows contains pictures of all except the bunkers in 10D, and messages of varying levels of neatness and competence, some beautifully illustrated and others almost illegible.

'Thanks', she shouts upstairs. 'I love my display.'

She blinks back the tears as she remembers the little pizza party, in the hot sun on the athletics field, where the rogues had been as delightful as they'd never ever been. Even the immovable Year Head, Garfield Porch, had wandered along to ruffle a few hairdos and kneel down to be photographed in front of a barrage of strictly banned mobile phones and the odd digital camera. It had been a day of compromises. Ella smiles. She reckons it's good for pupils to occasionally see the human side of their unyielding teachers.

After receiving a huge bunch of flowers in assembly, Ella had enjoyed announcing that 10D were the best form in school, except the world didn't know this yet. The fun of this was soon eclipsed by the euphoria of finally extricating herself from the stresses and strains of teaching.

'Now what?'

At home now, her words have rung out in the eerie silence, interrupted only by a blackbird in the sunny garden and Rick's gentle snores from upstairs. Snoozing late after reading into the early hours is a luxury in which, as a retiree, he can now indulge with impunity.

But Ella can't just stop doing - or being. You'd think after teaching all kinds of pupils in all kinds of places in all corners of the world she might be ready to put her feet up on the sofa and watch Countdown between chapters of War and Peace, as she had told her colleagues at the (recently out of special measures) comprehensive school.

2

Without her secret dream, the future would be stretching bleakly ahead, bereft of challenge and silently boring. A germ of an idea from a throwaway comment, 'I bet she doesn't write that book she says she could write about us,' has taken root in her brain.

In an attempt to move on, she begins to empty the bottomless giant carpetbag cum schoolbag her pupils had dubbed 'Miss's Mary Poppins bag'. Inside, nestling among the paper clips, glue, tissues, scissors and spare pens, she discovers the box, unopened, and wonders how she could have missed it. Had she been so discombobulated?

The box contains a coffee mug with a picture of a whole class, representing all complexions the world can offer in roughly equal numbers and all grinning. Printed in red is 'Good Luck Ms Fonseca 10D will miss you so much!!!!!!!!'

'Only for five minutes, I'll bet. They'll soon forget,' she says out loud to Pepper, the elderly cat who is demanding to be fed. However, there's a tear in her eye that refuses go away. She wishes she had opened the box and made a joke about still having the pleasure of seeing their ugly mugs every morning. She's always thinking of what she should have said in retrospect or, more often, what she ought not to have said.

All these years, all these children, all these places, all these memories and all these unspoken thoughts come flooding back.

It's time to set the record straight.

'I can do this. I can finally do this!'

As her enthusiasm wells up, every thought, feeling, face and action come together in one cohesive flash. She can jump right in there 'in medias res' and flit between the omniscient third person and reflective first person, flashing back over the years and back to the present and the words will just tumble out. If spoken, those words would have rushed out in a single breath. Ella has leapt over the barriers of practicality, suspended all pessimism and can see all the loose ends which, so recently, have been so inextricably tied in knots, untangling before her eyes.

The *'Not Quite English'* teacher, who, as a Scot herself, is not quite

English, has endless tales to tell of *Definitely Not English* pupils who are fluent in countless varieties of *Not Quite English.*

She places her new mug on the sideboard and fires up her old laptop. Then it dawns on her.

'Who am I kidding? People like me don't write books.'

Then, as she often does in moments of nostalgia, she reverts to her native Doric and announces to the cat, the birds and the silence, 'Noo, fit wye nae? Fa says I canna write a book?' Thrawn-ness restored, she makes up her mind.

She has to go back to school – writing school.

A Virgin Once More

August 2006

At fifty nine years, nine months and three weeks old, Ella's trundling up to Derby from St Pancras to become a virgin once more. The laptop and suitcase are a dead giveaway. She's feeling apprehensive but determined to write that novel by the time she is sixty.

'Are you a Penwicker?' A lady of similar age with a smaller suitcase and no laptop is behind her as they get off the train.

'How do you know?'

'Oh, you just look like one.'

'Really? What does a Penwicker look like then?'

'You - but you won't have time to use that,' the lady adds, pointing to the laptop.

'Oh yes I will,' Ella thinks from her 'in between' place for thinking and watching. Now this space has taken on a more exotic mystique. Ella Fonseca has adopted the persona of 'author' and needs to detach herself from the hurly burly of existence so that she can observe her surroundings in order to make deep and meaningful comments. Her feet, however, are still close enough to the ground for her to see the ridiculous side of this fantasy, so she allows herself a quiet chortle at her own expense.

'I hope that's good - looking like a Penwicker I mean.'

Ella is assured that a Penwicker is the very best thing to be and that her activities for the next thirty years will be centred on the Penwick Writers' Summer School. She reserves judgement but doesn't comment.

Derby station is filling up with suitcases coming from all directions accompanied by a variety of ladies of all shapes, sizes and ages and a few men with expressions varying from panic-stricken to that of the cat who thinks he is about to lick the cream.

A coach trip later, three hundred delegates have congregated in the Main Conference Hall. From teenage creative writing students to novelists in their nineties, the collective talent must be mind-blowing. Ella, however, is feeling uncomfortable. Her stomach lurches as her mind turns to the insecure days of stepping off a plane into her home country with a new and very brown husband. Here, at writers' school, there are only three non-white faces. However, her heart is warming to the fair number of Scots voices she's picking up in the crowd.

The 'virgins' are the first timers and they're wearing white name tags so that the old timers, who have yellow badges, will know who to bother to make an effort to speak to. Rick, Ella's poor husband, isn't too impressed with her first phone call home.

'How's it going then? Ready for the bestseller yet?'

'Not quite but I'm having a great time. Everybody keeps asking me if I'm a virgin.' Feeling mischievous, Ella decides to leave any explanations until she gets home at the end of the week. Meantime, she's going to learn all she can about writing and perhaps one day, that pipe dream will be real. Her brave face hides her turbulent 'in between' place. She's the gliding swan paddling like mad to keep afloat.

Tuition turns out to be superb, catering like clockwork with all the right ingredients for physical and spiritual comfort, and delegates are cocooned away from TV, radio, newspapers or the internet – unless they make a big effort to find them - a tried and tested formula to kick start the imagination and clear the writers' block. Delegates feed on each other's inspiration, or not, depending on their interests. Penwick's magic begins to work.

Aggie, aged seventy eight, is imparting her unsolicited advice. In her view there is a formula for success if you want to be a writer for a well-known publisher of romantic stories.

'You need a good story with a problem and a solution and you don't want too many o' them big words that people need a dictionary for,' she expounds in an indeterminate northern accent. 'You don't want any rape, like, or abortion or suicide or anything like that and none of your characters should be Asian or black. They don't publish that. But most important, there's no (how shall I say it?) hanky panky anywhere below the chin. Ye have to make it all in the mind – and ye'll be all right.'

Ella thinks she might have discovered where her talents *don't* lie. There is also that sinking feeling caused by the perceived rejection of Asian or black characters. Could this possibly still be true?

There are, however, endless gems to be discovered. After laughing until she cries at the anecdotes of Janet, a fellow Scot, she tells her next day,

'Your wee stories have been buzzing round my head all night!'

'If Ah find any o' mah wee stories in a magnificent novel, I'll sue.'

Another strange lady, dressed in flowing tie and dye and exuding an intoxicating mixture of exotic perfume and cigarette smoke, takes Ella to one side and says, 'Are you writing something now? If you are, you *must* finish it. I can see an aura of success around you.'

Ella wonders if this woman is a plant engineered by the tutors to get people to believe in themselves.

'I'd better try my hardest then. Thank you so much for that.' This is something else to buzz around in her insomniac's head and make her dig deeper for feelings and ideas.

Homework tasks require some thought and the synopsis for 'that' book is labelled as waffle with nothing but ideas. Ella swallows a mixture of indignation and distress and accepts that her literary gem is destined for the slush pile never to be read and prepares to start all over again. It needs to be story world, action, conflict and resolution with issues hiding in the background and coming out all by themselves. However, Ella is stubbornly sticking to her title. It will now be 'The Not Quite English Teacher', wisely no longer 'Memoirs of a Lap Teacher', and will have stories about these multinational children on the mug she will always treasure, the gift from Form 10D. It will also tell stories of her pupils in the different parts of the world she has taught. Her main aim is to illustrate the universal truth: 'They're 'a Jock Tamson's bairns'.

Today, Ella's getting over one of the worst moments of the week - seeing a big red line through 'They're a Jock Tampson's bairns' with the comment '*Distortion of language difficult to understand and does not contribute to the plot'*. She feels the heart of her masterpiece has been gouged out, leaving it, frankly, dead. How could anybody not know Jock Tamson is God and this means we're all the same? When is a dialect a distortion? How can a story be just plot without any ideas? She's coming to terms with the impossible task of getting people to understand what she means. Why should people have to write to please the masses? Why should writers listen when other writers twist their ideas to make them fit the 'market' whatever that is?

'What's up, Ella?' her new friend Janet asks.

'I'm just thinking I can't do this – write a book how they want me to, I mean.'

'Of course you can. On the other hand, why should you write what *they* want you to? Why don't you write what *you* want to? Mind you getting somebody to read it might be a problem. Time for a glass of red wine, I'd say, and we can share sob stories.'

By the time the week ends and after the pantomime, 'Jack and the Queenstalk' where Jack brings home a thinking cap and laptop instead of beans and has his manuscript accepted by his long lost father's International Publishing company, she's feeling more hopeful of success.

Armed with the technical skills to tackle a double-spaced manuscript she goes home to recraft her precious novel – and to produce a stunning synopsis which will bowl over even 'Glance and Binnits' the International Publishers.

More significantly, 'The Not Quite English Teacher' finds its own voice when Ella finds the courage of her convictions to be true to herself and steer clear of the constant intervention of well-meaning critics,

That voice quite often speaks in a North East Scots Doric accent.

Defining Not Quite English

For forty years Ella Mackay Fonseca was a Not Quite English teacher. For much of that time, while imparting the joys of Sir Walter Scott, Shakespeare and Dickens to unwilling British teenagers, or discussing the merits of Achebe and Ngugi with enthusiastic African youngsters, she considered herself a plain English teacher.

She didn't quite know when being a Not Quite English teacher had begun. Maybe, being a Scot, teaching Scots pupils, many of whom didn't want to be posh, was the beginning. Or could it have been her arrival at a secondary school for the cream of Kenya's girls, who desperately wanted to be posh? Perhaps it had been the day when Rick and she had bumped into a character walking along Piccadilly wearing a sandwich board advertising English lessons for foreigners.

Yes, that was the start. From that point on, Ella has been analysing the concept of Not Quite English. In her new persona of 'writer', many years later, she began doing some research, on the www.com of course, as all good 21st century authors do, before moving on to tell the tales of a few of her many multinational pupils who are all different all equal and all special. It soon became apparent that a clear definition of Not Quite English was going to be elusive.

Acronyms abound: ESL, English As a Second Language, E2L, the same but sounds better, EAL, English as an Additional language (for multilingual learners), ESOL, English for speakers of other languages, EFL, English as a Foreign Language (not to be confused with ELF, English as a Lingua Franca) for those who want to keep their first language, EAP, English for Academic Purposes, ESP, English for Special Purposes for businessmen, lawyers, street sweepers, teachers or whoever. Then there are LAP teachers in Tower Hamlets. Ella's consideration of the title 'Memoirs of a LAP teacher' for her masterpiece perhaps might have raised expectations which she 'couldn't possibly fulfil'. In East London LAP teachers are merely working on Language Acquisition Projects.

Put a T for Teacher in front of them and you get TEFL, TESOL etc. and Ella's done a bit of them all in her time.

Consider the language attrition caused by all these globetrotters beavering away, persuading the world to speak English. Of the world's 6000 languages, half will be victims of linguicide before too long, so someone came up with the Endangered Language Fund, to pay for a spot of language revitalisation.

Ella could say, as a Scot, that she's not English at all. Linguistically speaking, she must concede to being not quite English though a bit more English than if she and her classmates hadn't been harangued with, 'There will be *no* broad Scots in *this* classroom,' by a prissy teacher 'wi a bun in her hair an a plum in her moo.'

Such schoolmistresses were the first step towards the Standard Scottish English spoken by educated fowk in the North East. The Doric, the language of the rural 'teuchters', began to lose ground as the more urbane 'toonies' of Aberdeen or Inverness wouldn't dream of uttering a cheery 'Aye Aye' instead of a polite 'Good Morning'. Thankfully the dialects have survived. Youngsters reared on the comic bothy ballads and cornkisters (songs sung by farm workers sitting on a chest (kist) of corn) as well as the rich literature of Queen's English mixed with dialect such as 'Beside the Bonny Brier Bush', viewed the vernacular as the language of fun.

Expensive elocution lessons aimed at turning Scots into North British were for the more serious. Upper class Invernesians boast of speaking the purest and best of English as declared by Dr Johnson on his 1773 journey with James Boswell to the Western Isles. Ella suspects that, after an incomprehensible dose of Aberdonian teuchters and a *skalk,* an eighteenth century pre-breakfast knock on the head with whisky, a dazed Dr Johnson, expecting wild highlanders, made this comment because he was pleasantly surprised at the genteel level of their language.

Ella's cradle songs and verse were from both the Doric and the Gaelic as one of her grannies came from Skye. The pronunciation was *Khalik* not *Gaylik*. The Gaelic lilt and melodies haunt her still. Only the meaning has escaped.

In the nineteen sixties Aberdeen University sported one professor, one lecturer and two students in the entire Gaelic faculty for at least the four years that Ella was there. Today, over forty years later and due to a great deal of effort, a wide range of university courses in Celtic and Gaelic studies is on offer, more children are learning through the Gaelic medium and the rich linguistic and literary heritage of Highland Gaelic is being preserved and developed.

Throughout Scotland attempts to ding the Queen's English intae the heids o' the locals may have succeeded but most Scots communicate through a peculiar form of bilingualism, soaking up accents like leaches and adapting like chameleons to different social groups. Occasionally they 'fa thraoo themsels fin they're tryin tae be posh' – but that's fine if they can still laugh.

Are these rich dialects fast becoming endangered species, in the written form at least, as Anglicised speech and writing and the mass media wear them away? Alarmingly, in 2008, only 306 school pupils in Scotland said that their main home language was Scots. 681 spoke Gaelic, 4677 Polish, 4622 Punjabi and 1,506 Cantonese to name a few. Mercifully 653,731 named English as their home language so it is to be hoped that some of them might also speak a form of Scots. Many cross dialects like Galwegian (Gaelic mixed with Glaswegian) have all but disappeared already.

However, the death of the Doric and many other Scots dialects has not come about. As long as people enjoy 'The Scots Quair', Lewis Grassic Gibbon's cracking good read of a trilogy, the rich, rural dialect of East Scotland will live on. Words like stammy-gaster, clamjamfry, clishmaclaver and feuch could never be surpassed by flabbergast, plaster with mud, noisy chat or ugh!

Hats off to the stalwarts who are fighting for the survival of the Scots language. Let's hope their call of 'Let's get yokit wi writin Scots' is heeded. And here's tae 'Itchy Coo' an imprint of Edinburgh's Black & White publishing, who have brought out "Braw books for bairns o Aw Ages" with original stories in Scots, books such as "The Eejits", a translation of Roald Dahl's "The Twits" or

"Blethertoun Braes" Manky, Mingin Rhymes fae a Scottish Toun. We are invited to slip into our baffies and settle down to enjoy the humour. Here's tae the new generation who can celebrate a return to written literature in their mother dialect while still being part of the global community. The two sides needn't cancel each other out.

Dundee University has digitalised all ten volumes of 'The Dictionary of the Scots Language' and made them freely available on the internet. Ella discovered, while looking up the spelling of teuchter, that there's been an explosion of revitalisation of all things Scots or Scottish – through a website aptly named Rampant Scotland. The language and all things cultural are going worldwide; eleven million Americans claim Scottish ancestry, for example. Who knows where it's all going to lead?

Ella stopped surfing when she discovered that the winner of the National Tartan Day Poster Art Competition somewhere in USA was a young South Korean girl, Youngeun Kim, with her entry 'A Piece of Music for America's Quilt'. There were some bagpipes in the picture.

She needed a pause for reflection. *I'd better climb down from that wave before visions of teaching the bothy ballads to Glaswegian Punjabi speakers with pink turbans start to take root in my brain.*

Here I am, a Scot, therefore Not Quite English (NQE). I've spent much of my life teaching Undeniably Not English (UNE) students to speak enough NQE to communicate with all English speakers, only one in four of whom speak Definitely Native English (DNE) – and I'm contemplating the ramifications of the whole procedure.

A global lingua franca is undoubtedly a marvellous ideal. But does it have to be English? The French would think not, 'sacrebleu!' (Is my attempt at French as bad as Tony Blair's when he announced, 'I desire your Prime Minister in many different positions'?) They say Spanish will soon be the majority language in USA or is that Spanglish? Why not Brazil's Portagnol? Why not Chinese? What about the Doric? Now there's a thought.'

Ella gets back to the www and discovers there are six official UN languages, Arabic, Chinese (Mandarin), English, French, Russian and

Spanish in alphabetical order. However if the world wide web is to be trusted, the most widely spoken language is Mandarin, followed by Spanish, English, Hindi-Urdu, Arabic, Bengali, Portuguese and Russian to name a few, with Germany at ten on the list and French at fourteen. So who decides what an official UN language is?

What happened to the dream of Esperanto? The web reckons there are only one thousand native speakers from birth so it looks like it needs a touch of TLC from ELF, the Endangered Language Fund.

The consensus, it appears, would agree. The chosen foreign language of communication is English. From Spanglish in the West through Maltish, Zamenglish, Singlish, Australish, Chinglish to Japlish in the East, all continents are covered. Since the internet emerged, a gigantic vacuum cleaner seems to have swept the earth sucking up English and spewing out endless varieties of Patois, Creole and Pidgin, some simplistic but others with whole new and complex grammatical systems.

English, however, before the electronic age, was the enormous, wandering hungry caterpillar who guzzled up words from many foreign languages; they say these words were 'borrowed' but how can you give them back? Pyjamas are Hindi but we haven't gone back to calling them sleeping suits.

English has become a global lingua franca but the phrase lingua franca is not English. In Arabic lingua franca meant the language of the Franks who were all those people who didn't speak Arabic; it later developed into a mixture of Italian, Greek, French, Spanish and Arabic for trade purposes. Today it means any language which acts as a common language in a diverse group.

Long before globalisation of language via the internet, 'English' words we take for granted have been firmly planted. We use bananas from Senegal, coffee from Ethiopia, gherkins from Poland, biscuits from France, lager from Germany, admiral from Arabic, ketchup from China, ukulele from Hawaii, robot from Czechoslovakia, hooligans from Ireland, penguin from Wales, cider from Hebrew, coconut from Portuguese, cauliflower from Italian, sauna from Finland, karaoke from Japan and avatar from India's literary language Sanskrit – to name but a few.

In fact English has stolen so many words that it now has far too many. A brief glance at a thesaurus shows half a page of words which all mean 'big'. Who needs them?

It's all very confusing; DNE, Definitely Native English, is chock-a-block full of UNE, Undeniably Not English vocabulary.

To cap it all, some Frenchman called Jean Paul Nerriere has come up with 1500 words to save us all from the total 'confusion of tongues' that resulted from the crumbling Tower of Babel so many centuries ago. Could he be right? He calls this 1500 word communication tool, Globish. Lots of people reckon it's a good idea and one fellow, Madhukar Gogate, has developed his own form with different spelling.

M. Nerriere claims that Globish is correct English but accessible to all as long as there are no jokes! He might be right but it doesn't sound much fun.

Ella emerges blinking from too much surfing and confounds her poor husband.

'I wish this guy had discovered 1500 words of Globish forty years ago and all these English teachers needn't have wasted their time.'

Wee Haimish

1968: Altnabervie Secondary School, Caithness

Many years before the innumerable acronyms from ESOL to EFL - all meaning Not Quite English - had come into Ella's young life, there was nonetheless that peculiar bilingual situation in Scotland's classrooms which had been ongoing since the King James's Bible had relegated the Scots language to the realms of the less educated. If you counted the dialects such as Doric, Laland, Glaswegian or Dundonian to mention only a few, and the hybrids like Galwegian (Gaelic mixed with Glaswegian), the situation could be described as multilingual.

Ella Mackay did remember, from her schooldays, some attempts to introduce some poetry in the Scots dialects, like 'The Twa Corbies' and 'The Puddock' which were fine. However books like 'Kidnapped' by Robert Louis Stevenson and 'Rob Roy' by Sir Walter Scott were usually read to pupils when they were too young to appreciate them, or killed off by over-analysis. By the time she was doing her teacher training she was beginning to think that not everything about her education in English lessons had been for the best; she would do better. Lessons would be fun and include the Doric.

Somewhere amid all these memories, Ella recalls a wee lad who turned up in her first lesson as a trainee teacher at her own old school, and sorely tried her patience.

Wee Haimish arrived at school with one sock, two battered shoes, worn trousers which revealed his lack of underpants, no shirt and a half-darned woolly jumper. His straggly, mousey hair might have been blond. Apart from the dark circles under his big, blue eyes, he looked about eight years old. He was eleven, and it was his first day at the big school.

It was decided that he couldn't go to class until he was 'sorted'. A phone call to a comparatively affluent mum and a rummage around the second hand uniform cupboard produced a more or less suitable outfit for the 'poor wee soul'.

Then there was the painful business of getting him under one of the new showers in the boys' PT changing room. He struggled and whimpered but eventually succumbed to a much needed shampoo and rinse. Once dry, warm and dressed in his new (to him) uniform, he calmed down and even managed a wan little smile. His fair hair shone and his freshly laundered socks, pants and shirt looked smart. Only the oversized shoes and blazer looked odd. He spoke in his broad Doric accent.

'Fit's that queer lik smell?'

It was cleanliness.

To save him any more embarrassment, Haimish was allowed to stay out of class until the next bell went.

It was an English lesson and the teacher was Miss Ella Mackay, who had been fully briefed and entreated to handle the situation with the utmost of sensitivity.

'Ah'm nae deein' ony o' yer readin' an writin'.'

Ella was sorely tempted to reply in similar vein with a 'Fit Wye Nae?' instead of 'Why not?' but memories of an old teacher 'wi a bun in her hair an a plum in her moo', and the thought of losing the battle before it was begun, prevented her.

'Can you tell me why you feel like that Haimish?' she whispered in her most cajoling manner.

'Ma mither says ye dinna need ony o' that for fairm work and she's needin me to start bringin the siller hame for the wee bairns.'

It dawned on Ella that she knew this family. There was mother, eighteen bairns at the last count and probably as many fathers. They were known as the mixed drops in the area. Ella's classmate Ally (Haimish's big sister) had escaped via a shot gun wedding as she had proved as fertile as her mother.

'I know Ally would like you to read and write.'

Haimish's shocked expression changed to a cheeky smile and a sidelong glance. Maybe there was a glimmer of a chance.

For a while it seemed that it was a vanishing glimmer. Haimish would sit in the front row of the classroom and fart as robustly as he could. This was his way of testing the student teacher and getting in

16

with his new classmates. It didn't work. Ella sent him to sit in the back row and carried on as if she hadn't noticed.

Gradually, over the six weeks of teaching practice, the wee lad realised his antics were going to be ignored so he decided to try getting attention for doing good things. But he still didn't engage with lessons.

Then, one day, Ella decided to have an entire lesson in the vernacular. Light bulbs went on all around the room and wee Haimish was positively flashing. Out came everybody's Grannies' wee songs and stories from 'Coory doon ma dearie' tae 'Chin cherry, moo merry' and Haimish's favourite poem, 'The Puddock' which he could recite from beginning to end as if he were 'the verra McPuddock himsel'.

From then on Haimish's popularity grew, as did the use of vernacular, which, sadly, didn't go down well with everyone.

'Excuse me, young man. Please speak properly in the classroom.'

The reply, 'But Miss Mackay says it's fine,' landed her right in the soup. The young teacher, however, defended her corner robustly, highlighting how disaffected pupils, when allowed to use broad Scots in lessons, had come back into the 'body of the Kirk', some even with enthusiasm.

Soon Haimish's "Ah'm nae deeing it" had changed to "Ah canna dee it" and then "Ah niver thocht ah could dee it!" His subterfuge had turned out to be a cover. He hadn't ever been slow at reading and writing; he just hadn't wanted to admit it.

Why do 21st century educationists think they've made a new discovery that boys don't think it's cool to be literate or posh?

Ella's best, but most surprising farewell present at the end of her stint at Altnabervie was a box of black magic chocolates from Haimish

'Ahm sorry a wisna awfa good. Ye're ahright ye ken.'

'Well thank you, Haimish,' and in a whisper, 'ye're ahright yersel, ye ken.'

Soon after that, by August 1968, young Ella had astounded the isolated community and traumatised her family by getting herself down to London for an interview and leaving for an adventurous new job in Africa.

Evelina Vegetable

After Wee Haimish there was Evelina Vegetable

Between them was the most exciting, life-changing journey for Ella, from remote Caithness to bustling London by train, to hot, exotically cosmopolitan Nairobi by plane and to once again remote, but very different, Kericho, 300 miles into highland Kenya. As her white-haired new headmistress from Solihull, Haidee King, drove her VW Beetle along the bumpiest of roads, she informed her new recruit about the role that teachers were expected to play in post independent Kenya while bombarding her with a running commentary on the sights and sounds along the way. There was no need of any more induction.

After a sound sleep in crisp white sheets at Haidee's house and waking up to the smell of wood burning and the sounds of African songs, goats bleating and wood being chopped, it was off to the dormitories for Ella, to meet the first of the privileged new arrivals for the new term at boarding school.

Evelina Vegetable was round, smiley and curly, a bit like a cabbage. This made her teachers, including Ella, wonder if that was why her parents had named her Mboga, which is Swahili for vegetable. Babies in Kenya are often named according to the time or place of their birth so Evelina could have been born in a cabbage patch. For example in the Kipsigis language 'Chebet' means a girl, or 'Kibet' a boy, 'born during the day'.

In the 1960s and 70s, African children also had English names related to days, times, places, people, virtues, moods, feelings, states, items or anything else associated with their birth. The name Evelina was straightforward and Marys and Elizabeths were so numerous in school, they had to be numbered.

However, many names were definitely NQE in the British sense (NQBE?). Girls and boys could be named Soon, Late, Early, Monday to Friday, January to December, Morning, Noon, Afternoon, Evening or Night. Sometimes the names of the colours were used; Brown,

Black and Green for boys and Red, Purple and Pink for girls. Happy, Precious, Hope, Sunshine, Gladness, Curiosity and Goodness could all be found on the class lists at the girls' schools while Bold, Strong, Wisdom, Brave, President, King, Proud, Rich and Honourable were listed at the boys' schools. Biblical names were there in abundance as were Jomo (Kenyatta) Winston (Churchill) or Cassius (Clay). Less common were Pencil, Book, Mercedes, Dictionary, Concorde and Ruler, the latter having two meanings. There were a few foods, like Peach, Honey or Sugar, many flowers, like Hibiscus, Lily, Rose, Orchid or just Flower but there didn't seem to be another Mboga or Evelina Vegetable as Ella and her colleagues at Kipsigis Girls' School named her. Evelina loved the joke but flatly refused to say why she was called Mboga. In that way, she always had one over her teachers.

Ella, arriving for her first ever job as a fully-qualified English teacher, had been in Kenya for one day when she met Evelina, who had spent the previous four days walking to school. Evelina had eaten and slept but not bathed along the way and Mrs King, the very English headmistress, wasted no time in getting her showered and into a long nightdress before she was measured up for her school uniform – a bespoke outfit, for each pupil, created and stitched by Mrs King herself, sometimes with the help of other teachers of the domestic science variety which Ella definitely wasn't.

Ella remembered wee Haimish being subjected to a shower and a change at Altnabervie School a few months before. Why did that memory make her cringe with shame at his humiliation? Evelina, on the other hand, adored her shower and change. It was part of everyone's experience – the best part of the arrival.

Another little girl, one of the Elizabeths (Cheptoo 'born when there were visitors'), had arrived earlier and the two of them were perched on a pristine bed, with the tightest possible corners, beside themselves with excitement at the prospect of their new school uniform.

'When weel eet be leady, Meesees Keeng?' (NQE, Kipsigis-style.)

'Leady soonee – maybe tomollow – I'm not a magician!' laughed Mrs King, more pussy cat than tough headmistress, confident that no

20

offence would be taken. To keep them busy, she armed the girls with old newspapers to 'shine' the windows of the long dormitory.

Evelina, like the other girls, knew how privileged she was to be one of the 2% of boys and girls in Kenya to have a place in a secondary school. Her family had sold a cow to pay the fees, which was remarkable as she was the third child of a fourth wife. But she was an extraordinary child, clever, funny and enthusiastic about everything that had to be done.

'I'm a good investment. When I get my O-levels, I'll get an educated boy who can pay my father many more cows than the one he paid for my schooling.'

The incentive was there. Evelina hung on to every word uttered by the teachers and five minutes after class her nose was in a book.

In post independent Kenya there was an explosion of education, for which there were not enough teachers to cope, so anyone who knew a little was employed as a primary school teacher. This meant that there was a huge amount of NQE at Kipsigis Girls' School. The girls were multilingual, speaking English, Swahili and their home tribal language - and were being taught French by a charismatic M. Jeanne Pierre Sédou. The linguistic experience for everyone was rich.

Add to this, Ella, with her broad Scots accent, being given the task to prepare two poems and two dances (one of African and the other of non-African origin for each category) to enter into the choral verse and folk dance competitions at the Nairobi Music and Arts Festival, a colonial event which was hanging on by a syllable, step and note, poised on the edge of the cliff of Africanisation. Another teacher, an American, was handling the solo singing and choirs.

Evelina could sing and dance beautifully and led her fellow pupils in the preparation of a traditional African dance and was to sing a traditional African song as a solo. That took care of the African side and Ella managed to teach them a passable 'Hamilton House', a Scottish Country Dance, as the non-African folk dance.

The choral verse was the problem. None of the pupils could come up with a suitable African poem in English so Rudyard Kipling's

21

'Boots', which at least mentioned Africa, was suggested, and Ella thought Hilaire Belloc's 'Tarantella', one of her favourites, would be perfect. It was a decision she would regret.

In the languages of the particular area of Kenya, there are: a b/v sound confusion, an l/r confusion, only five vowels sounds, a (apple) e (egg) i (see) o (hot) and oo (foot) and every word should end in a vowel sound, usually i (ee). So 'Boots' by Rudyard Kipling became 'Bvootsee' bahee Ladyadee Keepringee and 'Tarantella' by Hilaire Belloc turned into 'Talanterra' by Heerellee Berrocee. And these were only the titles. When, after hours of practice, the girls still produced

'We ah footee, srogee, srogee, srogee

Srogeeng ovah Afreeca

Footee, footee, footee, footee,

Sroggeeng ovah Afreeca

Bvootsee, Bvootsee, Bvootsee, Bvootsee,

Macheeng ap an dan agenee

Der ees no deesschajee in da war'

And

'And da heepee hoppee happee

Of da crapee of da hands', Ella was in despair. How in the world or Africa was she going to polish this? The whole thing had to be analysed. She appealed to the choral team.

'What in the wurrild are we going to do?' When they laughed, she realised she had spoken in her broadest Scots accent with its most heavily rolled r, something the girls were highly amused by. There was her answer. They could hear the difference. If they took one word at a time and worked on "top of your mouth le, le, le, and rounded tongue r, r, r and shut your mouth b, b, b, and bite your bottom lip v, v, v", they might get somewhere. Then there were the new vowels sounds and the words which ended with consonants to practice.

It took six weeks but they produced a passable

'We are foot slog slog slog slog

Slogging over Africa

Foot, foot, foot, foot

Slogging over Africa
Boots, boots, boots, boots
Marching up and down again
There is no discharge in the war.'

They excelled themselves in Tarantella
'Do you remember an Inn, Miranda?
Do you remember an Inn?...
...And the hip, hop, hap
Of the clap of the hands
And the twirl and the swirl
Of the girls gone chancing, glancing, dancing
Backing and advancing
Snapping of the clapper to the spin
Out and in
And the ting, tong, tang of the guitar.'

The sounds were crisp and they had added their own rhythm and movement as only African children can. They were ready for the adjudicators.

The choral verse team had risen to the occasion, done their best and Ella was sighing with relief. But she hadn't reckoned on Evelina Vegetable. Evelina stepped forward on the stage and held up her hand.

'We want you to know how hard it was for our teacher, so please listen to how we used to say our poems.'

Before the adjudicators could cry 'foul', the team launched into a rendition of Bvootsee, Bvootsee, and heepee, hoppee, happee of da crapee of da hands. They made such a parody out of the whole thing that nobody could stop laughing for long enough to disqualify them. Evelina had probably saved the day. They won. They got an excellent critique which ended with a question. Had they realised they had recited their poems in a distinctly Scots accent?

Evelina could act as well. Ella had been dubious about the whole idea of African school children studying British literature, feeling that they should be studying the many African writers who were by then writing in the English medium. She was particularly horrified at Robert Bolt's 'A Man for All Seasons' being on the syllabus and thought 'Romeo and Juliet' might have been a better choice than 'The Merchant of Venice'.

When Ella arrived in Kenya, rehearsals had been in full swing, with an all girl cast, for 'A Man for All Seasons'. How weird that had seemed. Despite her fears, she had to admit, the performance was good and the themes well understood. Why shouldn't a polygamous society discuss the merits and demerits of Henry VIII's many wives?

However, she was very glad not to be responsible for a performance of 'The Merchant of Venice', shared between Kericho Boys School and Kipsigis Girls School - a huge and complicated project. The boys and girls rehearsed separately at their respective schools and in the end had only three joint rehearsals before the final performance on the hockey pitch at Kipsigis Girls' School.

Portia was resplendent in the bridesmaid's gown Ella had recently worn at her brother's wedding and needles had been flying to create brightly coloured costumes for all the characters except Shylock, who was conspicuous in his unique black costume. Three hugely oversized boxes painted gold, silver and lead dominated the stage, as excellent caskets for Portia's suitors to choose from, thus hammering home the significance of 'all you desire', 'all you deserve' and the 'virtue of sacrifice'

Cast, production team and audience had a firm grasp of Shakespeare's timeless and universal themes of prejudice, cruelty and the quality of mercy, no longer surprising Ella, who had soon abandoned the pre-conceived idea that such 'western concepts' were alien to and therefore beyond the local Kenya populace.

The audience, consisting of the staffs of several nearby schools, some local dignitaries, a few parents and various members of the public, were spellbound.

Most impressive was the performance of the girl who played an imperious and confident Portia, Evelina Mboga. (Certainly not vegetable by nature.)

24

In fact, Evelina was one of the 60% of her class who went on to study at University: She gained a first class degree in African Literature in English from Nairobi and followed that up with a law degree and a PhD in Politics in America.

Ella has never found out how many cows made up her bride price.

Somewhere along the way in Kenya, another life-enhancing event took place in Ella's life. She met and fell in love with a spy, with a degree in Political Science, masquerading as a Science teacher called John Francis, whose real name was Ricardo John Francis Fonseca. If it hadn't been for the profound effect this had on her, she might have gone back to Scotland to marry a Wellington-booted farmer 'wi a big hoose and a combine harvester' and that would have been the end of this particular story. As it turned out, by 1971, she found herself in Zambia after a hopeless attempt at trying to fit back into village life in remotest Caithness, with all its parochial tendencies.

Ricardo John Francis Fonseca, now Rick, rescued her, as he keeps telling her, by finding her a job at a girls' boarding school which just happened to be a few miles away from Mpika Boys' School in Northern Zambia, where he worked.

Philomena

August 1971, Zambia

Philomena, Ella forgets her other name, was a beauty. She was in her last year of Lwitikila Girls' Secondary School in Zambia which was run by Sisters of Mercy with the help of a couple of White Fathers. They ran a tight ship but not without humour. Philomena didn't appreciate being hemmed in and couldn't wait to get on with the business of living, which was going to start with her wedding, she declared.

Philomena's parents were educated and affluent and she was articulate and fluent in high standard NQE. The academic stuff she could cope with, but this wasn't her first priority. He was Ayub, the son of a rich businessman.

Beautiful 'Philly' sorely tried the patience of the nuns, especially Sister Scholastica whose duty it was to keep hemlines well below the knee and preserve the virginity of the 'girls'. One day, Sister Immaculata, the Headmistress, was watching Sister Scholastica trying to make 'that Philomena' turn the waistband of her skirt down, yet again, to a decent level.

'You do realise, Sister, as far as Philomena is concerned, the horse has well and truly bolted.'

'That's as may be, Sister Immaculata, but uniform is uniform.'

Within minutes of rolling her waistband down for Scholastica, Philomena had rolled it up again, opened the top buttons of her school blouse and was wiggling her way along the 'cat walk' corridor to her next class.

Ella had Philomena in her English class. This was more a pleasure than a problem as Philly loved African literature in English and was a vociferous asset during class discussions. She couldn't be bothered with grammar so she simply sulked quietly - until Ella hit on the idea of getting her to explain the correct versions of the common mistakes that were too wrong to be NQE, which her less accurate classmates kept making. Philomena rose to the spotlight. Ella had to admit she

26

could quite often do a better job of explaining what was wrong than she herself could, because she knew how translation had caused the errors. Before long the Not Nearly English, NNE was becoming a respectable NQE for most of the girls – at least in written examples for Cambridge Overseas Examinations.

What Philly most wanted was to be the centre of attention so, when it came to the school play, 'The Black Hermit', by Kenyan James Ngugi, Ella cast her in the female lead as Jane, the white Australian girlfriend of an African student. She loved it.

Lwitikila Girls' School had an amazing outdoor 'theatre in the round' carved out of the ground, built of hand made bricks and smeared with mud which was hardened in the sun. It had plenty of seating in a semi-circle, a labyrinth of tunnels for entries and exits, different stage heights including a 'distant' hill for weighty speeches by Tribal Chiefs and a wooden shed hidden behind a wall which provided changing facilities. The theatre's own electricity generator provided various spotlights, as well as lighting in the changing room. In the heat of the evening, after dark, the atmosphere was magical.

The school play was a whole staff project, so costumes were stitched to a high standard, make up was handled by two glamorous young Irish teachers, sound and lighting were expertly handled by a young Liverpudlian science teacher and elocution lessons were given by the sister in charge of the Queen's English, so NQE was hardly allowed to slip into the dialogue.

Ella's job was to make sure the girls understood the story and learned their lines. Philomena was the prima donna who had to be transformed. First her face had to be painted white with poster paint – and she wanted her hands painted too, complete with red nail varnish. Then she had Irish-coloured pan stick foundation make up clarted on top. Then came pink rouge, bright blue eye shadow and oodles of red lipstick. Topped with a blonde wig, the effect was startling. Philomena could have been an Australian; she even managed to sound like one. In fact the local African District Governor was overheard asking who the new, young teacher was that he hadn't met.

27

One Philomena story involved Sister Immaculata, who'd heard that the wayward girl had been creeping out at night for various romantic assignations. She always found out after the deed was done, so to speak, but was determined to catch her out before there was a race between exams and the maternity ward. The dedicated Sister decided to tour the dormitories every hour, on the hour, throughout the night, until she caught Philomena in the act of 'escaping'. It took some time. One night, in a state of exhaustion by now, she took a second look at Philomena's bed. It was an artistic creation that looked like a body, right down to the wig on the ball on the pillow – but it wasn't Philomena! Sister was so tired, she emptied the bed of its rumpled up stuffing, crawled in and fell fast asleep. Philomena got back at 5 a.m., just after the nuns had begun their morning prayers, she thought.

The kerfuffle that followed included summoning a furious mother and an amused father. This, for Philomena, resulted in a week of feeding the pig named 'The Pig' and two weeks of weeding the vegetable patch for an hour a day with a rusty old hoe – pronounced [hoey] in NQE. Infuriatingly, despite the blisters, Philomena loved the limelight.

Needless to say, soon after getting a good set of O-levels, which was never in doubt, Philomena was the mother of one, married just in time, and mother of two within eighteen months. Her comment was: 'If you educate a man, you educate a person but if you educate a woman, you educate a family.' That old chestnut.

Meanwhile, Rick and Ella had had their own wedding. It wasn't the quick registry office affair with two witnesses they had planned because the nuns weren't going to be done out of a good wedding at the mission. The domestic science department were co-opted to make a wedding dress (rather like a nun's habit), a veil (out of net curtains) and a beautiful three-tiered cake.

'What a wonderful learning experience for my girls,' the domestic science teacher was heard to exclaim. So a reception was held in a parched garden surrounded by tall maize plants and banana trees. Having been brought up as a Wee Free in Scotland, which was traditionally sceptical of Roman Catholics, Ella had reservations about marrying in the Church at the Catholic Mission.

'If you don't want them to make a Roman out of you, don't let them,' an Irish priest told Ella. 'I'll marry you.' So there was an ecumenical service.

Rick and Ella seem to remember there were more gate crashers than invited guests.

After the wedding and the honeymoon visiting Rome, Scotland and Kenya to check up on the Pope and both families, Ella took up residence and a new job at her new husband's school, Mpika Boys' School.

Berrington Bwalya

1974-1977, Zambia

Girls swooned over Berrington Bwalya. He was the tallest, most handsome boy in Mpika Boys' School in Northern Zambia, and probably the oldest, though nobody was certain. He had probably exceeded the upper age limit of sixteen for entry into Form 1 and it was not unusual for there to be no birth certificate.

No one minded. Like Philomena along the road at Lwitikila, he came from an educated family. He could never reveal to his classmates that he'd had the dubious benefit of attending a very English prep school in London for a few years while his father was studying. The likelihood of there being no birth certificate was remote, but such a clever and athletic boy would be an asset to the school, so this was overlooked.

Berrington was an anomaly. There were flashes of DNE (Definitely Native English) delivered in an English Public School accent. Those were quickly followed by some utterance in the local Bemba NQE. Ella couldn't help thinking this was the equivalent of rural teuchter Scots trying to speak toonie posh English and then 'faain thraoo themsels' – except the other way round. Berrington didn't want to appear posh. She decided to tell him he was rumbled and was treated to a loud bass-toned laugh.

'Please, Madam.' Teachers in Zambia are respectfully called Madam, even when they are younger than their students which, in this case, Ella probably was. 'You will keep my secret.'

'Yes, Berrington, but can *you*?'

'I'm going to try, Madam.'

Berrington was the best English student in the school. His father was a journalist and politician whose son had inherited his way with words. Berrington was full of anecdotes and the confidence to tell them, both orally and in the written form. He was an inspiration to his class mates and hit on the cunning idea of telling them that he enjoyed mimicking the upper class Brits.

Just as at Lwitikila Girls' School, Ella had to work on the common confusions which had become ingrained in the Zambian NQE.

Berrington would deliberately make mistakes, though he knew they were errors, then sit back with a grin and watch how Ella coped with them.

He'd either say, 'That was good, madam,' or, 'Why don't you explain it this way?'

One common mistake when asked the question, 'How did you come to school?' was to answer, 'Footing,' or 'By foot'.

Ella would say, 'You should say, "Walking" or, "On foot".'

Berrington, who very well knew this, would say, 'But why do you say "By bus" and "By car"? It must be right to say "By foot".''

"But it isn't.'

'Why?'

And Ella was scuppered. 'Just because it isn't,' wasn't a good enough answer so she went away, to mull over her lack of experience and come up with a better one.

She came up with the usual answer of common usage making language correct which of course didn't wash with Berrington.

'Then this is in common usage here so it must be correct in Zambia.'

Ella had to agree, so it was the beginning of an ongoing project which lasted for the five years she was in Mpika. Led by Berrington, of course, who claimed the idea, the pupils began to compile a Zamenglish dictionary of words and phrases alongside their more colloquial British English equivalents – or occasionally American, Australian or even UK regional equivalents, even Doric inevitably. It was a fascinating project. A black, hardback, foolscap notebook with a red spine, blue lines and a red margin was kept in the school library for entries. These weren't in alphabetical order as that would be too complicated. One day, when the book was filled, 'someone' could put it all in alphabetical order ready for publication.

That day and that someone hadn't come along before Ella and Rick, her new husband acquired along the way, had left in search of

31

new experiences, leaving Mpika Boys' School to its new batch of graduate African teachers conjured up by the process of Africanisation.

Berrington, the actor and raconteur, made his mark in both fields. He starred in two plays, as Oba Danlola in 'Kongi's Harvest' by the Nigerian Wole Soyinka, and in a Zambian adaptation of 'The Government Inspector' by the Russian Gogol, in which all the characters were given appropriately satirical Zambian names. This caused a good deal of hilarity among the local dignitaries who could laugh at their own inadequacies which were identical to those in the small Russian town where Gogol had originally set his tale.

Ella's lasting memory of Berrington's acting was his delivery of traditional African leader Oba Danlola's bitter criticism of Kongi, the modern, westernised leader turned corrupt dictator:

"Ism to ism for ism is ism
Of isms and isms on absolute ism
To demonstrate the tree of life
Is sprung from broken peat
And we the rotted bark, spurned
When the tree swells, its pot
The mucus that is snorted out
When Kongi's new race blows"

This was a glimpse of Berrington the man, who would grow out of Berrington the boy, who might one day fight the dark forces in his continent. The conviction in his performance was chilling, especially when he fixed his young English teacher with a steely eye, checking whether she understood exactly what his point was. There was a mutual respect.

What his classmates most enjoyed about Berrington, however, was the way he could tell a story. He had some tales they wanted to hear again and again.

'Tell us about your fada's erections, Bellington,' one boy said one day which alarmed Ella until she realised that it was the same old l/r sound confusion she had come across in Kenya. A quick lesson on

32

roof of the mouth le, le, le and curl the tongue r, r, r followed, while Berrington looked ready to bubble over with suppressed amusement.

'And while we're at it. Let's try, between your teeth th, th, th and behind your teeth and the back of your throat d, d, d, . Right. Shall we have your story now, Bell – ah – Berr – ington?' Ella was learning. Thank goodness for Tarantella and the Kipsigis girls.

The boys loved the story; it had just the right ingredients of skulduggery, subterfuge, incompetence and finally shrewdness leading to the triumph of the virtuous, in the shape of Barney Bwalya, MP, Berrington's honourable father. It involved the squeaky clean, idealistic politician,(Barney) having to outwit the greedy, incompetent opposition, through decoy ballot boxes filled with newspaper, cut into the shape of voting slips, mad dashes through crocodile-infested rivers, keeping boxes above head-level, while the real ballot boxes had a comfortable journey by helicopter to the returning officer to be accurately and fairly counted. The embellishments changed with each telling of the tale. Ella thought it sounded just like a Zambian James Bond story and told the students so – which pleased them enormously.

Her favourite Berrington story, which he told many times and he insisted was true, was the one about the over-anxious primary school headmaster who had been told he was to be banned from his school during the exams after his antics of the previous year while trying to 'assist' his little darlings.

This man, Berrington would say, had a plan. His pupils knew about this plan too, and he might have got away with it if the invigilator, A Britisher (NQE, Zamenglish, now accepted), had not noticed the strange behaviour of the pupils. Pens poised, at exactly the same moments, pen on paper at exactly the same moments. This was repeated at roughly equal intervals, so Mr Britisher had come out from behind his airmail Manchester Guardian and actually looked at what the pupils were doing. All the questions were multiple choice with four answers A B C or D, except for the last question which required a bit of free writing. Mr Headmaster could do nothing about the free writing but he could, he felt, get 100% for the rest. How? He had rehearsed the candidates carefully, down to telling them not to look as if they were listening too carefully. He had a copy of the exam paper and had settled himself on top of a hill with a drum. A rapid drum roll would start the proceedings and God help any idiot who missed it. Then, methodically, he started to beat out the answers from questions 1 to 100. One beat was A, two beats B, three C and four D. The stress must have been unbearable for the poor little souls. Then, Berrington would continue, the invigilator shouted, 'STOP!' in a very loud voice and 'PUT YOUR PENS DOWN AND LISTEN! Can you hear something?'

'Nothing,' the little innocents said.

'Well I CAN HEAR SOMETHING. We'll just wait for a few minutes and then you can continue answering the questions. Is that all right.'

'Yes, sir,' was all the students could muster as their hearts sank. Nothing was ever proved, even though the whole group got every single one of the first twenty answers correct. Perhaps Mr Britisher should have sent someone out to the top of the hill where the drumming hadn't stopped

Ella had followed this up, the first time it was told, with the question, 'What do you think the moral of this story is?' and got some unexpected answers.

'Madam, the invigilator was stupid. He should have let them finish so he could have the proof.'

'The headmaster should have drummed more quietly, Madam.'

'What about learning that cheating doesn't pay,' Ella suggested.

'But sometimes it does, Madam.' Madam didn't comment. It was not her country.

For Ella and Rick, the days in Zambia were coming to an end. Rick, as acting head, had, with great difficulty and some subterfuge, managed to keep the students fed before the final exams, once by redirecting a lorry load of kapenta (dried fish) in the direction of the school kitchen. The boys were extremely grateful but some members of the local government were far from pleased. Rick didn't mind that.

34

He was glad the boys would be fed for a little while – at least until the exams were over.

What Rick did mind, as did everyone else, was when a government lorry came to pick up the boys as soon as their last exam was over. The school staff and students were 'informed' that there was a short meeting for them to attend and they would be returned soon.

They didn't return to school that evening.

Zimbabwe had to be freed with the help of as many young Zambian men as possible. Were these special young men given a choice or was it conscription? Their devastated parents and teachers were never 'informed' but they did learn the shattering news that many young men from all over Zambia had died soon after.

Berrington Bwalya was one of them.

Giovanni Vendola Togliatti

Summer 1977, London WC2

Haunting memories of those final tragic days in Zambia scarcely left Rick and Ella throughout their travels to London via Mauritius, India, Caithness and the Outer Hebrides. It was as if their raison d'être had been wrenched from their guts leaving them asking, 'What was all that for?'

The June 7th street parties to celebrate the Queen's Silver Jubilee, although hugely inspiring despite the Sex Pistols' attempts to whip up anti-monarchist feelings, failed to uplift the young couple.

Then a fateful walk along Piccadilly knocked them out of their doldrums. Rick realised he was going to have to speak up to establish that his English was as good as any DNE (Definitely Native English) around, if not better, despite the widespread prejudice that brown people don't speak the language.

Rick and Ella had bumped into a bearded character walking along Piccadilly wearing a sandwich board advertising English lessons for foreigners.

'Excuse me, Sir,' he said to Rick, 'do you need English lessons?'

'Excuse *me*, Sir,' Rick replied. 'I think I have enough of the language to cope... (pause for effect) ...thank you very much.'

Ella had decided to rapidly restore dignity and cash in on the situation. 'You don't happen to need any teachers, do you?'

'Desperately. What are you doing now?' This reply was no surprise in 1970s London, where the teaching of English to foreigners was becoming a thriving and necessary industry.

'Not a lot. Looking for jobs and trying to stay alive.'

'Listen. Can you go round to this address and tell Kate that Jack sent you?' young beardy said as he scribbled an address on a piece of paper. 'The nearest Tube station's Covent Garden but you could walk it.'

Within an hour, the two had presented themselves at the untidy table which passed for the reception desk of *The London Co op School of English* in Longacre, Covent Garden. A flustered young woman glued on a wide smile in their honour.

'Hello. Welcome to London. Can you fill this form in for me, please?'

'We're not students, but I believe you need a teacher,' Ella said and watched the glue melt.

'Oh thank God. We've lost two teachers this week. I'm Kate, by the way.'

'What d'you mean you've 'lost' two teachers?' Rick asked.

'Well, um, they just moved on.'

Alarm bells should have been ringing, but then Kate asked, 'Could you take the class in that room over there? It's 'if' on the list,'

'Do you mean the conditional tenses?'

'Exactly. If I can, I will... If I could I would and if I could have, I would have but I didn't... They're the advanced class so they just need to practise them all. Do you mind if I observe?'

Rick and Ella exchanged glances, picked up a pile of Tube maps from the chaotic desk and waded in. Ella knew how to teach that, and Rick could be her glamorous assistant.

After, "If I go from Covent Garden to Leicester Square on the Tube, I will take the Piccadilly line and if I get there I can ...go to the cinema... have a meal... meet a nice boy/girl...buy a silly hat," and its endless combinations of places, Tube lines, stations, and things to see and do, had generated hilarity and enthusiasm, Rick and Ella were both offered jobs, starting immediately.

Rick quickly declined the offer, wisely as it turned out, while Ella jumped into the situation with her usual optimism, agreeing to present herself at 8.30 a.m. prompt the following day.

Rick had been observing green hair and safety pins in ears and had come to the conclusion that he wasn't prepared to tackle the younger generation in 1977 London, inside or outside a classroom. He had replied to a cryptic ad in The Times Educational Supplement aimed at the 22,000 jobless teachers and got himself employed as a commission only sales consultant. Commissions are a long time coming for rookies so Ella would have to work. The days of seeing London in all its glory through the starry eyes of tourists were numbered and bills had to be paid.

So Ella got herself to Leicester Square station by 8.00 a.m. next morning, early enough to sort out which of the four exits would get her to Longacre. She breezed in just in time for 8.30 with no trace of the fog of confusion she'd had to struggle through. – or her longing for the simplicity of remote regions with only one road to a destination.

London Co op School of English was unique. It was housed in a partially converted greengrocery with a huge conveyor belt between the basement and the ground floor which had once moved fruit and vegetables up from the chilly basement but now carted outdated books donated by various schools and libraries.

After a quick tour of the stock and the one classroom warmed by a single bar electric fire in the basement, two classrooms and open plan chaotic office/reception area on ground level and three classrooms, kitchen/staffroom, bathroom and separate toilet above street level, Ella was ushered into a classroom with nine eager beginners.

'What's your name?' and 'Where are you from?' yielded 'I'ng from Colombia' to 'I oom from Angola' and revealed clientele from Chile, Peru, Cuba, El Salvador, Spain, Russia and Czechoslovakia.

During coffee break in the staff 'kitchen', unchanged from being part of a rented flat above the shop, Ella felt the eyes of a giant Che Guevara staring at her from the wall. 'Rock Against Racism' 'Amnesty International', 'It's Class Not Race That Divides Us' and a request to join the Asian ladies on the right to work picket line at the Grunwick Film Processing factory all twinkled at her in bold letters. It was going to be tricky for Ella to maintain her preferred apolitical aloof persona. Sad memories of lost boys in a fight for freedom brought back tears and she determined, however noble the causes, she was not yet ready to become embroiled. Her five colleagues, one for each classroom, had plans for her – which she managed to side-step politely. She told them the story of the Zambian boys they had taught for four years, only for them to die for Zimbabwe before they had got home to their families. Ella's colleagues said they understood.

After a happy and successful day with the students, Ella went home to report to Rick, who reported attempts to motivate him to become a millionaire in a month by selling his company's products. They laughed at the contrast and came down somewhere in the middle.

As Ella arrived at work next morning (via the wrong Tube exit again) a vroom and a screech of brakes announced the arrival of a yellow Ferrari which now straddled the yellow lines and half the pavement outside the school door.

'Buon giorno Bella,' he called showing perfect white teeth. He rifled through some papers in the glove compartment and stuck an envelope under a windscreen wiper. 'Insegnante di inglese?'

'Si,' Ella replied hoping it was the right answer, but pointing with a questioning frown at the car.

'Putta yesterday park ticket again. Notta more today?' His loud laugh echoed along Longacre so Ella shrugged her shoulders and spread her palms outwards. Her Italian allowed no more communication.

'Oh, Ella,' Jack said as this character followed her into the school. 'We met Giovanni in the pub and he wants to join the beginners' class.'

'Fine.'

This was the tenth member of the beginners' class, Giovanni Vendola Togliatti, aged 20, who was proud to say he was di sinistra, liberto e cattolico and a proud member of the successful Partito Comunista Italiano. Where the Ferrari 308 GTS fitted in was not clear.

'No hay problema,' Giovanni was saying to Kate. 'I pay you how much you want' while Jack was explaining to Ella that wages for teachers were paid according to the number of students registered and how much they could afford for lessons. Giovanni was therefore a very welcome addition to the beginners' class.

Before class, he handsomely paid a 'new friend' (a random passer-by) to look after his outrageously parked Ferrari and watch out for traffic wardens. Then, the lesson was enlivened by his enthusiastic gesticulation which enhanced the whole process of acquiring survival English. He was also on a serious Italian charm offensive. His teacher became "Bella Ella" as soon as he realised students were on first name terms with their tutors.

At one point his young 'watchman' rushed in and Giovanni rushed out and the class could hear the roar of an engine disappearing and, after ten minutes, returning, presumably to the same spot after the warden had moved on. Giovanni tumbled in cheerfully, 'I get 200 park tickets no problema. I go home soon. But no takeaway car please.'

'In New York you getta yellow boot. Denver boot on wheel. Not can move car,' Eduardo from El Salvador informed Giovanni for the benefit of the class, describing the American forerunner of the wheel clamp which had yet to hit London.

Whatever his political views, Giovanni had oodles of joie de vivre as he hurtled through life at breakneck speed with a freedom of spirit that could only come from being disgustingly and gloriously rich. Ten minutes before the end of the third hourly morning class, he jumped up out of his seat.

'I gotta go. Lunch, con mio zio – Reetzee.' (This was no cheap restaurant; it was *the* Ritz.)

And he was gone amid the roar of an exhaust pipe.

There was a hush in the classroom before the muttering began. 'Muy rico', 'Pokrytec bogatyr', 'Ipocrita', 'No good man'. There was no need for translation of much of the muttering as the disgruntled expressions of the struggling, insecure students said it all.

'His family not died in conflict,' one said.

'He not in danger when he go home,' said another.

Finally, one kind Cuban soul conceded, 'He OK. Very funny. And he pay good to escuela. Us not pay so much, no? I'ng happy.'

Next day Giovanni agreed to hide the Ferrari round the corner where it could collect another parking fine without offending any of his impoverished classmates.

'I sorry I miss lesson yesterday. Mio zio eez very important man, leader of Partito Comunista Italiano. He say I go lunch so, I go lunch.'

'Hey Giovanni. You don't know problems. Okay. We know real problems,' Juan from Chile added. This was accompanied by the nodding heads of the rest of the class, while Ella kept aloof and quickly dragged the students back to a structured lesson, involving lots of pictures and miming, on the old favourite: 'What do you do every day?' With a list including: I get up... I clean... I brush... I comb... I eat...I drink...I walk... I listen... I speak... I read... I write... I have... I go... I come... I go to sleep... and another list to match up with: early in the morning... my hair... a shower... my teeth... coffee... tea... whisky... coca cola... chocolate ... to the teacher... to my friends... to my class... the newspaper ....

This was followed up by: Do you ... every day? Yes I do or No I don't. A whole hour went by and the class discovered how much they had in common.

Despite the irritating disadvantage of his obvious wealth, Giovanni, the shampanskoe sotsialisticheskogo, limousine liberal, gauche caviare or whatever you might like to call him, had enough charm (and spare cash for the pub later) to allow him back into a classroom full of students of a certain hue, politically speaking. The animated learning atmosphere continued and Giovanni lasted the full five hours of the day, having no rich uncle to take him to The Ritz again.

After three more days, Ella finally cracked the exits from Leicester Square tube station and thought perhaps she ought to produce some credentials, although nobody had asked her for any. There didn't seem to be any hierarchy amongst the six teachers as everyone took turns with marketing, buying equipment, reception and fee collection or any other admin that seemed to be necessary. Somehow it worked. Students came, paid, studied and went home. With Giovanni around, there was enough money for the teachers to be paid a little after all the other expenses had been covered.

'Don't you want to know if I'm qualified?' was Ella's question.

'No. You might have a PhD in Education and still not be able to teach. We watched you in action. That's enough. What have you got anyway?

'A PGCE and nine years experience in Africa.'

'Blimey. I bet you move on soon.'

'Why d'you say that?'

'Because you can, and most of us here can't. Are you sure you won't come to Grunwick's on Friday afternoon – to join the picket line?'

'I'm afraid I'm busy and I don't really understand what's going on,' was Ella's definite reply. She realised that her quick response had probably cooked her political goose. As it turned out, the television news of the violence and 84 arrested pickets that day prompted Rick and Ella to buy several newspapers in an attempt to cover all viewpoints. They felt a little ashamed that they hadn't yet found out about the plight of the exploited workers who were mainly Asian women.

'I thought we'd left racist exploitation behind,' was Rick's disappointed comment. 'What kind of country have you brought me to?'

'At least all kinds of people, black and white, are sticking up for them,' Ella said, defending the country she had brought her Portuguese Indian, born in Africa husband. 'Even Shirley Williams the M.P. has been picketing.'

'We'll see how far they get,' Rick answered. 'Wherever you are in the world it's the rich who have the power. I bet these poor women stay bullied. They won't get what they want.'

Meantime, as student numbers dwindled, two more teachers decided they couldn't survive on low pay, and for one week no pay, so went home to Mummy or wherever, but Ella managed to cling to the job until the student numbers dropped sharply at the end of summer, about a week after Giovanni had dashed into class, kissed everyone on both cheeks and scurried off out again with 'ciaos', 'arrivedercis' and 'grazies' peppering his conversation.

42

'What's happened to all the English you learned?' maestra di Inglese Ella asked.

'Grazie Bella. I won't need Eenglish in Italy. I'm going home now before I am immerso in park tickets.'

'Prego Giovanni. But you should say 'parking tickets'

'Si si. Ciao Bella Ella, Ciao tuti!'

The breath of fresh air was gone forever but not everyone was unhappy.

London Co op School of English, however, would be the poorer.

Mumtaz Mohseni

September 1977, London W1

Ella didn't expect to get the job, having arrived late and laden via Foyles Bookshop, having spent the last of Giovanni's donation to London Co op on graded readers, and picking up a lump of chewing gum on her smartly dressed bum from, perhaps, the previous candidate's chair.

She must have been the best of the bunch and was asked to get prepared for the beginning of term at *LTC College of Secretarial and English Studies* in two weeks time. This had been in the nick of time for Rick and Ella's survival in their 21guineas a week bit of basement in Hampstead. Commissions were still low to non-existent for Rick and the Co op was dwindling towards extinction – although the school could probably survive a teacher's flat with a couple of tutors and some books. Hence Ella had invested in readers – but she wouldn't be one of the tutors.

LTC was everything that the *Co op* wasn't; it had a tall, greying distinguished principal, serious staff with many letters after their names, wealthy students and vast resources including a state of the art language laboratory. Salaries were paid regularly, could be lived on and included London weighting. Ella had been employed on the strength of her nine years in Africa as a large number of the new intake of students came from Nigeria.

The rent could be paid and Rick and Ella wouldn't have to choose between steak and cheap sausages to go with the celebratory red wine. And Tottenham Court Road Tube Station was clearly signposted.

LTC was huge and expensive, providing language lessons for all kinds of learners. The EFL department provided general English for all levels of foreigners. The ESP department taught English for specific purposes such as business, medicine, hotel work, retail, travel agency, in fact most things anyone could talk in English about. The ESL department was experimenting with students who had been learning non-standard English as a second language, for most of their

44

lives.

Ella was employed as an English teacher in *The College of Secretarial and English Studies* where the students, a mixture of EFL and ESL learners, studied English at various levels and also learned shorthand and typing. The exciting innovation which was being introduced as Ella was arriving was something known as 'word processing'. The secretarial teachers couldn't quite believe that carbon paper, correction fluids and Gestetner copiers would soon become a thing of the past.

Ella's biggest beef was that learning English as a foreign language and learning Pitman's shorthand at the same time tended to end in disaster. She campaigned to ban shorthand until her students had learned enough English to cope with it.

LTC would have been a ladies' only college, were it not for Abdul, a young man from Yemen, who said he wanted to personally assist a rich, bisexual businessman so he could look after all his needs and get plenty of perks. Working from East to West, there were students from Japan, Hong Kong, Singapore, Malaysia, Palestine, Israel, Yemen, Iran, Egypt, Libya, Lesotho, Nigeria, Greece, France, Germany, Switzerland, Brazil, Ecuador, Argentina and other countries. Hong Kong girls tended to have phenomenal typing and shorthand speeds, Middle Eastern girls were rich and Nigerian girls, of which there were many, were rich and had attitude.

January 1979

Ella's biggest ally in the campaign against shorthand for new to English students didn't appear until Ella had made herself unpopular with the older members of staff, who couldn't envisage a boss without a secretary with a small pad and a poised pencil. She was about to give up in disgust, but in the knowledge that things were going to change despite all these fossils, when Mumtaz Mohseni arrived, as a casual entry student, in January, 1979, having missed the first term of the academic year. There was speculation in the staffroom as regards a possible interesting background. She was a beautiful, fragrant Middle

Eastern girl with perfectly coifed and sprayed hair, plucked and pencilled-in eyebrows, blushered cheeks and shiny lipstick. Her English was almost fluent so all she wanted was to learn how to type and get her Cambridge Proficiency English Certificate. She was also the proud owner of a Dictaphone.

'I will never, never learn this stupid shorthand. My boss will speak in my Dictaphone, always, always.' She had a point.

One chilly January morning, as Ella was walking to work along Oxford Street, a black cab drew up and out stepped a woman dressed in black from head to toe. This was not unusual in London in those days of the oil boom. What was unusual was that this woman rushed into *LTC* and disappeared.

There was no sign of her after that so Ella forgot about the incident. Three days later on January 11th she spotted her again. There was something familiar about her eyes. It was Mumtaz. In class she was a fashionable young woman, well groomed and mini-skirted - but only after a quick change out of her all enveloping Islamic dress. It turned out that Mr Fairhurst, the principal, was in on the secret and had put a small office next to the front door at her disposal.

Mumtaz seemed relieved to have been recognised and wanted to talk.

'I have a very small flat in London but please come for my food with your husband,' was how she put it. She had written the address and phone number on a scrap of paper. 'Would Saturday evening at 7 be good?'

Ella decided to say nothing to Rick about Mumtaz except that she was her student so he was somewhat reluctant to accept the invitation as he imagined a scruffy pad with unhealthy student food but he agreed to come, as long as he could wear his jeans and a sweater. Ella was a tiny degree better with jeans and a nice top.

As they entered the apartment block with its fountain and giant exotic plants, these preconceptions evaporated. Mumtaz's 'very small' London flat probably meant she was used to a palace. Rick was frisked and Ella's bag searched before the concierge rang up to

Mumtaz's flat to see if they were expected.

After their bit of a basement in Hampstead, the split-level reception room of the luxury flat seemed enormous to Rick and Ella, however tiny Mumtaz considered it. And Mumtaz had a husband, Bashir. Together they had a story to tell.

'There's no number on your door,' Ella commented inanely. 'Why's that?'

'So nobody can find us,' Bashir answered with a twinkle in his eye, but a sideways glance at his wife, who seemed anxious.

After the small talk, aperitifs, delicious spicy lamb, lentils and a tower of rice in three colours, washed down with expensive wine, Mumtaz wanted to explain her double life.

'Bashir, my husband, is a follower of the Shah – or he was until a year ago. His family are very rich and they own a big shoe factory in Tehran. Well, we think they still own it. We came here to London very quickly in December. Things are not good in Iran right now. Even in London we are not safe.'

'Is that why you wear a burka?' Ella asked.

'We don't call it a burka. That's the full cover for even eyes. I wear a chador, like a coat, and a headscarf - we call it a rusari. I stopped wearing it at home when the Shah banned it. Do you know he got the vote for women?'

'But,' Bashir interrupted, 'for all his reforms in our country, he is hated by the landlords he took land from and the clergy who feel he has betrayed Islam and, to defend his monarchy, he's turned into a bully, so all that means nothing now. I don't think it will be too long before he's out.'

'I don't think so. SAVAK is too strong and dangerous.'

'What's SAVAK?' Ella asked.

'Isn't that the Secret Police?' Rick had never quite shaken off his interest in political intrigue, despite his promise never to become embroiled again.

'What my wife doesn't realise is that these thugs could turn on Pahlavi ...sorry that's the Shah, any minute.'

47

'I know that, Bashir. Any one with a bit of money is not safe in Iran, or even in London.'

'So that's why you wear the chador?'

'No no. You see Bashir follows the Government religion, which the Shah thinks brings unity between different Muslims. They call it Din-i-Dawlat.'

'But Mumtaz's uncle is an important member of the Ulama, the scholars of Islam. They feel the Shah has betrayed his country and will do all they can to change back to traditional Islam.'

'Which means women must wear modest dress or be punished. I never know when someone is going to take news of me back to Tehran. This block is full of Iranians – and maybe some are supporters of a new Islamic Republic.'

'So Bashir,' Rick began, 'what happened a year ago to turn you against the Shah?'

The question opened the floodgates. Bashir and Mumtaz had been supporting the westernisation and modernisation in Iran for years, and like many Iranians were either unaware of, or didn't want to believe, the stories of brutal repression by SAVAK. Then Jimmy Carter warned Iran to stop its abuses of human rights – humiliatingly, in the eyes of the world. When Carter came to Tehran, hundreds of demonstrators protested against his visit. People hated how Reza and Farah had made themselves Emperor, King of Kings, and Empress of Iran and spent their time with western monarchs, and especially the American president, who had the cheek to criticise Iran's human rights when his own CIA were SAVAK's best teachers.

Then the Shah, or his police, made the big mistake. On February 9th 1978, in Qmm, they shot and killed 70 students. That was already the end. There was no turning back. Forty days later, in Tabriz, 100 more people were killed. Again, after forty more days, 100 more people died in Yazd.

The Shah called for demonstrations without violence, but on Black Friday, September 8th the troops shot hundreds more people. He made more calls for no killing and in December, during Muhurram, when

Shi'ites remember the martyr Husayn, there were mass demonstrations.

'I remember all these young men, dressed in white, the sign of martyrdom,' Mumtaz added. 'They wanted to die. But the soldiers wouldn't fire. They wouldn't. I was there and I might be dead now.'

'I feel ashamed,' Ella said. 'We hear news of troubles abroad and switch off. It's as if it hasn't happened. Now when I listen to you, it feels real for the first time.'

Rick and Ella looked at each other, knowing that their thoughts had returned to these boys, whose minds they had nurtured for four years, only for them to die in a war that was not of their making. They also knew that they had deliberately turned away from thinking about the troubles in the rest of the world, so the pain would not return, or they could pretend these things weren't happening or wouldn't affect them.

But things do happen and they affect the entire world. Rick shook his head imperceptibly. He was right. This was not the time for Ella to tell the tale of massacred Zambian schoolboys. It was a time to listen. These young people were in the middle of a revolution. Mumtaz put it simply.

'We have two Irans; one wants to be westernised with a monarchy at the head and the other wants to be islamised with Ayatollah Khomeini in charge. What is bad, they both blame the other side for what is wrong – and they're ready to die or kill for what they believe.'

'It isn't even that clear,' Bashir added. 'There are all the different groups in between. Even those who want only unity are attacked.'

'Like the Baha'i?' Ella asked. 'I can't understand why a faith which includes all beliefs should be a victim of such persecution.'

'You know about the Baha'i?' Mumtaz eyebrows rose, while Bashir's withering look revealed what he thought of this British woman's naivety.

'We met an impressive follower of Bahá'u'lláh in Mauritius. He inspired us both so much when we needed some hope,' Ella continued, her eyes on her less optimistic husband.

Bashir sighed loudly, blinking sadly. 'Perhaps in thousands of

49

years, the evil powerful will let go and let the world be good and harmonious. It is not happening now.'

'But we have to hope,' Ella persevered, 'or nobody would try to fight against repression or prejudice or persecution or greed.'

'Let's see what will happen in Iran,' Bashir added. 'I am afraid one repressive regime is going to replace another. Both think the other is evil and that they are good.' 'I have to agree,' Mumtaz said, 'with both of you, Ella and Bashir. There was a young man, Ali Shariati who died in Southampton in England two years ago. He disagreed with the evil in both Islam and westernisation. He said there was nothing in the Koran which allowed such repression that there is today and he called the love of the west *gharbzadegi* which means like a disease or frostbite – like westoxification. Some say SAVAK murdered him but some say the Islamists killed him. SAVAK may die with the Shah but it will rise with a new name. It is hard to hope.'

'Anyway, Mumtaz,' Ella went on in an attempt to move the conversation away from the crisis, 'What are you planning to do with your new diploma from LTC?'

'I'll be Bashir's personal assistant when we set up a business outside Iran, perhaps here or maybe America. If the Shah goes, sadly, it may not be safe for us to return.'

'Meantime,' Bashir announced as he presented a tray of brandy glasses and a bottle of Remi Martin, 'we are alive, in London and we can drink to the 12th Imam, the Mahdi who, with the Messiah and Jesus, will bring peace to the world when he comes.'

Despite the incongruous mixture of Islam and brandy, the four raised their glasses to peace and harmony.

The two couples said good night amid cheerful banter about Mumtaz and Bashir's luxury flat and wonderful food and Rick and Ella having to go back to their tiny box and fish and chips the next day.

The following Tuesday, the front page headline of The Times read: SHAH FLEES INTO EXILE.

On January 16th, 1979 Shah Mohammed Reza Pahlavi and his wife

Empress Farah left Tehran and flew to Aswan in Egypt.

The couple's three youngest children were flown to USA yesterday. ...

This time, Ella and Rick did not simply let the story wash over them.

Mumtaz did not appear in class that day or the next or the next.

On the following Monday morning she appeared, dressed in bell bottom jeans, a flowery blouse, long, woolly, grey sweater and a big leather jacket. No scarf topped her new scruffy hairstyle which was successfully hiding her face.

'We've found a new flat in Holloway and this time it *is* small. Those rich Iranians will never look for us there. How do I look? Can I pass for British?

'You'll do. Now let's get on with getting you this diploma.'

Mumtaz passed her Cambridge English proficiency, typing and business studies with flying colours. She was awarded her diploma despite her refusal to learn Pitman's shorthand.

The last Ella heard from her was a postcard from New York where Bashir had set up in business. She was distraught at being unable to visit her ailing mother in Tehran but delighted to say they had a baby boy.

One more pupil had moved on. The Not Quite English teacher carried on, though a little sad that she and Rick still had no news of any baby.

Leonora Alves

1981

Leonora Alves, from Lisbon, was one of those well read, widely travelled graduates who feel the need to improve their English with the help of a native speaker and she came into Ella's life just when she was needed. Apart from strange syllable stress and the odd confusion with tenses and idioms, her English was nigh on perfect. She had a degree in History of Art from Portugal but wanted to add an English degree and teaching qualification to her portfolio. But mainly she was fun and that's what Ella needed.

Rick and Ella, having got their respective bosses to provide them with inflated payslips so they could get a mortgage, had bought themselves a £12,000 bijou flat in the less classy end of Hampstead Garden Suburb. Some of the deposit came from forgotten National Savings Bonds that Ella's father had been hiding for a rainy day.

'Every Friday, the teachers used to collect half a crown, five bob, fifteen bob or even £1, if you were rich, and put a sticker in a savings book,' Ella told Rick, smiling at the memory. 'Can you imagine teachers having the time to do that these days?'

They loved their little ground floor flat with its veranda overlooking the park; at long last they felt settled and secure. It had one long corridor leading to a hexagonal living room, two bedrooms overlooking the park on one side and, off the other side of the corridor, a bathroom, huge linen cupboard and tiny kitchen with a door leading to a balcony overlooking the A1.

However, after nine years of marriage, they were beginning to resign themselves to a life without children of their own. Ella wasn't coping. For a while, gaining a further qualification in TEFL and throwing herself into teaching and extra curricular activities with her multinational students had kept her going – even after rent and rate hikes had driven LTC out of Oxford Street into smaller premises near Gloucester Road.

Long journeys, stress and monthly disappointments were taking their toll and to make matters worse, Rick was busily enjoying work, badminton and his new hobby of golf, apparently unaware of Ella's inner turmoil. He barely noticed her loss of weight and the dark circles under her eyes – until he came home one early Saturday afternoon to find his usually bubbly wife, apparently asleep in a darkened room.

'What's the matter?' was all he could say.

'Have you only just noticed that everything's gone wrong?

He didn't know how to handle this. He had thought that if nature had meant them to be childless, so be it, and that Ella would be content with her lot. He had seen no need to have a fertility check so had refused to go. He admitted that he was scared of the prospect of babies. It was hard enough making his way in a new country and he worried about what kind of future any baby of theirs might have. After all, he was a man. Ella, on the other hand, was a woman with a ticking biological clock. The thought of a future without a child was breaking her heart so she had gone to bed and was never going to get up again. She had been through a barrage of tests and a laparoscopy which confirmed that all tubes were open and everything was in working order but, without Rick having tests, the whole procedure had been pointless. She pointed this out to a horrified Rick, who was beginning to realise just how insensitive he had been. Tests were arranged, much to Rick's embarrassment, and once again, everything appeared to be swimmingly in working order. Their doctor sent them off with instructions to eat healthily, take more exercise and for Rick to cut down on cigarettes and booze. Ella was advised to avoid stressful situations and all alcohol.

'Why don't you give up that job?' Rick suggested. 'Try something else without such a long journey.'

Ella was too tired to argue. She handed in her notice, stuffed herself with healthy foods and walked for miles around leafy Hampstead Garden Suburb. This seemed to cure the insomnia and anxiety which had been feeding off each other and she slept for what seemed like a week before arising reinvigorated. She set about painting the flat from one end to the other. That done, she paid 10p to put a postcard in the newsagent's window, advertising English lessons for au pairs, with her phone number.

'If I don't find something to do, I think I'll have to go out and paint the A1!'

One phone call flooded in from one au pair girl who wanted one lesson a week, but it would have to be at her 'lady's' home. Her name was Leonora Alves, she was from Lisbon and she sounded articulate. Next day, Ella put two copies each of intermediate and advanced English texts in her back pack and walked to the address in Bishops Avenue, known locally as Millionaire's Row, to find that Leonora's 'house' was a huge mansion behind tall gates with a double front door flanked by ornate columns. Ella stood on the marble doorstep and rang the bell, trying to avoid the highly polished brass around it. It seemed like the kind of house where you wiped your feet before entering.

A pretty young woman opened the door; she had intense brown, smiling eyes and long, dark hair scrunched into a hair band behind one ear and pulled to the front.

'Sorry, my lady is out so I must look after the house – and the son,' Leonora explained and then added in a whisper, 'who is seventeen. Can you believe that?' Her English seemed good so Ella felt her job was going to be easy - probably proficiency exam preparation.

'It's fine by me. I've often wanted to see inside one of these big houses.'

'I will show you the house another day, when the son is out.'

They sat in the vast kitchen in which everything from the ceilings to the floor, including the cooker and even the sink and taps, was gleaming cream and smelled of the lilies in the huge vase. There wasn't a sniff of anything having been cooked there.

Teacher and student were just getting to grips with Leonora's reasons for wanting to learn English, which included getting into university and training to be an English teacher in Portugal when a whimpering voice emanated from somewhere.

'Leono –o-o-ra! Any chance of a cuppa tea?'

'Okay!' shouted the au pair, raising her eyebrows and stifling a

54

giggle. It was no surprise to Ella that the mugs from the perfect cupboard were cream. By the time the cream kettle had boiled, an overweight, spotty teenager had shuffled into the kitchen clad in a baggy grey shell suit with purple trimmings. Not colour coordinated.

'Any Mars bars left?' he said, diving into a shiny cream biscuit barrel.

'Only you eat them,' Leonora snapped only to be greeted with an arrogant look that suggested she had dared to come close to insubordination.

'Benjamin, this is my English teacher, Ella.'

'Wot for? She *can* speak English, you know. She don't need no lessons.'

'Yes, but she wants to improve her English. We can *all* do that.'

At that, he ripped off the paper from his Mars bar, took a bite, picked up his tea with two sugars and shuffled off to his corner of the mansion.

'He says he is studying but he's watching TV and listening to music.'

'And eating chocolate?'

'Yes. Very spoiled.'

Ella located the advanced text and Leonora took most of the first lesson, a difficult diagnostic cloze test, in her stride. She would need more of a challenge.

'What are you reading?' Ella asked, taking a chance.

'I've nearly finished "The Thorn Birds" then I'd like to read "Watership Down" if it is in the library. Have you read them?'

'As it happens I have. I can lend you "Watership Down" if you like.'

"Oh good. There aren't any books in this house – only magazines like "House Beautiful" and "Woman's Weekly".

Ella decided she had better read "Watership Down" again to make sure she'd understood it clearly; she was beginning to wonder who was going to be teaching who … or was that whom?

As Ella was leaving, the lady of the house arrived home, laden with shopping bags, no doubt with contents to dress her tall, slim, beautiful body in. How on earth had this woman spawned Benjamin?

'How *lovely*! You're going to teach Leonora. She is *such* a clever girl. Not like our Benjamin. He's turning into *such* a waste of space. I'm Suzy Green, by the way.'

'Ella Fonseca.'

'Now, I don't mind paying for some lessons but I *do* need Leonora to stick around the house. And she has to be near a telephone or the alarm button. Bishop's Avenue is *such* a target for people who want to steal things.'

'I can understand that.'

'But if she wants more than one lesson a week, she'll have to pay for that herself.'

'Yes of course.'

'Have you seen the house? My *dear*, haven't you shown your teacher, sorry what's your name – around the house?'

The tour began with the spacious lounge which, *again*, had a cream carpet and curtains although the luxurious suite was chocolate brown – with cream cushions. In the dining room, a glass table and light wood chairs and sideboard sat on a patterned carpet, 'in autumn hues', Suzy said, so that any spills wouldn't show. Suzy's blonde hair almost matched her house. Her brown suit and gold shoes and handbag completed the coordinated picture.

It was a different story when it came to the seven bedrooms each with its own garish bathroom with gold taps; there was the orange bathroom, the green bathroom, the purple bathroom and so on through the most lurid shades of pink, blue and yellow.

'My husband and my son both *love* bright colours but I put my foot down for my own bathroom.' It was cream, with shiny gold taps.

'You have a lovely home,' Ella felt obliged to say, but without too much stress on the word lovely. 'You must have to work hard to keep it so well.' Stupid thing to say.

'Oh my dear, I don't *do* cleaning. I have a cleaner and we have a gardener and a chauffeur too.' Ella wondered why they needed an au

56

pair. 'We've *always* had an au pair for Benjamin since he was born but he doesn't need so much care now so Leonora does the ironing and answers the phone when we are out – as well as being on guard, of course.'

After a few more polite noises and a polite amount of time, Ella started to make her escape.

'I'm afraid I have to go now. Things to do.'

'All right dear. I'm sure you have lots of other students. London seems to be *full* of foreigners.' Leonora was stifling a giggle so obviously hadn't taken offence.

Before she could lie about all these students she had (not), Ella bumped into a short, fat, balding man who had just thrown his car keys on the hall table.

'Oops, sorry,' he said. 'I'm Bernard, the husband and father. You must be the English teacher. Our Leonora seems to have a hankering for the more intellectual, doesn't she?' It was clear how Suzy had spawned her short, fat son but not why such a pretty woman had married this man or why he had married such an airhead. Or wasn't it? Ella put her pack on her back and walked past the three Mercedes cars outside the mansion, on her way home to what, for a brief moment, seemed like a rabbit hutch, rather than a cute and comfy little flat.

Over the following weeks, while Leonora's English was developing with Ella as a mere facilitator, Ella's mood improved and the two women shared a sense of humour, much of it lampooning Suzy the trophy wife and her spoilt son. The two soon became confidantes.

Leonora, who, at twenty seven, had survived a broken engagement, was searching for a new beginning, perhaps a career, but preferably a relationship.

'The best way to really learn a language is to find a boyfriend who speaks it. "Le meilleure temps pour apprendre une langue étrangère, c'est la nuit,' Ella gushed and the two dissolved into giggles.

Leonora listened as Ella unburdened her sadness about being childless and somehow life didn't seem so hopeless.

'It's easy to show your scratches,' Ella told Leonora, 'but much harder to show your wounds.'

'Especially to those who are closest to you,' was the younger woman's wise reply.

Slowly, Ella was relaxing. Rick was relieved to hear his wife laughing again and for a time the ticking biological clock seemed less intimidating, except for when Ella remembered to take her mid-cycle temperature. Rick, with less alcohol and nicotine in his system, was grumpier but perhaps healthier.

A few new to English au pairs had telephoned, some wanting lessons at the luxurious homes where they were working. These lessons were usually conducted with little children around, which wasn't ideal. Others wanted to come to Rick and Ella's little flat where they had peace to make progress. None, however, were as interesting as Leonora.

In a while, Benjamin the 17 year old 'child', though he failed to get into university, moved out to his own 'pad'. Suzy was happy to keep Leonora on to do the ironing and answer the telephone but, being a virtual prisoner in a mansion, was not doing Leonora's social life any good.

One Friday evening, soon after Rick and Ella had been away on a company convention to Bermuda for a couple of weeks, Leonora arrived on their doorstep with a friend, a handsome young Scotsman with unruly dark hair and a mischievous smile.

'This is Rory. You told me to find a boyfriend to teach me English.'

'I had to meet this teacher who said the best place to learn a language was in bed.'

'Now, hang on. That wasn't quite what I said but, ah well, nice to meet you.'

'I've got a new job too. What is it Rory? Gopher?'

'Dogsbody, maybe.'

'What? Don't be rude. I'm your Personal Assistant.'

'And a waitress in the café next door to my studio. I went for a coffee and she attacked me with her charm and beauty. I didn't have a chance so I gave her a job.'

'You needed someone efficient to sort out your life, you mean.'

'And you needed somewhere to rent.'

It transpired that Leonora was renting a room at a reduced rate in Rory's flat in return for organising his business.

'But we're just friends,' Leonora claimed.

Not for long, Ella thought.

'Well, I'm glad to see your English is improving, Leonora. You should always listen to your teachers' advice.'

'Red or white wine,' Rick asked, ripping open a big packet of crisps and pouring them into a wooden bowl. He was glad of any excuse to stop being too healthy. And Ella's rounding figure was looking hopeful.

'Are you...?' Leonora asked.

'I think so but I'm scared to go for a test.'

'You must go – tomorrow. Promise?'

'Monday, I Promise.'

But Monday's visit to the doctor didn't come about. Instead, on Sunday, after six weeks of excitement and apprehension, nature had decided that this pregnancy should end. Ella wasn't ill so didn't go to the doctor.

'I should have drunk that glass of wine after all,' Ella told Rick before dissolving into sobs. Had it not been for Leonora calling to find out the result of the test, Ella would have sunk into another deep depression.

'Don't worry; it's going to happen one day. Listen, we've got four Monday last minute tickets for 'Cats'. They're like golden dust. Can you and Rick come?'

'I'll ring him at the office. Yes, we'd love to come... And it's gold dust.'

The buzz of rushing to meet Rick after work and getting to The New London Theatre by 6:30 in time for a glass of wine with Leonora and Rory stopped that ticking clock for a while. Ella had even remembered to put a copy of T.S. Eliot's 'Old Possum's Book of Practical Cats' in her bag for Leonora's edification.

Over the next few months, Ella taught survival English to various au pair girls, while Leonora got an A in Cambridge Proficiency English, which she attributed to Ella's teaching. Ella felt Leonora had done it herself.

Rory and Leonora's relationship blossomed and it wasn't long before they announced their wedding. Rick and Ella were invited to join a few members of Leonora's Lisbon family and Rory's Dundee family on a two hour canal boat cruise from Camden Lock to Little Venice.

A Catholic priest conducted a short ceremony on board before the boat set off and he joined the guests in a glass of champagne and canapés to get the celebration going. He hadn't been sure he had time to come on the cruise but thought perhaps he could, as he eyed up the tempting cling-filmed buffet. It had taken ten minutes to pronounce the two Man and Wife and follow it with a hastily chosen, unaccompanied rendition of 'Give me joy in my heart, keep me praising' which was Rory's mum's favourite. Luckily she could sing so the 'Sing Hosannas' were as enthusiastic as any to be heard inside a Dundee Kirk. It turned out that, through Rory and Leonora, not only had Scotland and Portugal been joined together, but the differences between the Portuguese Catholic Church and the Church of Scotland had been overlooked. Rick and Ella had much in common with this couple.

The lasting memory was of the bride and groom leaping from one side of the boat to another in opposite directions. The wedding barge was in fact two boats clasped together which could be separated when they got to a narrow bridge. The newlyweds hadn't wanted to be separated so soon after making their vows but, after their double leap, they found themselves still on different boats.

Perhaps Leonora hadn't become the English teacher in Lisbon her parents might have liked her to become. Leonora and Rory would be going to California where Rory had got a job as a film animator on the strength of the successful publication of a children's book which he had been commissioned by the author to illustrate. They said their good byes to family and friends that day.

Within a week, they had gone.

Ella and Rick, once more, were overwhelmed by the transience of the friendships in their lives. Perhaps one day in the distant future, their paths might cross or perhaps not.

Keiko Takahashi

1983

Keiko Takahashi found Ella through another postcard advertising English lessons. She was the first of many Japanese 'ladies who lunched' while their businessmen husbands were at work, who became students of Ella. If one lady had a home 'resson', 'one on one' as they described it, they all had to have one.

By this time Rick and Ella had sold their £12,000 flat for £35,000 with no difficulty after they, mostly Rick, had fought and won a battle with the landlords over service charges. Many of the residents in the block were pensioners and very happy to have someone fight this battle for them. Another pensioner bought Rick and Ella's ground floor flat within three hours of them putting it on the market so they were free to sign a contract on a three bedroom semi in a leafy Hendon cul-de-sac. Ella had viewed around fifty houses and dragged Rick along to three.

They had both fallen in love with the Hendon house with its big thru-lounge, bay windows and French doors leading to a garden. The fact that the grass was high enough for lions to hide in didn't deter them; they would have their own bit of land. The price was reasonable because the young owners were desperate to sell as they were off to Australia with their two children, for dad to start a new job.

The bottom of an upstairs bay window had collapsed just before the purchase so the vendors had paid for it to be fixed and reduced the selling price to £42,000 as it was suggested that there might be other hidden problems. Rick and Ella were feeling lucky until Ella pulled back the living room carpet and promptly fell through the floor. An expert was quickly called and he confirmed that, unfortunately, cowboys had done a great deal of damage to their lovely new home and it was going to cost a pretty penny to sort it out. The rubble from the wall between the two downstairs rooms was still under the floorboards, along with cigarette packets, milk bottles and a newspaper from 1953. The air bricks for under floor ventilation had been blocked so the whole floor was rotten. Otherwise, apart from giant orange circles in a bedroom, thick hessian wallpaper and cork wall tiles in the long living room, a bottle green kitchen and an avocado bath suite, the house was liveable in.

Rick and Ella worked hard to clear out the rubble and managed to pay for workmen to replace the wooden floor. It was, however, some time before they could afford to put a carpet down and replace the furniture they had brought from the flat, which looked silly in the bigger house.

The day the beige (not cream) carpet was laid was wonderful. Ella celebrated by putting another postcard, advertising English lessons, in the local corner shop – the one Keiko found.

Ella jumped in the little orange Datsun Sunny she and Rick shared and set off on her new venture, full of optimism. When she arrived at the Golders Green semi, she was met at the open door by a tiny, exquisite doll of a lady carrying a plump bundle of a toddler who looked almost too big for her. This was Keiko Takahashi and she had been looking out of her bay window, eagerly awaiting the arrival of her teacher.

Keiko bowed her head quickly several times and said in a sharp little voice, 'Bow head, Saori, bow, bow. Good girl.' The little girl quickly shot off a couple of small bows in Ella's direction which made Ella feel she had to return them.

'Hello Saori,' she said, smiling broadly. 'And you must be Keiko.'

'Yes and you Mrs Fons … um …'

'You can call me Ella.'

'Hokay … Erra.' This sorting out of l and r would be the first lesson. However, there were a few things to attend to before the lesson could begin.

'Shoes here, prease,' Keiko said indicating a shoe rack in the porch and handing Ella some fluffy slippers.

'Thank you.' Thankfully there were no holes in Ella's socks. She'd have to be more careful from now on though.

Next Saori was settled with a biscuit and some toys on the floor.

She was soon placidly engrossed.

'Saori always happy when biscuit. Now I make tea.' Before Ella could argue, a tray with small lidded cups and a plateful of purple bean curd cakes was placed on the flowery tablecloth on the dining table.

'Now we have resson. I have text book from bookshop and I finish read Resson One but not understood all.'

'Would you like me to use this book?' Ella asked. After checking its suitability, she added, instinctively reverting to ESL speak, 'I will go to Foyles and get a copy for me too.'

The lesson went well. Saori was well behaved, Keiko understood Lesson One on 'Introducing Yourself' she said and had been left to tackle her 'l and r sounds' and practise some little dialogues with her husband and friends.

'I very happy with this rrr...lllesson.'

Within a week, after a couple of ladies' lunches, Keiko's friends were queuing up for rrr...lllessons. The husbands had been given company allowances for their wives and children to have English lessons, so instead of £5 an hour, Ella could charge £10 an hour.

This helped to buy a cheap dining set from The Houndsditch and a new seven-seater lounge suite which was Rick and Ella's pride and joy. They could now entertain the large extended Fonseca family who were now settled in Peterborough.

Mum and Dad Fonseca, who had come over from Goa, had finally moved into their own house complete with the furniture from Rick and Ella's previous flat, after discovering that it isn't easy to mix the generations in one house, especially when there has been such a cultural upheaval and new grandchildren keep coming along. Their stay at Rick and Ella's flat had proved cramped and stressful. Without meaning to, they had added to Ella's misery by constantly asking them when they were going to start a family.

There had been no sign of any pregnancy since the disappointment after Leonora and Rory's visit so Rick was carving out a life by joining The Rotary Club and looking for a golf club to become a member of. They had been on a list at an adoption society for too long without hearing from them to be hopeful of finding a suitable child.

Ella, meantime, in between lessons, had signed up for a correspondence course in journalism and was busy filling her empty hours with writing exercises and sending off stories to newspapers and magazines. Her very first light-hearted article, entitled 'Scrabblemania' was accepted by the Lady magazine and sending a story to 'The Northern Scot' in August, about climbing Mount Kenya at New Year and finding similarities to Cairngorm, was the right time for it to be accepted for the Christmas Magazine.

At the back of her mind, however, was that constant sadness. Rick had used the health care insurance provided by his company to find private medical care for Ella. A kindly Doctor Gordon prescribed some pills to cheer her up and told her to go away and write about how she felt and do some research into rates of infertility, treatments and how couples come to terms with childlessness. This led to Ella publishing a series of articles in 'SHE' magazine, under a pseudonym. This had the desired effect of making Ella feel less alone and persecuted; she hadn't known that one in four couples had problems with conception. She could survive – if she really, really had to. At her last appointment, Dr Gordon had said, 'Go and have a good time; drink, smoke, go dancing but just don't get pregnant.' Then he had added, 'But if you do, ring me straightaway.'

Life as a travelling English teacher of Japanese ladies was good. There was a mini tea ceremony before or after every lesson and each lady had her own speciality to offer. Lessons were easy to prepare as all the ladies insisted on using their special text book, strictly from one page to the next and they had always done their homework perfectly. This left Ella with little to prepare except some simple conversation; she was putting on a little weight and feeling healthy.

Keiko's husband Susumu wanted lessons in business English. Keiko must have been feeding him as well as she fed Saori, because he was tall and well built, verging on plump. Part of his job was translating business articles from Japanese newspapers into English.

This, for Ella, was a challenge but he seemed satisfied.

Ella continued with the happy pills and the temperature charts and kept herself busy. One morning she woke up feeling convinced something was happening in her body. She rang Doctor Gordon but he was in the Cayman Islands. She booked an appointment with the local GP.

'We'll see,' he said. 'Women of your age often mistake pregnancy for the menopause.'

Finding Ella in tears and hearing what the GP had said sent Rick into a spin. He got on the phone and demanded the blood test which Dr Gordon had said could detect pregnancy within a few days of conception. The result was positive and Ella was terrified. What if she lost a baby again? This time she'd never get over it. She couldn't wait for Dr Gordon to get back and had left a message for him to contact her as soon as he had got back.

'Congratulations Ella. I'm so pleased for you.' Dr Gordon's voice was such a comfort.

'Thank you but I'm so scared it doesn't last.'

'You won't lose this one. Your hormones are balanced now – but you must stop taking these green pills right now. You don't need to stimulate your hypothalamus for the moment. It has done its job.'

Ella was paralysed. She wasn't at all sure that this baby wasn't going to disappear so she was almost scared to walk. She made Rick promise not to tell anyone about the pregnancy and faked flu so she could cancel all her lessons and rest. And she read and read and read and wrote and wrote anything to help her escape from the anxiety. She played Mozart, Bach and Beethoven to her bump, ate fruit, wholemeal bread, and all things healthy and avoided eggs, soft cheeses, coffee, tea and alcohol. Rick told her she was being daft but was secretly anxious. A phone call from Rick to Doctor Gordon generated a call to Ella telling her to get the hell back to work before she went crazy. Reluctantly, she obeyed.

After twelve weeks, the expectant couple found the courage to tell the world their news and hoped for the best. The family were pleased and the Japanese ladies were ecstatic and immediately started baking special cakes that were good for pregnancy and insisted on coming to Ella's house for lessons 'to keep the baby safe' as Keiko said.

As Ella grew bigger, she had to find someone to take over her lessons and Patsy, a teacher neighbour was showing some interest. She wanted to meet some students. This was the perfect opportunity to invite Keiko, Susumu and Saori for a promised traditional Sunday lunch along with Patsy and her husband Jack. Ella cooked Scotch broth, roast beef and all the trimmings followed by apple pie and custard and/or cheese and biscuits. This was no light lunch.

Everything seemed fine; nothing was burnt, no lumps in the custard and everyone was tucking in, especially Susumu. In fact, his appetite was voracious. Ella had cooked enough for leftovers next day but the food was disappearing. For some reason Susumu had got it into his head that it was rude to say no if he was offered seconds. The combination of this and Ella's over exuberant hospitality had a painful outcome which, uncomfortably for the polite Susumu, caused him to miss work the next day.

Saori was the one to blurt out, 'My daddy was velly sick after your dinner.'

'Oh no. Why?' Ella was horrified.

Keiko, who would have been too polite to say anything, was left to explain. 'He thought that to say no more you think he doesn't like your food but he liked it too much so he was greedy.'

'Poor Susumu. I feel terrible.' Ella said, hand to mouth in horror, after she'd recovered from the complexity of Keiko's not quite English sentence. 'Tell him he can come again and say no whenever he likes.'

'He say he never want to see loast beef,' little Saori piped up and wondered why her mum and Ella couldn't stop laughing.

'Out of the mouths of babes,' Ella said when she got her breath back.

'What's mean that?'

'It means children always tell the truth.'

'So sorry.'

'No. I'm the one who should be sorry. I have learned something today.'

'What you learned?

'Never offer a Japanese man more.' And the laughing started again.

'Please, Keiko, you must tell me if I am not being polite.'

It was time to start the lesson:

Now. Today's lesson is about asking what things mean. We say, 'What does this mean? or What does that mean? or What does "embarrassed" mean?' Ella, the teacher began.

'What's mean "emballassed"?'

'That started well,' Ella said in mock exasperation, but with a smile. 'What does "embarrassment" mean? is correct. And *not* 'what's mean "embarrassment?",' she added waving her palm at Keiko to emphasise 'not'.

'Then it not start well when you say it started well.'

'That was sarcasm - when you say the opposite of what you mean.'

'In Japan, we don't like sarcasm. We think it lude. And Erra, we don't show palms to people. To say 'no' you wave back of hand. And when you laugh, it is polite for ladies to cover the mouth.'

'And now I am embarrassed because I have been impolite – not polite. I am not happy because people think I have done something wrong. That is what embarrassed means.'

'And I am emball …embarrassed because Saori was lude.'

'Yes. But take care. Rrrrude usually means not polite but with the l sound it's like l-e-w-d, lewd, which means rude in a bad, sexy way.'

'Like polnoglaphic.'

'Yes, exactly.'

And so it went on, without it being clear who was learning from whom.

By now, Ella's baby was almost due so, one by one, Patsy took on the Japanese ladies, although they would often check in on Ella on their way to lessons. Keiko, however, kept coming until, though early, the first contractions came.

'We phone Lick now,' she said briskly in Japanese staccato. Was she *never* going to master her 'r' sounds? Lick was phoned, panicked and brought home ASAP but the contractions had stopped.

'Blaxton Hicks,' Keiko said.

'Huh?'

'Baby knocking on door but not leady yet to come out. Saori did to me.'

'*Is* knocking and *is* not ready yet, Keiko,' Ella moaned with a pained expression on her face. Then she smiled to let her student know she wasn't *too* irritated.

'Erra ... Elllla, is that a happy smile or an angry smile?'

'Not too angry.'

'Japanese people smile when, happy or sad or angry or embarrrrrrassed.'

'Well done. Embarrassed is hard to say. You are a very good student.'

It crossed Ella's mind that Saori's English would soon be better than her mum's.

After a week or two of shuffling around like an overfed hippopotamus, Ella had an urge to wash the kitchen floor on her hands and knees, but there was still no sign of this baby. By 4 a.m., however, a sleepy, befuddled Rick was driving a puffing Ella to the hospital near his office, where the contractions promptly stopped.

'Go to work,' a midwife told Rick. 'We'll ring you if anything happens.'

Fat Ella lumbered along Oxford Street and window shopped in Mothercare where her Scottish superstition wouldn't allow her to buy anything until the baby had arrived safely; still nothing was happening.

'You can take her home now,' a nurse said when Rick arrived after work, just before Ella stood up and landed in a pool of amniotic fluid.

The baby arrived at 8.14 p.m. on November 21st on the cusp of Scorpio and Sagittarius, just before a huge clap of thunder, a flash of lightning and a heavy rainstorm. This all seemed very significant but probably wasn't. It was a girl and she had been born on her maternal granny's 76th birthday. Both mothers had been 38 years old when their daughters had been born. This was significant. Three Scorpio women in the family could turn out to be a problem. Rick certainly thought so.

The first people, after the family, to visit Ella and baby Molly at home, were Keiko and Saori.

'You give me English lesson and I give you baby looking after lesson,' Keiko said. So, when Saori went to playschool, Keiko came for a lesson while baby Molly slept in her big, green pram by the dining table. When she cried, she was breastfed and Keiko insisted on the lesson carrying on.

'We women all same,' she said.

Tikva and other Playgroups

1987 North London

'Tikva' means hope in Hebrew, Molly's mum discovered, when Molly was two years old. When a baby comes along, especially an extra special, long awaited one, mum's identity is submerged under nappies, nipples and night feeds. She rapidly becomes somebody's mum so Ella was now Molly's mum and didn't she love that.

After a couple of years of total immersion in 'brain left in the maternity ward' motherhood and Molly's maternal granny's 'Give me a child until she is five and I will give you the woman ...' , for Ella, it was all beginning to wear a bit thin.

Molly's dad, on the other hand, was still very much Rick and his activities at work and on the golf course hadn't been much curtailed. Molly's first sentence had been, 'Daddy gone goff,' which reminded Ella of her farmer brother Jamie's son Hughie's first sentence, 'Buddy tacter boken agane', no doubt with the same tone of despair in his voice as there was in Molly's. Just as she thought she would have her bouncy, funny daddy for the day, he was piling his golf clubs in the car and driving off at speed.

The other NCT (National Childbirth Trust) coffee morning mums were equally immersed in baby talk and paraphernalia so Ella felt her only link to brain food was loyal Keiko who hardly missed her weekly English lessons which now, after some years of not exactly successful grammar lessons, consisted of discussions about all things British, from Shakespeare, Dickens, The Royal Family from Henry VIII to Elizabeth II, to what was currently showing at the West End Theatre. Keiko came up with her own unique critique of the smash hit musical, 'Cats', which hadn't hit the spot for her.

'I watch half and then I want the dogs to come,' she peppered out in Japanese intonation. The lesson in the past tense, which ought to have followed such a grammatically inaccurate sentence, evaporated amidst the giggles, Keiko with a demure hand over her polite Japanese mouth.

But Susumu's contract in London was over and it was time for the Takahashi family to go back to Japan. But Keiko wouldn't stop fussing over Ella and had told some Japanese ladies that she knew a teacher who would teach them English in a group at a synagogue where their children, including Ella's Molly, could attend a playschool called *Tikva*. There was no 'might' about it, so, before the Takahashis left for Tokyo, amid exchanged promises and addresses, Ella and Molly were propelled into a synagogue where Ella taught twelve delightful Japanese ladies for two hours on a Friday morning, while their children and Molly were deposited at the playgroup called *Tikva* where they had a wonderful time learning blessings and songs for Shabbat. There the little Jewish and Japanese children, and Molly, were bewitched by the candles, tiny glasses of apple juice, in lieu of wine, and the challa bread which Molly called the bumpy bread that you pull bits off. *Baruch at Adonai* was all that Ella could remember but her baby daughter was quite the little expert in both Hebrew and Japanese.

Sadly the situation didn't last beyond the summer. The playgroup had moved to Wednesday and, soon after that, the Japanese families moved house from leafy areas near the Northern Line to leafy areas near the Central Line, when the Japanese school relocated from Camden to Ealing. This left Ella without any ladies to teach and Molly without the apple juice and bumpy bread of Shabbat.

It was time to move on. Perhaps it was time to get into the real mainstream world of the London that Molly was going to grow up in, and that Ella and Rick were going to grow old in. But, hang on, what was that?

There were several playgroups around. Molly chose the nearest one which was also the one with the friendliest mums. She also liked the big notice outside which read, 'A Church for ALL Nations'. The church hall had a kitchen where, on day one, mothers were expected to hide from their little darlings in case they were needed. The group turned out to have formidable leader called Mrs Gorski who didn't have a first name as far as anyone knew. After a few days, she would decide which mothers were allowed to escape from their children, and which ones had such difficult offspring that they had to stick around. It became a source of anxiety for some and amusement for other mums, depending on how tired they were or how much sense of humour they had managed to dig up. Molly was in the group whose children were quite happy to dump their mothers so Ella got away as long as she took her turn to help out with the setting up and clearing away, which had to be exactly according to Mrs Gorski's instructions. Some mums decided they couldn't hack the stress and left. The survivors could watch their toddlers blossom into confident children, ready for school.

In between times, Ella the teacher, and her guitar, got roped into running a mother and toddler singing group as someone, who was much better at that job, had left the area and there was no replacement. The children seemed to like it and Ella hoped the more discerning mums hadn't noticed that she only knew six guitar chords. When Molly grew out of all these lovely songs like 'Who is wearing red shoes? Can you see who it is?' and 'A great big crocodile is washing his clothes', Ella grew out of it too, and hoped that someone with greater talents would take over the group.

When it was time for Molly to go into the reception class at the 'big school', Ella had done some sick leave cover for a teacher at a local school called Brentgold Comprehensive and was considering applying for part time work there. The cover had been a happy experience (most unusual) as the sick teacher had been the Head of English and his classes had probably been either cherry-picked or well trained, and she'd been able to impress the GCSE class with her knowledge of why Steinbeck's 'Of Mice and Men' had been given that title. Thank you Robbie Burns.

When the sick teacher recovered however, there was no job in the English Department. The school, however, needed a part time Geography teacher and offered Ella the job.

Meantime Rick's career had been forging ahead and he and Ella had decided they could have a loft conversion built so that an au pair girl could move in and replace the childminding they needed for Molly before and after school.

Stephanie, a 17 year old French girl, became a second daughter in the family. She dropped Molly to school on her way to three hours of English lessons, went home to do her homework and a little housework, collected Molly from school and was free after Ella got home. It was a perfect arrangement.

Ella became a teacher again, though of Geography rather than Not Quite English, though she could still be Molly's mum.

Hawa

Brentgold Comprehensive, April 1990

It was during one of those Geography lessons when Ella was discovering that Natural Regions were now Ecosystems and that Time Zones and The Solar System had been stolen by the Science department, that Ella discovered Hawa.

It was the last lesson of the day, a little after the beginning of summer term. There she was, hidden at the back of the classroom, an exquisite little doll of a girl with delicate, high cheek-boned features, enormous brown eyes and shiny, nut brown skin. She was wearing a conspicuously new uniform for Year 8, the second year of secondary school, and a big smile.

'Hello,' Ella said after the class had settled into a task. 'You must be new.'

'Yes.'

'What's your name?'

'Yes'

'Ah. There's an elephant under your chair, isn't there?'

'Yes,' and the smile was even wider.

'Mi a iss.' (It was nice to be rejuvenated to Miss after all these years of Madam while in Africa.) 'She's supposed to show you her passport. It's her first day and she's been in withdrawal all morning. I'm supposed to be her helper.'

'Thank you, Jessica. What's her first language, do you know?'

'Somali, Miss, but nobody in Year 8 speaks it.'

'Right, let's see what we can do.'

Withdrawal was not from drink, drugs or anything else; it was from mainstream lessons, and Ella recalled an announcement made by Justine Samuels, a capable, comfortable woman from St Lucia who was in charge of Language Support. Justine had caused a few titters by saying that the withdrawal method didn't work. After a pause, she went on to say that ESL students would be coming into class with a passport and a helper, a teacher if possible, but more likely a willing pupil.

The 'passport' that this little girl was carrying had a red, cardboard cover and the following information with blanks filled in, in Justine's handwriting:

My name is <u>Hawa Hussein</u>

I am in Form <u>8R</u>

My Form Tutor is <u>Miss Jones</u>

The language(s) I speak: <u>Somali, Arabic and Swahili</u>

My English level is <u>BEGINNER</u>   LEVEL 2   LEVEL 3

My student helper is   <u>Jessica Wright 8R</u>

Staff Mentor: <u>Mrs Samuels, Room F15</u>

<u>Please encourage Hawa to interact naturally with the others in the class. She could hand out books, organise equipment, or do tasks such as copying from the blackboard, drawing diagrams or maps, colouring etc. Don't worry if she is silent. She has to go through a listening period. Smile a lot. If she is happy, she will learn more quickly. Contact me in F15 with questions, problems.</u>

There was also a temporary timetable tucked in the booklet, and a couple of picture worksheets to help Hawa to learn the alphabet and the numbers 1 to 20.

Ella went to work. 'Jina iangu ni Mrs Fonseca. Jina iako nani?' she tried in her best Swahili which was pretty rusty and had never been much good.

The girl's face lit up even more as she almost shouted out, 'Jina iangu ni Hawa!!!' Then Ella quickly added that she knew Swahili, kidogo, kidogo, which meant a very little and that there would be only Kiingereza at school and teacher and pupil practised 'What's your name?' and 'My name is' a couple of times while the others finished drawing their graph.

'Miss, I never knew you could speak African,' class clown, Wayne, called out.

'I can't really. That was Swahili – and I don't know much.' The teacher in Ella couldn't help adding, 'Did you know there are more than 3000 African languages, 69 of them in Kenya and 70 in Zambia, where I used to teach?

'Blimey, Miss. How many can you speak?'

'I know a tiny bit of two Kenyan languages and two Zambian languages but not enough to speak properly to people. I know how Hawa feels.'

'I'll help her, Miss,' Jessica chipped in.'

'Me too, Miss.'

'Can *I* help her, Miss?'

Suddenly Hawa was surrounded by willing helpers so Ms Fonseca had to assign one at a time for each subject where Jessica wouldn't be in the class, leaving Jessica to help her in Geography and in Form time. Wayne wanted to help her at break time. That would probably mean Hawa learning every swear word known to North London teenagers, so the Not Quite English teacher's reply was,

'She'll probably need her break by then, Wayne, but thank you, anyway.'

Hawa, now seated at the front, quickly finished her alphabet and number worksheets and copied out a list of the contents of Jessica's pencil case and Ella's handbag. She also managed to colour in the areas of tropical rainforest on a world map, with Jessica's help, and put a big red dot where London was and another where Somalia's capital city, Mogadishu was, with Ella's help. This little girl was smart and, though quiet, was soaking up vocabulary like a sponge. She was also desperate to learn enough language to communicate with her peers.

After the lesson, Ella went round to find Justine Samuels, in Language Support. She thought she had better tell her about all these volunteer helpers she had appointed. Justine was in the thick of after school Homework Club and promptly put Ella to work on explaining something from Science to a small boy from Angola. When Ella eventually managed to tell her about Hawa's helpers and give her the list, Justine was over the moon.

'I could hug you. That was my next job but we've got so many new ESL pupils, it's hard to keep up. Thank you *so* much.'

'No problem. I enjoyed having her in class.'

'I wish I could say the same for the other mainstream teachers… but that's another story. Hey, how would you like to help out regularly at Homework Club, maybe at lunch time?'

'Perhaps for one day. My timetable's pretty full.'

'You'll have to brush up on all the subjects on the curriculum though, and put up with teachers that don't seem to understand that some homework is just too hard for most of our kids.'

Within a few weeks, Justine was realising that she and Ella could work together and the workload was growing with so many ESL, now E2L pupils coming from various corners of the world.

'Why don't I ask the Head if you can have half a timetable of Language Support from September?'

'I think I'd like that.'

'But you'd need to learn how to use a computer. We might be inheriting the old office Acorn BBC, which is better than nothing, I suppose.' Justine warned.

The thought terrified Ella.

Come September, two days before the beginning of the new year, Justine handed Ella a frighteningly thick instruction manual and pointed to a large trolley, with wheels, bearing a square monitor, a long box, a keypad, a labyrinth of wires and some small boxes on the top shelf and an oblong metal and plastic contraption plus a box of paper with peculiar holes punched along the edges and perforations to allow easy tearing. Ella had been studiously ignoring the monster, but the time had come to confront it.

'Do you see that socket in the wall over there? Well, wheel this trolley over there and plug this in and do what the book tells you. I've got a meeting to go to.'

'What?'

'Don't worry. It hasn't got WIMP but at least it's got floppy discs instead of these stupid reel to reel tapes that keep breaking.'

'Wimp?'

'Windows, Icons, Mouse and Pointer.'

'Huh? I'm glad it doesn't have WIMP then. What's a floppy disc?'

Justine opened a box and took out a flat thing about 7 inches square and pointed at a slot in front of a big box which was under the computer screen.

'If you put it in here, THIS way up, and follow the instructions, you'll be FINE.' At this, she put the disc back in the box, closed it with a loud snap and flounced off, announcing that she was going to be late.

'Have fun!' she yelled without a backward glance.

Tentatively, Ella opened the instruction book and began to read. Much of it seemed indecipherable but there was a diagram which looked vaguely like the equipment in front of her. She wheeled the trolley over to the wall plug. The contraption finally creaked into life as the murky green screen lit up. She was afraid to touch the keys because they were the only means of control, and they could just as likely do something wrong as do something useful.

After what seemed like all day but, in fact, was two hours, she managed to produce the following on perforated computer paper, which is now framed for posterity:

The Final Straw.

The day I was offered
the chance of 'amusing' myself on
a computer, was rather an
alarming experience for a
technowally such as I am. Not
only could I not load the
infernal contraption, I couldn't
even open the box which
stored these things they call
floppy discs. As you can see
this goes beyond mere 'phobia'
----
to the realms of genuine

'walliness'. However, having
got as far as this, I am now
extremely proud of myself and
indeed, have planned in my
mind, exactly where to place
my new home-computer which
I can't afford to buy. This is
all very silly but no one will
ever know because I'm
incapable of finding out how
to store or print this.
September 1990

Ella had cracked the word processing and printing bit, and had more or less joined the computer world, though she still hadn't heard of the internet, which as yet only a tiny 0.9 of the British population had access to.

Unfortunately, this computer was practically useless for teaching purposes, having no graphics or sound, so it was used to store long lists of pupils with their countries of origin, mother tongues, levels of language acquisition and any special educational needs they might have which were not related to language. This was important as all the mainstream teachers had to have access to this information, although some didn't find time to read it. Funding, to cover teachers and equipment, was also based on these documents – and, of course, there was never enough money. The E2L pupils kept arriving and they had to be helped.

Hawa had made huge progress over the five months she had been in England and could now talk about how she had been found alone in the desert having run away from the fighting in her village. She could say how happy she was to be safe in England and she had unlearned all the swear words – or at least found out when not to use them. With help from her peers and teachers, her handwriting was improving and she could understand more and more in each of her lessons. Most importantly, she was accepted. At her London home, things were tough financially, but she had come with her mother and an aunt, both of whom had been widowed during the conflict and had fled over the border to Kenya, where they had been sent to Nairobi and eventually to London. Now, Hawa was happy in school and would hopefully have a better future.

Team Justine and Ella hoped that this was the same for all of their new to English pupils but they desperately needed more people in the Language Support Department. The ongoing campaign to find new teachers, teaching assistants and strategies for mainstream teachers continued.

After one particular lesson where the mainstream teacher didn't feel comfortable with a Language Support teacher 'disturbing' the lesson while helping an E2L pupil, Ella's frustrated comment was, 'I feel like a whispering radiator.'

The Not Quite French Teacher

June 1992 'French Farmers Blockade Euro Disney'

In the bad old days when E2L pupils were shoved in low ability sets because lack of language was equated with lack of ability, Ella Fonseca found herself supporting Masako Tayama, a shy Japanese girl, in her French lessons. The rules dictated that Masako had to learn French, and no amount of protestation that English was Masako's second Modern Language made any difference.

9C2 on a new timetable struck fear in the hearts of Brentgold teachers. It was usually a sink group for disaffected pupils, sometimes intellectually challenged, often streetwise and usually blessed with a fluency in the use of urban slang, heavily peppered with 'cusses'.

'Miss, he cussed me,' was a common complaint.

This was exactly *not* the class for sweet little Masako. She did however quickly learn that fuck was the commonest word in this new language English that she was obliged to learn in order to survive. She found out it was a verb if followed by off, me, you, them, it, this or that, an adjective if ing or ed were attached to it or a noun if er was added and that the word was often preceded by stupid. If ing was joined to it and it was followed by Hell, it could show surprise, delight, disgust or anger. With off it meant go away, be quiet, leave me alone, I just don't believe you or no I *won't* do as I have been asked. Followed by you, it seemed very rude and abusive and you had the feeling you weren't liked.

Then she learned that this was a very bad word which you should never use so Masako, being Masako, checked the meaning in her state of the art electronic translator, in the safety of the E2L department. She was streetwise enough to keep it well hidden inside a concealed zippy pocket in class; she had also learned the meaning of the word nicked. When she discovered that fuck meant sexual intercourse, shock spread over her face and she looked as if she was about to cry; then she laughed hysterically, her polite little Japanese hands covering her mouth and nose.

'In Japan, my teachers never allow this word. I will not speak it.'

'Good,' Mrs Fonseca said. 'I don't say it either… or at least, you will not hear me say it.'

Scott Innes, the French teacher and a bit of a maverick, was amused when Ella reported this conversation.

'If we ban the F word, we'll cut that lot's vocabulary in half. Fuck knows why we're being asked to teach them French. They don't give a fucking monkeys about it.'

'You're as bad as they are, Scott. If you showed a bit of disapproval they might at least try and find different words to express their feelings.'

'Nah, it's ingrained into them by their upbringing.'

'Well, we could try and show them there are some alternatives, or teach them where and when to be polite.'

'I'll leave that to you, Mrs Hoity Toity.'

'Oh f…fly off.'

Ella landed up helping 90% of this class of fifteen pupils. James was usually almost asleep and after a great deal of persuasion might get as far as writing his name on a piece of paper because he had forgotten, or probably lost, his French exercise book; he sometimes had his own Special Needs teacher. The Murphy brothers were willing but had huge gaps in their education, like not exactly having a handle on the alphabet. They weren't twins but their Irish twang gave rise to a bit of bullying, so they were in the same class to look after each other. They did, however, disapprove of the F word, having had the benefit of a good Catholic upbringing. Dwayne, a jack in the box, should never have been asked to sit in one place and listen, far less read or write, without some rap music bopping around in the background. The educationists had a name for him; he was a kinetic learner so could only learn by 'doing'. One skinny Bangladeshi boy looked constantly spaced out and the aroma around him wasn't exactly of curry. Unfortunately, he had never been caught with any 'stuff' on him in school and the school hadn't got around to fixing up dope tests.

The rest of the class had mainly just given up and couldn't wait to get going with life, doing something practical and useful, like hairdressing, bricklaying or working just about anywhere to make enough money to live on and perhaps escape from a dysfunctional home. One physically well-endowed girl, Tracy, declared she couldn't wait to have a baby so she could get her own flat. Even Scott was shocked by this sad declaration but later on confessed to Ella that he had almost made an appropriate facetious comment.

'What was that, then?'

'Fuck you, then.'

Ella responded to this puerile comment with a pff and set off in the direction of Homework Club feeling disheartened.

Thank goodness for E2L Homework Club with its happy, motivated kids, pulling themselves up by the bootstraps, desperate to learn enough language and keep up with their homework to please their teachers and their parents and to do well in this new country they had adopted. Ella often felt that their parents must be strong, bold people to travel the world either to escape danger or find a better life; this adventurous attitude seemed to have rubbed off on their children and Ella and her colleagues had nothing but admiration for them.

Masako seemed to have developed a philosophical attitude towards 9C2 French and had managed to detach herself. She surrounded herself by an ocean of serenity and acquired French a little more quickly than the others. Ella was hoping to get her moved up a set when there was a bit of a 'development' within the class.

'Sir, why the f.... should we learn f....ing French?'

'Well,' said Scott. 'You might visit France one day.'

'Never. We'd never get to France. What would we do there?'

'Sir. We could go to Euro Disney. I saw it on the tele. That's wicked, man.'

'Okay,' said Scott recklessly. 'I'll take you. Mrs Fonseca, you'll come too, won't you?

'Er...,' Ella said in a state of shock.

'But we'll only take you if you spend the next year learning real

84

French that you could use to speak to real French people. Deal?'

'Deal!'

'Hey, that would be f....ing brilliant, Sir! You're ace.'

By the time the class had left the room, Ella had calmed down a little. She'd moved from, 'Has the idiot considered the implications for one second?' to, 'This just might be a brilliant idea,' to, 'How can we get this off the ground?' to, 'We can't possibly let these kids down now that he has promised them a trip to Euro Disney.'

Scott was there already.

'Look we'll have to get the Head on our side. Most of these kids are on free dinners so they can't afford to fly and they'll even need funding for the cheapest option. There's a bus from Golders Green to Paris and there are plenty of youth hostels if you don't mind slumming.'

'My God, you've been planning this.'

'Not exactly, but I *have* been racking my brains to find a way of getting those kids to enjoy French – and this just sort of ... happened. You wouldn't mind coming would you? I'd need you for the girls, especially.'

'How can I say no?'

Ella decided she'd drop into the head teacher's office to pre-empt any refusal to comply caused by Scott Innes sounding too impulsive and scatter-brained to take 9C2 to Paris on a bus, using, no doubt, precious school funds from voluntary contributions.

To her surprise, Barry Latimer seemed happy with the idea.

'The way you put it, Ella, it would be dreadful to disappoint those children. And it sounds as if the prospect of the visit is very motivational. As it happens, I do have a fund that can be used. Mind you, it isn't often that a whole group need subsidising but I suppose it's a small class.'

'Fifteen, including Masako Tayama,' Ella replied and she couldn't help adding, 'who shouldn't be there.'

'You're not going to give up, are you Mrs Fonseca?'

'No. Mind you, she has certainly learned plenty of language in 9C2

85

– mostly bad.'

'Hm. Perhaps you could ask her if she'd like to move, now that she's made such good progress.'

'Really? Right, I will, but now I suppose she'll want to go to Euro Disney.'

'We can't have everything in life, can we?' Mr Latimer said, rather smugly.

That was how *'la plume de ma tante'* or any such useless phrase was abandoned and Mr Innes's French classroom was turned into *un café, un restaurant, une gare routier, un magasin ou un boulevard* where nobody understood English. Total immersion was the technique. Everyone started to have fun pretending to be *'à Paris'*. Dwayne was nearly always *le vendeur* selling something or the *le serveur* at a restaurant describing what was on the menu so he was happily busy, and learning.

Masako was having a wonderful time because she had learned more French than most of the others so they appointed her the 'French Dictionary' and she wanted to go to Euro Disney so certainly didn't want to move up a set.

Scott and Ella decided to cash in on the new *'régime'* to ban the f word, and by the way the b, sh, and h words on the grounds that they weren't used *'en Paris'*.

'What do they say for f…. in Paris, then?' wasn't considered a valid question because it wasn't asked *en français*.

Sadly some wise guy came up with, 'It's *merde,* innit. That's shit.' So the 9C2 classroom was then enhanced by sprinklings of the *m* word.

'That's okay, Sir, it's *en français,* innit.'

Total immersion was impossible to maintain but motivation levels in this little class of 15 pupils, who knew that a free or cheap trip to Euro Disney depended on their progress, remained delightfully and exhaustingly high. Scott and Ella had to constantly come up with new scenarios, such as *'Nous irons à Paris,'* and *'Allons-y,'* or

'Maintenant, nous sommes au supermarché' or *'aujourdhui j'achete un gateau chez le boulanger'* or *Allons-y à Euro Disney'*.

Classroom motivation was the least of Scott and Ella's problems. Organising transport, accommodation, day tickets for Euro Disney and, horror of horrors, travel documents for the French trip fifteen turned out to be a nightmare. The only person in the class with a passport was Masako so there was a lot to do between January and June 1992. Parental contribution of information was a huge struggle; some parents were unwilling to reveal complicated family details while others opposed the idea of their offspring going anywhere south of the Thames far less a foreign country. One mother was happier when she heard her boy could get there on a bus; it was planes she didn't trust. Parental contribution of money was mostly out of the question so the total cost of the trip was limited to £100. Teachers would have to pay their own way but could claim for unexpected extras which involved the pupils.

Eventually, all fifteen pupils had passports or valid travel documents, enough French to survive – if they remembered it – return coach tickets from Golders Green to Paris, including to and from Euro Disney, via the Dover to Calais ferry, one night in a basic youth hostel and a plastic £24 day ticket for unlimited rides at the theme park. The coaches would pick the group up at Euro Disney in time to get back across the ferry overnight for their parents to fetch them from Golders Green bus station on Sunday morning. It would be tough but manageable and certainly memorable. There was huge excitement.

In the Fonseca household, Rick was none too happy about his wife swanning off to Paris on a school trip leaving 8 year old Molly with him, when he had an important golf match on the Saturday.

'Sorry, Rick, I don't often ask you to take charge, do I?

This was true and Molly was amused. 'Do you remember when I used to say, "Daddy gone goff"? I don't but Mum reckons I did.'

'No problem, Moll. We'll have fun as long as you don't drag me to Brent Cross Shopping Centre.'

'Aw, Dad.'

But it was Molly, hanging on to the phone as usual, who saved the day. 'Can I go and stay with Holly for Friday night? They're going to Chessington Zoo on Saturday.'

'Of course you can. You'll love that,' Rick said with a smug grin at Ella.

'They'll drop me home at 7 o'clock at night. Is that okay?'

'Fine.' He'd got away with it again.

The French trip fifteen's first bit of excitement was getting Friday off school and as the coach was leaving at 9:30 am it was a later start than usual. Everyone was on time and Ella had parked her jalopy nearby at a friend's house. A few anxious parents hung around to wave the coach off.

'Shore, I nivir thought we'd really be going Sir,' was Tom Murphy's comment as he settled into his seat and the bus set off towards Hampstead. 'I've nivir even been on that tube to the cintre o' London.'

Scott's reply was, 'Don't worry. Maybe you'll get there soon.'

'My mither says it's a dirty evil place. Is that true?'

'I wouldn't say that. There are plenty of good things, like museums and theatres and shops.'

'But ye need money so ye do.'

'Do you know, Tom, some of them are free.'

'But it's money ye need for that tube.'

'Maybe we should write to the Mayor of London and ask him to make it free for school children. What do you think?'

'Sir, you're ace.' Scott was now Tom's idol who could do absolutely anything.

Ella couldn't help overhearing this conversation as she was sitting beside little Chloe Smith on the seat behind. Chloe was beaming and wriggling with excitement.

'Are we really going to Euro Disney, Miss? I've never been to a Game Park with all them rides. My cousin has, like, you know, the one near the M25 - what's it called… Foap Park? She said they had a BIG roller coaster.'

'You mean Thorpe Park. They call it a theme park I think. A game park has lots of wild animals like lions and elephants, like in Africa.'

Chloe stared at Ella. 'Will Euro Disney have animals?'

'No Chloe, but plenty of rides and you can have McDonald's for lunch, if you like.'

There was an intake of breath before Chloe answered, 'Wicked, Miss – but I like animals.'

'I'll tell you what. Next year in school, perhaps someone can organise a trip to London Zoo or even Chessington Zoo which is like a Zoo and a theme park put together. Would that be good?'

'Yea, Miss. Do you think they would?'

'Maybe, if the school's got any money left.' Ella's face fell as Chloe's face crumpled.

'I'm only joking. Don't worry.'

'But I heard Mr Latimer telling Mr Innes that we were an expensive lot so he'd better take care of us.'

'Oh. Um. Don't worry, he was joking too.'

Ella's thoughts turned to how privileged her Molly was to have been to Thorpe Park and now, that day, was going to Chessington World of Adventure. She hoped she realised how lucky she was.

'Anyway, Chloe, you're going to have the best time ever at Euro Disney. And you'll use some of your new French.'

'Miss, I can only remember Bonjour and Merci and une coca cola s'il – what's the rest?'

'S'il vous plait,' Ella finished but she wasn't quite sure if coca cola would be une or un so she kept quiet.

9C2 had never been so grown up and well-behaved, seated as they were in twos scattered amongst the general public, apart from Tom and Chloe who had needed the reassurance of one of their teachers beside them. Masako was in her element as she had found a Japanese university student on her way to Paris. The two girls had spotted each other at Golders Green and were enjoying a good chat in their mother tongue with the added joy of knowing that nobody could understand what they were talking about. Ella wondered what Masako might be telling this Japanese lady about her experiences in 9C2 at Brentgold Comprehensive. They were laughing a lot so it was a bit disconcerting.

At Victoria, the transfer to the channel crossing coach was smooth. Insecurity kept the fifteen stuck like leaches to Scott and Ella and Masako was clinging on to her new friend who was called Yoshie. She chatted confidently to Masako's classmates and a couple of the boys were openly flirting with her. An older, very pretty woman presented an interesting challenge and she knew that. What the boys didn't know was that she was the one in complete control of the situation.

Spirits were high as the coach sped through south east London, Lewisham and Dartford and out into the countryside of Kent; the rural landscape beyond the A2 quietened down the group until the excitement of reaching the ferry terminal stirred them up again.

'Are we going on that big ship then?'

'The very one – we sit on the coach and it drives us on.' The excitement was reaching a crescendo but so too were the lunchtime stomach rumbles. 'I'm starving, Sir,' was dealt with after everyone had negotiated the narrow metal stairs and agreed on a clear meeting place at two o'clock on deck, to avoid loss of pupils. As it turned out, no pupil would let Scott and Ella out of their sight for long.

One or two had brought a packed lunch while the others tried a canned drink and a sandwich or a hot dog. They had been told to bring enough money for snacks seeing as the school had forked out for everything else for most of them; Ella and Scott warned them not to spend too much as they might find food at Euro Disney expensive. The two teachers had an emergency fund but it wasn't enormous.

They hadn't expected to dip into it too deeply.

The fifteen, plus Yoshie had been fed and it was up into the June sunshine on deck. The white trail of the wake stretched back towards England and the friendly chug of the ships engines was in tune with the exuberance of the group. A gentle breeze blew everyone's hair back and there was a sense of freedom on the wide empty deck.

'I love this, Sir. Like, you know, nothing's in your way.'

'What's them white walls, Miss?'

'Those are the white cliffs of Dover. They're white because they're chalk.'

'Is that where the chalk for the blackboards comes from?'

'Well, it's the same stuff, yes.'

Then there was the inevitable, 'When are we going to be there?' like a small child in the first five minutes of a long journey.

'Well, the ferry's an hour and a half and, Mr Innes, how far would you say from Dover to Paris?'

'I'd say about three hours but we might find it takes a while to get to the hostel.'

Tom's brother Sean Murphy was lost and it was time to go down to the coach. It was almost time to panic. Unfortunately for him, he was chucking up his hotdog in the gents so Scott sent Ella off with fourteen of the fifteen and tended to the invalid. Two very green looking faces, one washed and still wet, staggered on to the coach at the very last moment and the ferry disgorged its row of coaches on to French soil.

'Miss, they've got funny words all over the place.'

'Yes Chloe, everything's in French now.' Ella looked over at Scott who was still looking a trifle ashen and decided it wasn't the moment to remind him about the French only rule they were going to impose as soon as they reached France. Instead she tried, 'Okay guys and girls, *mes jeune filles et mes garcons,* look at all the road signs and adverts and see how many words you can understand and see if you can remember some of the things we have to say. Remember people won't understand us if we only speak English.'

'Oui madame - nous parlons en français maintenant,' piped up jack-in-the-box Dwayne.

'Merci, Dwayne, très bien.'

'I'll be all right in a minute,' Scott groaned with his eyes closed. Men don't deal very well with vomit.

Looking at signs kept the gang busy for a while and when they were bored they were weary enough to have a snooze. Late afternoon came quite quickly.

'Look it says Paris 30 km, Sir, Miss. Are we nearly there?'

'Interdit au chiens means no dogs - innit Sir.'

'How did you know that?' Scott asked. That hadn't been in any lesson.

'There's a picture of a dog with a big X through it.'

'Not rocket science, then.' Scott was back to his witty self.

'No Sir, just super smart genius.'

'If you say so.' It was good to see these kids gaining confidence - probably. The coach trundled on through the outskirts of Paris towards the Bastille district. Scott had told the class stories of the French Revolution so they were quite excited that they would be driving past the big old prison.

'Will we see one of them things what cut heads off, geeyo things.'

'No. No guillotines on the streets, I'm afraid.' Scott was enjoying himself and forgetting the French only conversation

'Here we are… um…voici… "L'Auberge Internationale des Jeunes"- International Youth Hostel for young people under 30.'

'Where are you and Miss going to sleep, then?' Dwayne piped up cheekily. 'Vous êtes interdit innit.'

'N'est-ce pas, please, not innit. Sorry, but school teachers are allowed. Mrs Fonseca is in the girls' dorm and I'm in with you boys.'

Ella thought she heard an almost f word which turned into *merde*, coming from the direction of the boys. The hostel was heaving with back packing youngsters with as small a budget as 9C2 and their teachers.

Masako was a little sad as Yoshie had stayed on the coach which was taking her on to her different hostel. She was soon her bubbly self by the time everyone had put their luggage in lockers and Scott had promised them a fun time in Paris by night. He knew the area but pretended he didn't.

'You'll have to ask directions to a place to eat,' he told them and watched the panic cross their faces.

'Ou est restaurant?' was the tentative question posed to an elderly lady.

'Beaucoup, beaucoup, par là,' she laughed, waving her arm and pointing in the direction of what sounded like a saxophone.

'Allons-y,' Masako shouted, still excited at having met a new Japanese friend and exchanged addresses with her.

The teachers followed the pupils and sure enough, there was a whole long street of different restaurants and a live jazz band busking in the warm midsummer evening.

'You wouldn't find this in Golders Green,' Ella chipped in, charmed by the ambience. Scott had done his homework.

'How about I treat you all to something very French for starters?' Scott offered, feeling generous. 'Latimer slipped in a bit for a snack,' he whispered to Ella. The kids tore round all the stalls and restaurants and landed on a small crêperie with an enormous variety of sweet and savoury fillings to suit all tastes. Little Ruwadya needed something vegetarian; Guiliano fancied Bolognese sauce with his if he could and Amit wanted chillies in his. Little Chloe's comment was, 'Miss, my granny makes these with sugar and lemon. It's pancakes.' Ella hugged her round the shoulders and laughed. 'Yes Chloe but they're *French* pancakes.'

'Française, Miss.'

'Sorry, crêpe française.'

Scott and Ella resisted the temptation of a glass of Beaujolais and joined the pupils in a *jus de pomme dans un verre à vin* which they ordered in French and Scott paid for. The wine glass for everyone was Ella's idea.

The little group sitting around three tables were soaking up the ambience of jazz music and loud French accents; they could have been languishing in L'hotel Champs Elysée sipping champagne, judging by the radiant faces.

Scott insisted on waiter service, with the youngsters summoning the garçon and ordering their food though the stall was usually a takeaway joint; it added a touch of class to the occasion and 9C2 loved it. The band started to play American and French singalong numbers and the Murphy brothers joined in. They seemed to know most of them, even "Sur le pont, d'Avignon".

'Our granny knows all dese owld songs. We used to sing them at Christmas time. Hoi there, can ye play Danny Boy then?' And the American trombone player in Paris obliged while Tom and Sean Murphy, sons of a travelling family, added magic to a Parisian street on a warm June evening, by singing Danny Boy beautifully and word perfectly.

'Why do we judge kids by what they can achieve in a London classroom?' Ella said quietly to her colleague, feeling choked up.

The crêpes had been enormous at Scott's request so fifteen exhausted Brentgoldians and their two teachers wound their way back to the *auberge* and collapsed into bed. That Beaujolais in a bistro for Scott and Ella with the youngsters safely tucked up was never going to happen. The coach was due to pick them up at 8 a.m. to take them to Euro Disney. Everything seemed perfect. The day passes were safely in Scott's pocket and there was a wallet with the emergency fund which might not need to be touched.

The bus arrived on time and miraculously everyone was ready. The driver, however, was running his hand through his hair and stepping from one foot to the other impatiently.

'Y a t'il un probleme?' Scott asked.

'Oui, il y a un probleme.'

A conversation followed in rapid French, incomprehensible even to Ella with her fairly decent Higher French. She picked out *fermiers, TVG ou RER, autobus, impossible, Euro Disney and what sounded like 'tracteurs'* and perhaps, *'La vie est blé'*.

'Miss, what's wrong?' little Chloe, Ella's shadow asked.

'I'm not sure. Maybe we're going to Euro Disney in tractors,' Ella replied quickly adding, 'not really,'

'*Zut Alors! Zut, zut et zut.*' As this was the polite equivalent of *merde* , this was not a good reaction Scott explained.

'The coach can't get to Euro Disney. The farmers have surrounded

94

the place with tractors; it's a complete blockade and traffic can't even get out of Paris.'

'Can't we take the métro? It's just round the corner,' Amit asked.

'It doesn't go there but this man says he'll take us to a station on another line so we can get the R.E.R. Come on, let's get on the coach before we waste any time; we've only got one day. Sit beside me Mrs Fonseca, please.'

'Bloody farmers,' Ella whispered. 'Why did they have to choose the one day we've come all the way from London?'

'We need to find a bank – unless you've got enough money to pay for 15 return tickets on the R.E.R. It's damned expensive. We can manage the métro.'

'I've got some old travellers' cheques in dollars and my new Barclays Connect card, but I've never used it to get cash.' Ella wasn't sure she knew how.

'Keep your eyes open for a foreign exchange place when we get to Gare de Châtelet.'

'Wasn't the journey to Euro Disney part of the pre-paid deal?'

'That was what I was saying to the driver. He says we should be able to claim that back, but there's no guarantee.'

'Whatever happens we'll get the kids there. Look at them. It's the best thing that's ever happened to them.' The fifteen were poring over leaflets they had picked up in a tourist information kiosk the previous evening, planning the unlimited rides they were going to get.

'I'm going on Big Thunder.'

'Me too - and Space Mountain.'

'I hope we see Mickey and Minnie.'

'And Pluto.'

'I'd like to see the Indiana Jones Adventure Park.'

'That's only in America. It says coming soon, innit.'

'I fancy a Big Mac and double chips.'

'Them's French fries in Paris.'

'Pig chav – and you had two big bun things – what ye call them – for breakfast.'

'Croissants innit. Who you callin chav?'

The coach drew up a street away from Gare de Châtelet so Scott decided the group should ask directions.

'But, Sir.'

'But nothing. You know enough French for that. No, don't ask Mrs Fonseca.'

'Bloody teachers,' was the mutter. 'Take us to Paris and they won't help us.'

'That was the deal.'

'Excuse moi,' Dwayne began, 'Ou … est … Gare de Châtelet?'

'Along there, first on the right. You can't miss it,' was the very English reply.

'Well that was helpful,' Ella said to Scott with a wry grin.

It turned out that one ticket would get everyone on the métro and the RER to Euro Disney within thirty five minutes and Ella and Scott had managed to cash travellers' cheques at a kiosk so the day was saved. The brand new RER train was pristine and had only two stops. Sadly the final stop was a mile from the theme park. The drivers had decided to go on strike in support of the farmers against Disney. They would have to walk. It was a sunny day so, along with some other parents and small children they set off through the French countryside. Perhaps it was at this point that Scott Innes, of the left persuasion had the inspiration to support the cause. The group arrived at the gate to find no queues so everyone was let in immediately to an almost deserted but fully functioning theme park. For fifteen under privileged London fourteen year olds this was a dream come true. Off they went with their tickets with instructions to stick together in at least twos and be at McDonald's at one o'clock.

'Ella, I'm off.'

'What? Where?'

'It's history being made. I'm going to see the farmers.'

'You're an idiot. That stroppy lot have been kicking off for years.-any excuse will do. You'd better be back here by two o'clock in case there are any problems with the kids,' she called out at his

96

disappearing back.

'I can't stand theme parks anyway,' he shouted and started running. Ella was furious. A whole six months of preparation and he'd left her in charge of fifteen children, other people's children. What if something went wrong?

'Miss… Mrs Fonseca, aren't you coming? I want to go to Fantasy Land. It's over here.' Her little shadow Chloe would take Ella's mind off her rage. And thinking about it, there was no real danger with so many employees for so few customers on this strangest of days in the history of Euro Disney which had only been open since April.

'Where's Sir? He said he was coming on a big ride with me.'

'Sorry, Dami, he's got a bit of business to attend to.'

'His loss.' And Dami was gone. If the pupils didn't miss Mr Innes, Mrs Fonseca wouldn't miss him either. The colourful kaleidoscope of fantasy land with all the brightly-coloured Disney cartoon characters and music to go with them cast its magic spell. Shiny faced youngsters were spellbound and if the truth be told, their teacher was captivated too. All the apprehension slipped away and it was soon time to meet the gang for lunch, now all pumped up by the thrills and spills of the big rides. The hungry bundles of energy raced around the food section, choosing where they would like to eat and plumped for McDonald's where they were served by Mickey and Minnie in full costume. Chloe was overwhelmed at first, and a bit scared, but managed to get over that enough to let Ella take a picture of her standing between them.

Nobody seemed to be missing Mr Innes. Eventually he sauntered along around two o'clock with an inane grin on his face.

'You wanna a chip, Sir. We've nearly had our lunch.'

'How were the farmers then?' Ella asked.

'In militant mood.'

'Stroppy then,' she replied tersely and then loudly added, 'We've had a great time haven't we kids?'

'Yea. Wicked.'

'Awesome.'

'Excellent.'

'Cool.'

'The best.'

'Fantastic.'

To which Scott replied, 'So you didn't like it much.' The laughter proved they'd grasped the concept of sarcasm. Chloe just looked confused.

'Where were you, Sir?'

'I went to see the farmers to see what they were complaining about.'

'What did they say?'

'They don't want this bit of America on their land where they should be growing wheat.'

'That's dumb, Sir.'

'Now,' Scott continued, taking charge again, 'you've got until four o'clock and then we have to get to the RER station to go back to Paris to catch the bus for home at six. Understand?'

'Yes, sir but where do we meet?'

'At the front entrance - so off you go and make the most of it.'

They melted away towards the rides, knowing that there would be practically no queues. French citizens who hadn't taken a coach from London to Paris had chosen to stay at home when they heard the news of the blockading tractors.

'I've just thought of a problem,' Ella said to Scott. 'There are two entrances.'

'No problem. We'll take one each.'

'But what if someone thinks it's at the entrance to the RER station.'

'They won't. They wouldn't remember how to get back there. Anyway there are trains every ten minutes.'

Four o'clock came and between them, Scott and Ella had collected thirteen pupils, some from each of the two gates. Beth and Tracy were missing.

'I'll take this lot to the station and see if they are there and you wait here between the two gates and maybe put a call out for them,' Ella said briskly, still irritated with Scott and deciding to take control.

There was no sign of Beth and Tracy near the station entrance so there was nothing for it but to stand around and wait. A roughly printed notice announced half an hour between trains due to lack of staff – or at least that was how Ella translated, "Greve: Euro Disney Blocus: Trains chaque demi-heure: insuffisance de personnel."

If Scott and the girls didn't get there by 4:30, they'd have to wait until 5:00 which was cutting it really fine for catching the coach home.

Ella was trying desperately hard not to look anxious but Masako had managed to translate the notice. 'Mrs Fonseca, we must catch the next train.' It was 4:20.

'We need them mobile phones you see in the films.'

'Who's rich enough?'

'There they are Miss.' And there they were, running across the wide esplanade towards the station.

'Right, let's start queuing for the train,' Ella shouted. Scott and the girls rushed up, just as there was more bad news. Their travel tickets had only been valid for the morning and they needed more tickets – and there was no money left to feed the kids. Scott with his better French would have to sort this out. Tracy and Beth were explaining that they couldn't find the entrance and they were really scared and had to ask somebody. Chloe, oblivious to the predicament they were in was showing them the little Minnie she'd been given as a present. Scott's French was flying quickly and he had a wad of new tickets in his hand. 'We'll have to put one ticket through the machine twice. I ran out of cash.'

They made it to the train within seconds; nobody seemed to have noticed Ella passing her ticket back to Scott. They were speeding towards Paris but were likely to be late at the bus depot. Scott had telephoned ahead using one of the attendant's brick phones while he had been waiting for Tracy and Beth. The company had promised to delay the coach for them, under the unusual circumstances. The depot was a ten minute run from the RER station and with their backpacks it was a tough old run for everyone. They got there at ten past six and the woman on the phone had allowed a fifteen minute delay, she said. The coach had left and there was now a man in charge. He wouldn't budge. Too late was too late.

Scott went into action again while Ella was finding it hard to ignore requests for food. He didn't divulge the threats he had used but the outcome of Scott's 'discussion' was a woman in a smart suit jumping into a car and speeding off.

'She's bringing the coach back. She hadn't told anybody to keep it back.'

'Thank god for that. Can you imagine making fifteen reverse charge calls to London to say we wouldn't be in Golders Green until Monday morning? And, guess what, they're hungry and we're all broke.'

'Miss, I've got some money,' Guiliano said. 'We could buy some biscuits. They're cheap over there,' and off he went and came back with 3 packets of what looked like French custard creams. Ella couldn't bear it and remembered her mother's healthier cure for hunger in an emergency.

'Does anyone not like bananas?' Everyone liked bananas so she bought exactly seventeen and spent all except a few francs of her money. 'This is for later,' she added.

'I'm thirsty,' someone just had to pipe up.

'Get a drink … a tiny one in case there's no loo, - from that water dispenser – and keep the cup or cone, whatever they call it. Everybody, do the same. The bus will be back soon. And make sure you go to the toilet.'

There was just enough time for Ella to spend the rest of her money on a bottle of water which she hid in her bag for emergencies.

If travellers' looks could kill, the Brentgold group were dead as they clambered on to the rescued coach. The driver was now stopping for nothing if he was going to catch the ferry. He was an Englishman so everyone who was English knew exactly what he thought of the

100

Brentgoldians. Scott explained about the French farmers blockading Euro Disney and he blamed them entirely for the delay.

'Aw roight mate, but there's no stopping for the bog or nothing until we get to Calais. Roight kids.'

'It's okay we've been,' little Chloe said.

Twelve biscuits in a packet meant thirty six and divided by fifteen that was two each and six over. The calculation was made until someone piped up, 'What about Miss and Sir?'

'We'll have one each,' Scott agreed. 'That leaves four for the best behaved people on the bus home. I'll hang on to them.' He'd found some money to pay Guiliano so that was considered fair.

'Does the best behaved mean the quietest?'

'No, it means the most entertaining. It's going to be a very long journey.'

Whether it was relief at finally being safely homeward bound or memories of live street music in a Parisian street, the next surprising thing that happened was a spontaneous sing song which put smiles on the faces of everyone, even the strangers. Everyone agreed that Tom and Sean should have the extra biscuits but they only wanted one so Scott and Ella had another one each – which was fair as Dami pointed out.

The ferry crossing consisted of sleepy visits to *les Dames* and *les Messieurs*; the bananas and the bottle of water were long gone but it would be time to sleep when they got back to the coach anyway. Nobody complained of hunger and nobody saw the white cliffs of Dover or the Kent countryside in the dark. The Victoria Coach Station transfer to the Golders Green bus went by in a daze and at last youngsters were disappearing with their parents amid thank yous and good byes. Only Tom and Sean had nobody to pick them up.

'I'll drop them,' Ella told Scott whose latest lady friend had arrived to pick him up. 'Their place is on my way home.'

'You don't think your mum might just be late?' Ella asked in the car. She knew there was no dad around.

'No chance. She's not likely to be awake yet, sure she's not,' Tom

101

said, 'and we've got the keys.'

Ella stopped the car to drop them off within sight of the big block of flats which was home to the Murphy family.

'Miss,' said Sean, usually the quiet one. 'That was just the best day I ever had in my whole life. Thanks for that.'

'Yea, Miss. Thanks. It was terrific,' Tom added.

'Good. I'm glad you enjoyed it. And thanks for the singing. It was great.' That reaction made the whole trip worthwhile.

As Ella drove home tired, scruffy, hungry and broke, she was ready for a shower, breakfast and a snooze under the duvet but there was a car in her parking spot.

'Visitors, that's all I need,' she thought. 'Hello, how lovely to see you,' was what she said to Rick's brother, Carlos, his wife Lily and their children Julie and James.

'We thought we'd drop in on our way to Heathrow tonight,' Carlos crowed. 'School's finished for Julie and James so we're catching the plane to Paris to catch Euro Disney before the state schools get out and it gets busy.'

(As long as nobody's expecting me to cook, Ella thought.)

'Mum, did you bring some French bread?'

'Sorry, Molly but I was lucky to be able to bring myself back.'

'I hear you've been on some school trip somewhere,' Lily added.

'Euro Disney, actually – but I must have a shower and if anybody wants to take us out to lunch, I'll tell you all about it - and Molly, you can tell us all about Chessington?'

As Ella enjoyed a hot shower, she thought of those fifteen appreciative children who had so much enjoyed what a more privileged bunch of teenagers might have described as a weekend from Hell. She was ready to smile – the glow of contentment was coming from inside.

Olga

Brentgold, September 1993

Olga Visteskic wasn't ready to go into any classroom at Brentgold Comprehensive. In fact, at aged twelve, she was hardly ready to leave her mother's side. She couldn't or wouldn't speak and spent a lot of time with her head down on a table. Her mother brought her to school after the pupils had settled in class, and Ella, Mrs Fonseca, had been left to coax her out of her bewilderment.

Her mother, a gentle woman with sad eyes, knew a little English and asked Justine and Ella to talk about happy and lovely things and never to mention Sarajevo. In time, she said, her daughter would be better but she needed to learn English and how to get along with other children. The children had not been able to go to school regularly because of the bombing, she said, although they had been given a few lessons in Music, Mathematics and English; they had also read many books in Croatian. Olga's father, she told them, had studied at Dublin University.

'We'll do our best, Mrs Visteskic,' was all that Justine could say.

Ella had tried flash cards, alphabet picture books, mime, simple questions and a couple of board games, but the girl simply stared into space.

Then she asked her to help her to staple together some documents. Still, Olga didn't react – until Ella put the radio on to break the silence. *Eine kleine nachtmusik* happened to be playing. There was a hint of a smile on Olga's face and she picked up the stapler and began to do a neat job of stapling the papers together. She still didn't speak but when Ella said, 'Do you like music?' she nodded.

A few minutes later Ella tried, 'Do you understand some English?'

Olga nodded again. 'I like Mozart but I more like Michael Jackson,' she said in a clear voice with only a slight accent.

'I like Michael Jackson too. Shall I bring *Thriller* to school tomorrow?' Ella asked and was rewarded with a broad smile that lit up Olga's face and, for the first time, she saw how blue her eyes were and how prettily her dark curls framed her face.

'I bring Guns and Roses? Olga asked.

'Yes, of course.'

'I am play the veeolin all days,' Olga added and was greeted with a wide, encouraging smile from her teacher.

'I played the violin when I was a child - badly,' Ella said, pointing to herself, miming violin playing and stretching her hand out palm down at the height of a small child and shaking her head at 'badly'. This E2L speak seemed to work because the traumatised girl almost laughed.

'Now?'

'Not now – but I play the guitar – badly.' The teacher pulled a face to show HOW badly. This generated another faint smile and a puzzled expression.

'Hitta?' Olga dug into her backpack and produced a small, brown, leather bound, gilt edged dictionary with notches differentiating the letters.

'That's a beautiful dictionary.'

'My father say we speak Bosniac now but this dictionary Serbo-Croatian and English to translate. Hitta?'

'GuitAR,' Ella repeated, emphasising the second syllable and reaching for the English as a Foreign Language teacher's best weapon, the giant picture dictionary cum encyclopaedia. There were four pages of bright pictures of musical instruments.

'Da... um yes... gitara but you say guitar. My father play piano but not piano in my house now and my brother...' Olga's head went down on the table again. Ella was mortified; she should have predicted that discussion of the recent past would rake up horrific memories. She could only watch as the distraught girl fought her emotions. She gently touched her shoulder afraid of what the reaction might be; little Olga threw herself in her teacher's arms and wept uncontrollably.

'My brother...'

'What?'

'My brother... He... he dead. He fifteen and he dead.'

104

After the wave of shock had washed over Ella and subsided and she had told herself how much worse Olga must be feeling, it was Olga who wanted to talk.

'His name it Jaca and he play veeolin and piano before he dead.

'I'm sorry. It was a terrible war.'

'Every family lose someone, father, son, uncle, sister mother – but we lose Jaca. When we come London we go in big house with big hole and steps and tunnel … down.'

'Really?'

'Yes. My father upset. We leave Jaca's veeolin…'

'Violin.'

'… violin at home. My mamica say stop – too dangerous - but my tatica run back through tunnel in bangs - shooting and get Jaca's violin. That why I play violin all days.'

'You play the violin every day so you can remember Jaca.'

'Yes. I make mamica and tatica happy.'

Swallowing the lump and blinking back the tears, Ella grabbed the opportunity of teaching question and answer in the simple present tense with every day, always, often, sometimes and never. At the end of the lesson Olga's response was, 'Thank you, Miss Fonseca. I like to learn this English. I teach you some Bosniac tomorrow, da?'

'Da.'

'Tomorrow, I will say zdravo, hello, but now I say dovidjenja, good bye.'

'Dovidjenja.'

'Good. Hvala Mrs Fonseca.'

'Is hvala thank you?'

'Da.'

'Hvala Olga. You are an excellent pupil.' This led to Olga's back pack coming off again and another rummage for the treasured dictionary.

'Excellent, you say very good?'

'Very, very good, Olga.'

'I happy now. I learn soon.'

Would the other pupils ever be so polite and enthusiastic? Ella wondered. Fat chance, she thought, while telling herself how much she loved her job.

This clever pupil, with a wide vocabulary in English but who had missed out on grammar teaching in the war zone, would learn quickly. After she had mastered the present simple tense, she would soon master the past tense and be ready to tell her story, then write it down and if, *and only if* she wanted to, she could tell her new class at Brentgold Comprehensive how she had survived the siege of Sarajevo. Like all New to English pupils, she was desperate to learn and needed to be accepted.

With lots of listening, speaking, reading and writing and many hours of homework, Olga soon graduated from 'I always brush my teeth in the morning' to 'I used to read by candle light in the war but now I appreciate having electricity in London.' Within two weeks, she had found the courage to go into classes with a 'buddy' to support her and was surprised to find that the other pupils were mainly friendly. Before long, her form were reading 'A Day in the Life of Zlata Filipovic' in the Sunday Times supplement, which Olga's educated father had sent in to school. Olga told her form that she had never met Zlata but she had lived through all those horrors she had described in her diary.

She agreed to be subjected to questioning by her classmates in an English lesson and perhaps it was a cathartic experience; the class watched the brave young girl face her supressed emotions. Yes, many children died, yes there was no water, electricity or food, no she didn't have to go to school when the bombs were falling, yes her *tatica* had rescued her brother's violin and her *mamica* had thought he was going to die, yes she had seen someone shot, yes Sarajevo was a beautiful city before and was now destroyed and yes, people had taken a long time to build a tunnel to the airport which had allowed many people to escape. She told her new friends what it was like to wake up in bed and see the flashes and hear the bangs and have to run to hide in a cellar not knowing when your house would be hit and the windows would be smashed and the walls would crumble.

'Wow!' was the main response of the London teenagers. And one girl, who had become Olga's new best, best friend, in true teenage girl style, echoed the main feeling. 'You're here now and safe.'

The French A-level class were reading *Le Journal de Zlata* which had recently been published in French and Olga couldn't wait for the English translation.

February 1994 came along - time for Brentgold School's annual International Evening, and Olga's claim to fame was a respectable performance of Brahms Cradle Song and Pachelbel's Canon in D on the violin. Many people were impressed but few fully appreciated the anguish that had driven this young girl along the road of perseverance towards perfection, in memory of her lost brother.

'Mamica and Tatica are proud of me,' Olga told Ella, her eyes shining with tears of happiness.

'And I have never been prouder of any of my pupils... ever,' Mrs Fonseca added.

International Evening

Coming up to February 14ᵗʰ 1996

'Miss we've found 100 languages.'

'Brilliant. Well done. Have you written them all down?'

'Yes Miss. Some of them, like, we just had to make them look like what they sound like, you know, Miss. We don't know Arabic or Chinese letters, like. We're going to type them all up and make a, you know, poster, like.'

'And put red hearts all round, you know.'

'That'll be lovely, Mercy.' Ella wasn't going to burst their balloon of bubbling enthusiasm by pointing out that they had too many 'likes' and 'you knows' scattered about in their conversation.

'Thanks Miss. Can we use your printer?'

'Sorry it's broken. Try the IT department.'

'Okay Miss.'

A group of year nines at Brentgold had found 100 languages to say 'I love you' in for International Evening which, this year, would fall on Valentine's Day.

Even some of the boys were interested. Who would have thought that there were 100 different languages in one school?

Mrs Fonseca had been given the responsibility, as the new Equal Opportunities Coordinator, of reviving International Evening which had dwindled to five items and twenty five parents the previous year. A violin recital, by Olga Viteskic had been one of the five. Ella's tactic was to hand over to the pupils for ideas, but still hang on to the reins in the background; so far it was working.

Ella was briefing the Student Council organising committee. 'See how many countries can be represented in song, dance, poetry or short story and tell them to prepare their items for audition.'

'Will we be choosing them, Miss?' said sixth former Mary, the reliable secretary.

'If we get lots of response, you'll have to weed out some items but, if possible, we'll try and include them all. International Evening isn't about perfection. It's about having a go and celebrating as many different cultures as possible. What do you say to that?'

'If something's really rubbish we won't tell you Miss. We'll bring only the stars to you,' said Idris, the charismatic Chair*person*, who happened to be male.

'Sounds like a reasonable plan.'

'And, Miss,' Idris continued, 'I've got a great idea of how to compère the evening.'

'And, of course, you'll be the compère.'

'Of course – goes without saying.'

'I look forward to your scintillating ideas. Now skedaddle, you're late for next lesson.'

Armed with the power of autonomy, the youngsters auditioned performers, aged 11 to 18, who could sing, dance, recite poetry, read stories, play musical instruments, perform magic tricks, juggle or do anything vaguely entertaining.

It soon became apparent that there were enough would be stars to fill up the programme several times. There was going to have to be some heartbreak. Wisely, Ms Fonseca left the weeding out, as far as possible, to Idris, Mary and the student council reps, with the help of a few criteria such as making sure every year group, both genders and as many cultures as possible were represented. This made it possible, although not easy, to reject some of the ten Indian dances, five Spice Girls and four Back Street Boys 'dance' groups.

Another criterion had to be introduced. Stories and poems had to be presented in English if too lengthy to translate. This caused a brief kerfuffle and there was one happy exception. Verse XXIV of *The Rubaiyat of Omar Khayyam* was to be recited in English, Persian, French, German, Spanish and Russian. This pleased those members of staff who were a little unsure about the change of focus from European international cultures towards world international cultures. The choice of verse, perhaps inappropriate for such a youthful audience, lay with Maryam, from Iran.

Ah, make the most of what we yet may spend,
Before we too into the Dust descend;
Dust into Dust, and under Dust to lie
Sans Wine, sans Song, sans Singer, and--sans End!'

Before reading the verse from a large, beautifully illustrated tome, Maryam explained that it was telling us to be happy every day and make the most of our lives while we can - a sweet philosophy.

The programme grew steadily to include traditional dances from Ethiopia, India, Nigeria, Indonesia, Greece and Ireland, five dancing Spice Girls and six girls dancing to Backstreet Boys, four mini Michael Jacksons moon dancing in hats, bagpipes and Indian drums played by Year 12 Indian boys, a harmonium and sitar recital by a brother and sister of the Jain faith who had recently arrived from India, a violin recital by, once again, Olga Visteskic from Bosnia, juggling by Kit from Israel, magic tricks by Jalal from the Kurdistan region of Iraq, a short dramatized excerpt from 'Blood Brothers' including a young Antony Costa of Blue fame, an extravaganza of ribbon twirling, plate spinning and diabolo from six Hong Kong pupils, one from each year group, a demonstration of Karate by boys of all colours led by Kaori, a sixth former from Kyoto and a rendition of *Greensleeves* by Clare, but only after she was assured that being 'only English' qualified her for International Evening.

At the last moment, Idris and some of his mates decided they needed to contribute, so they cobbled together a few numbers they had been practising in someone's garage and decided to call it a band and give it a name, which, tantalisingly, they couldn't decide on. Ms Fonseca wanted to get the programme printed but was forced to wait.

Meantime, spurred on by Ella's encouragement and the animated rehearsals going on around school, various departments started to get in on the act. Maths produced posters of beautiful geometric Islamic art; Art classes created something typical of the pupils' home countries and Textiles had lessons in tie and dye and batik. Teachers, pupils and parents joined together to put on a display to proudly celebrate the many cultures at Brentgold School. Surinder, who had

110

just joined the Science Department, had stitched forty flags to hang high above the Main Hall where the performance was to take place. Just outside the door, in pride of place, like, you know, surrounded by red hearts, was 'I love you' written in 100 languages.

Food Technology made arrangements to provide some of the food for the International Evening buffet to supplement the ethnic dishes that parents had been asked to bring. Guests had been asked to wear their national costume where possible. All that was left was to prepare a speech, worthy of such a splendid occasion and print the final copy of the programme, complete with the name of the new band. The speech was as follows:

Hendon School International Evening – February 14th 1996 – Vote of Thanks

I think these Brentgold School pupils who are here tonight are very special. Don't you agree?

Here at Brentgold, every culture, every belief and every colour is represented. And every day we watch those children crossing those cultures all the time in so many different ways. Young people have an uncanny knack of finding out what they have in common and have created a sub-culture all of their own.

Tonight we have tried to show you something of the spirit of the school. I must tell you that all the items came about as a result of the pupils themselves. Without their volunteering and without their enthusiasm, this evening would not have taken place. I have to say a big thank you to the School Council, especially Idris the Chairman, who was also our MC tonight and Mary, the Secretary, who did so much to help in spreading the word. Thank you too to all the teachers who helped out backstage and with the organisation beforehand, of the entertainment and of course the displays which I hope you will have a look at before you go downstairs for the meal which we have to thank the parents for. Of course the biggest thank you has to go to all these wonderful performers who have practised so hard for this evening. (So let's give them a big hand.)

111

It has given me a lot of pleasure to get out from under the huge piles of paperwork which seem so necessary for the running of schools these days and get on with something just as important. A school needs a heart and a soul as well as a brain to make it tick over and act as an adequate preparation for life in the real world.

Recently we had a Staff Training Day (We don't call them Baker Days or 'bidets' anymore because we know what to do with them – or think we do.) The speaker told the story of two bricklayers. When he asked the first one what he was doing he replied, 'I'm piling bricks.' But when he asked the second one what he was doing, his reply was very different. 'I'm building a cathedral,' he said. Mr Latimer went on to talk about a shared vision that we might have at Brentgold – and perhaps this, which follows, might be part of it.

'As well as the pupils finding out what they have in common, we feel it is important that each pupil takes pride in and celebrates his or her home culture. It is important too, that everyone learns a little about each culture so that we can all learn something new and also learn to respect all other cultures. There's a place for every belief at Brentgold School – and if that belief is not a religious belief, that's all right too – but we do ask that there is respect for the beliefs of others and a moral code which demands that we treat other people as we would wish to be treated ourselves. I think that most young people today have learned that lesson extremely well – and I'm sure that much of the credit for the bringing up of these open-minded, tolerant youngsters MUST go to YOU the parents. We teachers hope that this spirit will continue and develop and we aim to do whatever we can to foster it.

I'd like to end with a short quotation from a poem by Robert Burns from my own native Scotland. Over 200 years ago he made this prediction which is perhaps even more relevant today than it was then. It's taken from a poem called 'A Man's a Man for a' that'. ('For a' that can be roughly translated as 'when all is said and done'.)

Then let us pray that come it may
As come it will for a' that…

That man to man the world o'er
Shall brothers be for a' that.'
Finally, it's only fitting that I hand over to the pupils to have the last International word (or should I say song) of the evening. Thank you all for coming.
Ladies and Gentlemen: they were just named at 4:30 yesterday. I present
DEFUNKT'. (I hope that's not prophetic – at least before the night is out.)

Ella wasn't at all sure that this was a speech worthy of the occasion, or whether it was too 'worthy', or idealistic drivel, so she stuck a copy in Barry Latimer's pigeon hole with a note saying, 'Is this okay?' He seemed to be excited about how wonderful it was so she relaxed.

The day came and the team of teachers, pupils and parents went into action. Front of house gave out programmes, welcomed guests and showed them to their seats. Parents poured in with exotic dishes which would be devoured during an interval. Teachers hustled and bustled sorting out costumes, make up, lighting, sound systems and seating areas for performers.

There had been no tradition of charging for the show but Ella was beginning to think this would be a good idea for the following year as many more guests than expected seemed to be pouring in. Even the School Governors had put in an appearance and sat in the front row.

All the performers sat on the side of the hall near the door leading to the back stage door and were to be ushered out and in by a chain gang of teachers. Dancers had instructions to appear backstage with exactly cued cassette tapes and all performers had been told to familiarise themselves with the programme and be ready to move two items before their own. In theory it should have worked like clockwork.

Ella, confident that her delegation had created an efficient team, positioned herself at the back of the hall for an overall view and to keep tabs on restless back row spectators.

Abba's *'I have a Dream'*, an inspired choice of background music, settled some of the audience and the others fell silent as the lights went down and a spotlight settled on Idris, in dinner suit and bow tie, seated, front right, at a table with a snowy white tablecloth, on which were a champagne glass and a red carnation in a tiny, crystal vase.

'Welcome,' he began, 'to Brentgold International Evening. My name is Idris and I'm going to be your MC for tonight. Sit back and relax while I take you on a fascinating world tour of the many countries our pupils come from. We're going to begin with a traditional dance from Ethiopia.' As he raised his glass and faded off stage, lights settled on massive posters depicting scenes of Ethiopian mountains and people in colourful traditional costume. The pulsating music began, right on cue, and the dancers, two boys and two girls, rushed on stage to delight the audience with a lively, athletic Ethiopian dance.

Ella allowed herself a sigh of relief as Barry Latimer turned to her with an ostentatious thumbs up.

The chain gang were superb and the performers, bar the odd little fluff, were getting on and off stage smoothly. Then, suddenly, a loud young voice, inadvertently helped by a microphone, announced, 'Sir, we've lost the Michael Jacksons.'

This was followed by a calm but loud whisper, 'Okay, don't worry, we'll put the next item on. Find the Michael Jacksons.'

'Sir, they've had a fight. Ayub says he can moonwalk better than Joe, so Joe hit him.'

'That's not very good for international relations,' a half-amused teacher reprimanded. What he didn't realise until the audience, school governors included, had burst out laughing, was that every word had been relayed through the loudspeakers.

'Oops, sorry folks,' the young Maths teacher announced, 'Normal service will be resumed as soon as possible.'

Predictably, the Hong Kong pupils were ready to go on stage with their exhilarating display of ribbon twirling, plate spinning and diabolo, saving the day and raising the standards in swirls of efficiency.

Meantime Ayub and Joe had been persuaded that each was as good as the other at moon walking so the cutest little Michael Jacksons at Brentgold moonwalked with hats over their eyes amid loud cheers.

There was, however, a bigger cheer for Clare, who, accompanied on the piano by Sue from Japan, sang *Greensleeves* and then, not on the programme, *An English Country Garden*, and declared that she was proud to welcome so many people from so many countries to *her* country.

At this point, the lump in Ms Fonseca's throat was too large for her to make any speeches and tears were blinding her, but a speech she had to make.

In a daze, Ella Fonseca, the idealistic, not quite English teacher, delivered that speech from the bottom of her heart, convinced that old wounds would be healed and future hopes would be fulfilled. On a night like this, there was no other way to feel. In the audience she could see her proud husband and rather surprised eleven year old daughter, who would soon be ready for secondary school. They were Ella's biggest fans, she hoped.

Relief washing over her, she handed over to DEFUNKT who roused the audience to loud cheers and had the last word, but not before they had presented Ms Fonseca with the customary enormous bouquet of flowers as thanks for all her hard work.

Ella Fonseca Mackay, collapsing into exhausted euphoria, retreated into nostalgia. Sadly her father, Charlie Mackay, had died before his headstrong daughter could say, 'I told you so,' when it came to the triumph of racial harmony over bigotry, as she saw it. However, Ella wasted no time in posting off a copy of the speech she was convinced justified her marriage to Rick, a man of a different race and, more controversially, a Catholic. Secretly, she hoped that outspoken family doctor, Iain Falconer, who had expressed his disapproval, would read it. Her mother, now eighty six and in need of regular doctor's visits, would take great delight in making sure he did. Mary Mackay had always been proudly on her daughter's side.

Within a few months, Mary Mackay had slipped away, shrouded in her favourite crocheted, white shawl, hair brushed, having weakly waved goodbye to the family surrounding her.

Alban and Ilir

1999: Pristina to Brentgold, via Macedonia

'Uh, oh, here comes trouble.'

The trouble came in the shape of two, sturdy lads who were strutting through the door, clenched fists, oozing aggression, not happy to be where they were.

Ms Fonseca was ready with a disarming smile. She had been given some background details and could understand why two fourteen year olds had the haunted eyes of boys who had seen too much.

'You Missy Fonseca?' the slightly taller of the two asked.

'Yes and you must be Alban and Ilir. Hello. Good to meet you.'

'The form teacher say we must learn English before we go in classes but we learning English for six months.'

'We work very hard and we want lessons ... now,' the other boy barked.

'Yes, okay, but we want to help you first. Can you wait for just one day? Now which of you is Alban and which one is Ilir?'

'I'm Alban,' the slightly stockier boy said. 'He Ilir.'

'Are you brothers?'

'No, we are friends. Brothers all dead,' Ilir said.

This was a detail that Ella had not been given.

'The Centre has sent a letter telling us about how you are very good students so we will get into classes with the other students as soon as possible. But first, look at this list: English, Maths, Science, French, German, Spanish, History, Geography, R.E., I.C.T., P.E., Drama, Music, Art, Technology, Graphics, Textiles and Electronics. Do you know what they all are?'

'...No.'

'Some.'

'Then, that is why you must have one lesson of EAL every day for a while.'

'What EAL, Missy?'

'It means English as an Additional Language. You speak Albanian

117

and you now speak English.'

'How you know we speak Albanian?'

'It's my job to know that, and my job to teach you the English you will need in lessons and to do your homework. Shall we start?'

'Start,' Alban said. And both boys smiled as they carefully wrote their names on brand new, yellow exercise books. For students this is always a pleasure.

The boys' aggression was channelled into the fierce motivation to master English and get on with the business of living in the adopted country which was not of their choice.

'Tomorrow, Missy, what is first class?'

'You'll be going into English with Mr Sugar to study Romeo and Juliet.'

'That's Shakyspeary,' Alban called out triumphantly. 'We read story in Albanian. Two families they fighting and Romeo and Juliet died.'

'Where did you read it?'

'Refugee centre.'

'Excellent.'

Ella was relieved that someone at the centre knew what they were doing.

The notes sent to the school from the Refugee Centre revealed that Alban Nebihu and Ilir Ahmeti were classified as orphans of Albanian extraction who were the only survivors of genocidal massacre in a village near Pristina in Kosovo. The teenagers had escaped because they had been hiding in the forest smoking forbidden cigarettes. Further details of the atrocity had been withheld. The two boys, it was stressed, were inseparable and had walked for days until they had found a column of refugees escaping to Macedonia.

Ella Fonseca and her colleague Justine Samuels didn't need to be told to avoid all mention of the recent past, but there was no way that they could stop the youngsters from talking about their experiences if they wanted to.

Meantime Ella was helping Alban and Ilir to acquire the basic language, social and practical skills to survive in a rowdy comprehensive school.

'You call a male teacher Sir and a female teacher Miss (not Missy) and, if you want to speak, put your hand up and wait.'

'Thank you Miss.'

'Hokay Miss.'

'Fine. Now here are your timetables. The teachers have given us the lesson plans so we know what to prepare for and you will be in all the lessons together. Is that okay? And Miss Samuels or I or perhaps another helper will be with you but we're sorry we don't have an assistant who speaks Albanian.'

Ilir dipped into his crumpled Tesco bag which acted as his schoolbag and pulled out a small, tattered dictionary. 'This one has the same A B C as English but more letters.'

'Thirty six letters,' Alban was proud to add.

'Good. That will help. I think there is a big Albanian-English dictionary in that cupboard too. Now, the second lesson is Geography with Mrs Bernstein. Did they teach you any Geography at the centre?'

'We got words. Wait.' Alban dug into a blue plastic bag and brought out a cheap, but neat plastic folder stuffed with A4 sheets of paper. 'Look, many Geography words.'

There were five pages of key words for Geography listed in alphabetical order, from atlas to continent, capital city, mountain, river, town and winter to (so X, Y and Z could be used perhaps,) xenophobia (insensitively) Yugoslavia and Zambia. Alban had found the Albanian translation for most of them.

'It's map reading tomorrow,' Mrs Fonseca said reaching for two folded copies of OS Map 145, the area south of London around the Surrey Hills that Victoria Bernstein, Head of Geography had asked Ms Fonseca in E2L, now changed to EAL, to familiarise the two Kosovar boys with. One look at Alban and Ilir's bemused expressions confirmed that the lesson had to begin with a simple world map pinpointing Pristina, capital of Kosovo and London, capital of England and outlining their journey via Macedonia to Heathrow

119

which, sadly, was not on the intimidating OS map and had, in fact, been their point of entry to UK.

The boys seemed to understand latitude and longitude and soon grasped the concept of grid references. They were desperate to learn and driven on by what felt, to Ella, like hunger and anger. Teacher and pupils romped through key words for the Science and Maths lessons for the next day.

'That's enough for now,' Ella said.

'No we want internet. You got internet?' Alban asked and the two boys looked at each other. 'No internet at the centre. We never see in England.'

'We can try but it doesn't always work.'

'Try, try.'

Ella put this down to boyish eagerness to play so set them up on her pride and joy, a purple Apple i Mac with off line games on the desktop.

They seemed to know more about computers than she did, so Ella left them to it while she got on with some admin.

Silence reigned for a while. Eventually Ilir called out.

'Miss, see our village.'

Images of atrocities, dozens of them, were invading the serenity of the room that Justine and Ella had worked so hard to create. There would be no reminders of trauma. Instead, there would be a comfortable and comforting ambience with a reading corner with graded readers for easy access to EAL pupils, charts, pictures, writing and drawing materials, background music, videos or carefully selected TV programmes – but no reminders of war zones.

Now, the room seemed to be full of pictures of blood and body parts and Alban and Ilir were consumed with morbid curiosity, unable to take their eyes off the screen, willing her to share their pain, or was that excitement?

'These pictures are after all the beating and shooting. They no see soldiers in blue and green and brown with guns. We see soldiers but we hide,' Alban whispered.

'Cigarette save our life,' Ilir added.

'How?'

'Father say no cigarette smoke so we go in woods and the soldiers came.'

'What did you do after they had left?' Ella asked. From the pictures it seemed obvious that nobody had survived.

'We run. We scared.'

'You didn't check... .' The words evaporated as Ella realised what an awful thing she was about to ask those children – because children they were. 'You did the right thing. It was too dangerous to stay.'

'No, no, no!' Alban shouted. 'Bad thing! Bad. We don't know who alive or dead.'

'And now you want to find out from the internet.'

Ilir began reading, '... eighteen men, women and children were shot... Miss, what does indis ... indiscrim ...mean?'

'Indiscriminately ... without caring about who they were.'

'... believed to be terrorists ...

'Not terrorists, just people,' Alban interjected.

'... no survivors.'

Dejection spread across the faces of the two young boys and their shoulders slumped.

'I'm sorry. You shouldn't have seen those pictures.'

As the afternoon bell rang, Justine Samuels walked in, caught sight of the images and exploded, but not before she had logged off and dismissed the two boys.

'What the Hell do you think you are doing, letting those boys get on to that site? I'm surprised at you.'

'Sorry. I thought they were playing games off line and I took my eye off them for only a minute.'

'Don't you realise... ?'

'Of course I realise it will upset them. And I know I'll have to talk to them tomorrow. And do you know what?' Ella threw in, 'They would have found these pictures somewhere else if they hadn't seen them here. And at least we can talk them through it.'

'Face it Ella, you've stuffed up.' With that, Justine stomped off home, leaving Ella feeling like a worm. She reached for the Refugee Council file to find out who looked after Kosovar orphan refugees in London. There was a local home address for the boys but no name for a guardian which seemed strange. There was a phone number for the Refugee Council. A friendly voice replied.

'Can I help you?'

'I need to get in touch with whoever is looking after Alban Nebihu and Ilir Ahmeti. I'm their teacher at Brentgold School and I'm afraid they found some harrowing information about their home village on the internet. I'm wondering if they are going to react badly.'

'Hold on. I'll put you through to someone on the children's panel. What's your name?'

'Ella Fonseca, their English teacher.'

'Hello, Ms Fonseca? Alban and Ilir's teacher? I hear they might have been upsetting themselves.'

'Yes. They found some horribly graphic pictures of their home village and it was clear that they had run away before they fully realised what had happened to everyone. I didn't know what they were up to. I left them playing games off line.'

'Don't worry. They would probably have found them somewhere else in time. Our policy is to try to protect the children when they're still traumatised but these things happen.'

'Do you think I should warn their guardian?'

'We'll do that. They are being fostered by an Albanian speaking family for the moment – a couple with two small children. Their English is limited which is why they asked that their names be withheld from your school. One of our Albanian speaking volunteers can pay them a visit this evening, making it look as if it's on a casual basis.'

'My line manager is furious with me,' Ella confessed sheepishly.

'Oh dear. Ah well, these kids' reactions are unpredictable. Let's hope Alban and Ilir are tougher than we expect. Our volunteer will have a chat with them tonight and probably waylay the nightmares.

122

Good luck for tomorrow.'

That evening, the images of the atrocities floated in front of Ella's eyes. She couldn't bring herself to share her horror with fifteen year old Molly.

'What's up, Mum?'

'Oh, I can't get the two new Kosovar boys out of my head? I think they must have had a horrible time.'

'That's war,' Ella's blasé teenage daughter said, rather too coldly in her mother's opinion.

'I hope that we, you and I and your dad never have to suffer it.'

'Sorry, Ma.'

Rick noticed his wife tossing and turning in bed and wanted to know why.

'Oh, Rick, you should have seen those pictures. They shouldn't put such stuff on the internet. It's not like it's a cartoon game. These two boys might have seen their family all chopped up in bits. It was horrible.'

Rick and Ella cuddled up together like two spoons, he trying to lull his troubled wife to sleep, she desperately trying to conjure up pictures of warm tropical beaches to block out the blood spattered pile of limbs and a severed head. Whose head was it? She hoped not that of one of either Alban or Ilir's loved ones.

Next morning, Alban and Ilir breezed into the first lesson, which was on Romeo and Juliet, seemingly without a care in the world. A form member had given them directions.

'Hi Miss, we sit near you?'

'That's right. I'll come in a minute when I have a word with Mr Sugar, your English teacher.'

'We have two new pupils, Alban and Ilir, today,' Harvey Sugar began. 'Welcome. Can anyone tell the story of Romeo and Juliet so far for them?'

'S'okay, sir. We hear two families fighting and Romeo and Juliet dead. We understand. Thank you.'

123

'Well, that was a bit of a spoiler, but very good, Ilir. Now can we have some more detail? We need to slow down. Okay?'

'Yessir.'

Ella issued a copy each of a picture story version of the play to Alban and Ilir, surrounded by key words such as: Romeo MONTAGUE and Juliet CAPULET, Verona, feud, masked ball, young love ... The boys were soon engrossed in the adventure of reading a Shakespearean play about two fighting families in Italy. There appeared to be no trace of the trauma, the expected result of the carelessness of Ella allowing access to the internet.

Ella sought out Justine at break time to report her attempts at damage limitation and the apparent lack of distress displayed by Alban and Ilir.

'You aren't trying to tell me they haven't been affected, are you?' Justine snapped.

'Of course not, but I *am* saying they're probably more resilient than we think. I didn't let them on to the internet deliberately, you know. I just didn't realise how clever they were on computers. As the guy at the Refugee Council said, they were bound to find these reports sooner or later, especially as they were so desperate to find out more about what had happened.'

'Anyway, we'll have to watch them.'

The days went by and lessons progressed, with the two Kosovar boys soaking up all the language and facts they possibly could with an eagerness bordering on obsession. The less willing boys, used to slouching and skiving, were beginning to allow their jaws to drop in awe. One or two were plotting revenge. They started to take advantage of Alban and Ilir's desperation to learn. Before long, Wayne, Damien and Jake had taught their new friends, Alban and Ilir every foul swear word they could think of without telling them their use was unacceptable in certain situations.

One such situation was in a Geography lesson.

'Miss,' Alban was heard to say to delicate, elderly Mrs Bernstein. 'What's a fuckeen beetch?'

'Who taught you that?' she managed after a sharp intake of breath.

'I'm so sorry Mrs Bernstein. He really doesn't know what it means. The other boys must have taught him that.'

'Well take the two of them away to wherever you teach them proper English or something resembling it!'

Ella decided she wasn't quite so fond of the not quite so delicate Mrs Bernstein she had been used to. 'Come on, you two; let's go to homework club early.'

'Miss, why you laugh?'

'I'm not laughing.'

'I think you laugh.'

Back in the safety of the EAL Department, Ms Fonseca began the delicate task of teaching her two Kosovar pupils the meanings of all the new B, F and C words and W, it turned out, they had acquired and where, when and in front of whom they should not be used.

'Oh no, Miss. I asked Mr Sugar what a fuckeen wanker was.'

'And what did he say?'

'You.'

'Me?' Ella mischievously asked.

'No, no, no, not you miss; me,' an embarrassed Alban said; 'but he was not angry; he laughing too.'

'He was laughing because he wanted to show you he knew it was not your fault – but please don't use those swear words. They are very bad and make people angry. Only stupid people use them all the time. Sometimes silly people use them when they can't think of a better word. Oh S...ugar, that's my last pen and it's run out.' Ella said.

'Did you nearly say shit, miss?'

'I did, but I was too polite to say that in front of my young pupils.'

'Thank you Miss.'

'Now. It's time for your Geography homework. Let's show Mrs Bernstein how good you are.'

'She not laughing,' Alban said.

'No, she wasn't laughing. Repeat after me; she wasn't laughing.'

'She wasn't laughing,' the boys repeated in unison.

Ella made sure that they drew the best, most neatly labelled climate graphs possible to appease the offended Mrs Bernstein. Such are the tasks of an EAL Not Quite English Teacher in a London Comprehensive School.

Sometimes the careful teaching backfires.

'Miss Miss, come quickly. There's a big fight on the field. I think it's the new boys havin' a pop at Jake and Damien and Wayne I think.'

'Go and find Mr Simons, quickly, or anyone like him,' Ella shouted, naming the biggest, youngest, toughest male teacher she could think of before heading for the field and wading into the middle of the fray. Luckily the shock of seeing a pint sized female teacher stopped all five boys in their tracks.

'He punched me Miss,' wailed Jake.

'He called me a .... I can't say it Miss. You told us not to.'

'Ah. What did you say Jake?'

'He called them effen wankin bees miss,' a snitching bystander piped up,' but he thought they didn't understand it and he was laughing at them.'

'And why did you all start punching each other? How stupid is that?'

'Miss, Alban and Ilir were really mad, Miss. We had to fight back.'

'Well they now understand all the swear words, Jake, and you shouldn't be insulting them. It's really not funny. I'll see you three outside my room in two minutes. Alban and Ilir, come here. You must never hit anyone, no matter what they say to you.' The utter futility of such an order in the wake of the atrocities these poor boys had witnessed and survived, struck home, so Ella added, 'Here at Brentgold School, just like it is wrong to swear, it is wrong to hit people.'

'Sorry Ms Fonseca. We angry.'

'Mary,' said Ms Fonseca addressing the snitch. 'Take Alban and Ilir to Mrs Bloke and get those cuts cleaned and a plaster put on.'

'Yes, miss.' Mary was the kind of girl Ella knew would be happy to help and get one up on the three rogues, Wayne, Damien and Jake. Perhaps she wasn't the most popular girl in school but today she would feel useful.

The three rogues weren't so easy to handle. They had turned up outside her room but were still in an aggressive mood.

'That Alban hit Jake for no reason. We were only joking.'

'If I had a pound for every time I've heard, "I was only joking" I'd be rich. I don't want to hear you've been calling these boys names. They've lost their families and they are in a new, scary country. You should be helping them.'

'Are they orphans Miss?'

'Yes.'

'That's bad. I'm sorry,' Wayne said.

'Why did they have to come here though?' Jake added.

'Shut up, you wan... idiot.'

'Thank you Damien. Now sit here and write an incident report for your Year Head and think about how all this happened. It wasn't Alban and Ilir's fault was it?'

'No, Miss.'

Next morning there was a note from Barry Latimer, the Head in Ella's pigeon hole in the staff room. *'Please come and see me during break when you have a moment. B. Latimer.'*

Eventually, after coping with a hundred and one essential tasks, Ella tapped on the door of the ivory tower.

'Mrs Fonseca. Sit down. I hear you intervened during a fight yesterday. I don't think that was a good idea. I expect the younger male teachers to handle such situations.'

'But they were my boys and I felt sure they would respond to me rather than someone else and I felt I could understand their explanation. The fight stopped as soon as I got there.'

'You were lucky, this time. Please don't ever get involved again. Is that clear?'

'It wasn't luck, Mr Latimer. And I had to stick up for the Kosovar boys.' She didn't add that she was the one who had taught them to understand all the swear words which had made the boys lose their tempers. She suspected there might be a lack of sense of humour in her boss's attitude. 'However, I'll take your advice – if it ever happens again.'

'Can you wait, please? I've asked John Russell to come along.'

John Russell was Head of Year 9 and responsible for Alban and Ilir; he was also one of Ella Fonseca's allies in the current situation of rising numbers of refugee children appearing in classrooms to the annoyance of some mainstream teachers but fortunately providing a welcome challenge to the more robust and optimistic teachers.

'I can't imagine what's happened to him … ah here he is.'

'Morning, Mr Latimer. Well done for yesterday Ella. I doubt if anyone else could have diffused the situation so quickly.'

'Thank you, John.'

A grateful glance from Ella showed John he had taken the wind out of the Head's sails and established the truth of what Ella had been saying.

'About the punishment for these five boys, two of them from Kosovo I believe,' the Head began with emphasis on Kosovo.

'Yes. After reading all the incident reports, I've decided they should have break and lunch time detentions for the rest of the week.'

'Can I add something to that please, John?' Ella asked.

'Sure.'

'I want them all to come to after school Homework Club. There are a few bridges they need to cross, with some help.'

'Are you sure…?'

'Great idea,' John interrupted before the Head Teacher could pour cold water on the plan.

'I'll leave it in your hands Mr Russell,' was the Head's parting comment, leaving Ella feeling more like a not quite teacher than a Not Quite English teacher. She swallowed her umbrage and stomped off to her next class muttering, 'I'll show him,' under her breath.

It was a Maths lesson and Alban and Ilir were stars, now that they had mastered the necessary vocabulary to get on with it. Ella was helping Salim, a small Somali boy who had barely mastered the alphabet or the numbers 1 – 100. He was in class, doing different work with pictures and diagrams so that he could feel what it was like to be in a classroom and learn how to behave. Salim had missed out on school completely but he was anxious to learn. Copying his letters and numbers was a necessary task he had to master and the other pupils who were mastering the intricacies of Pythagoras understood this. Ella was also there to help with the odd difficulty that her Kosovar stars encountered. As she watched them outstrip the others in the class and move on to extension exercise, an idea struck her, for later.

As the five boys, the three English boys unwillingly, crawled into Homework Club after the last lesson of the day, Ella was armed with her jar of sweets. Experience had taught Justine and Ella that pupils new to English were collapsing with exhaustion by the end of the school day and needed a little boost.

'Come in. Would you like healthy squash or water? We don't do coke or anything sugary here, but you can have one sweet for extra energy.'

Refreshments over, there was still a strained silence. Jake's cut above his eyebrow was healing but he had a significant black eye. Alban too had a shiner and an incriminating set of bruises and scars on his right knuckles. The others seemed to have very few light bruises despite the fisticuffs.

'Right. This is what we're going to do: twenty minutes of how to ask questions and twenty minutes doing your Maths homework for Miss Ali. I want you to make up and write down ten questions you could ask each other, real questions about things you want to find out about each other. Then, you must ask them. Jake, Wayne and Damien, if Alban and Ilir get their words wrong, please teach them the right words. When you finish, you are all going to tell me two things you have learned about each of the other four boys. Do you understand?'

'Yes Miss.'

'Okay Miss.'

'How I ask where his house?' Ilir began.

'Don't ask me. Ask one of the boys.' Ella said going over to put the kettle on in the adjoining office. She'd have a welcome cup of tea if she was going to be a fly on the wall. It was a fascinating eavesdrop.

'Where your house?' Ilir tried.

'No, you have to say "Where *is* your house? or What's your address?' was Jake's reply.

'Yes,' was Ella's silent response as she punched the air.

'Hokay. Where IS your house?'

'I live in Green Street, near the school. Where do you live?'

'With an Albanian family in Abercorn Road.'

'That's near Green Street.'

'I know. I walk there to school. I don't see you.'

'Why do you live with an Albanian family?'

'They speak my language.'

'Where's your family?'

'Dead.'

'Oh, I didn't know. … I'm sorry.'

'Me too but that's war. Alban no family too.'

'Say "Alban has no family either".'

'But what means either?'

'Ms Fonseca. Can you help me here?' Jake was now involved. Similar conversations were developing in all directions within the group, and barriers were crumbling. Before long, the boys were making plans to play football in the park at the weekend, but falling short of inviting each other to their homes. A step too far as yet.

'Now, I want to hear about the things you found out about each other.'

Wayne, he like Arsenal,' Alban kicked off.

'Wayne likes Arsenal. Everyone, say "Wayne likes Arsenal".'

'Wayne likes Arsenal,' the five boys said in unison.

'Now Alban, say "Wayne likes Arsenal".'

'Wayne likes Arsenal.'

'Good.'

'Jake and Damien likes ManU,' Ilir continued.

'Aaw, Miiiiiss,' groaned Jake. Pause for an "I like, you like, he, she or it likes, we like, you like, they like" lesson.

'We all like football,' Damien called out. 'Alban likes fish and chips but Ilir likes McDonald's.'

'Wonderful!' Ms Fonseca shouted.

'Damien's mother is a hairdresser.'

'Alban's dad was a postman but he's ...,' Jake began,

'Lost in the war - like my family too - everyone in our village,' Ilir finished off, sparing this new friend, an English boy who was beginning to understand the trauma the Kosovars were going through.

Ella spotted a small tear trickling down Jake's face before a quick shirt sleeve wiped it surreptitiously. No one commented.

'Maths homework now and then we can all go home.' Ella had noticed that the two Kosovar boys had finished the task half way through the lesson earlier that day and that the other three had been struggling.

'Miss, I did it.'

'Me too.'

'Oh really. I didn't know,' she lied. 'Then you can help the others. Deal?'

'What means deal?'

'What   does   deal   mean?   Say   that.' Within minutes, Alban and Ilir had sorted out the homework for Jake, Damien and Wayne and it was all done, dusted and neatly written out.

'I didn't know they were so clever Miss,' Damien whispered.

'Well, now you do.'

Then the most surprising, unexpected thing happened. Away from the eyes of the crowd of peers and the street cred that had to be maintained, a very different Jake said, 'Group hug,' and soon, with a bit of gesticulation and demonstration, there was a five boy hug in progress. 'You too Miss,' Jake said so she joined them. How she wished Mr Latimer, the cynical head teacher had been doing his rounds at this point. Justine, working with some Chinese girls in

131

another corner of the room, had, however, witnessed this little triumph. Ella knew that day why she loved her job.

Come February, a new duet was added to Brentgold International Evening for the Year 2000. Alban and Ilir had got a hold of a *çifteli* (an Albanian lute) and some *gajde* (hessian bagpipes) and had belted out a lively Albanian folk tune they had learned in their childhood and perfected with the help of the Albanian refugee population in London.

Olga, from Sarajevo, now a leading light in Year 13, was proud to both compère the evening and play Mozart's violin sonata number 18 in G major, accompanied on the piano by her new, young Music teacher who couldn't believe his luck in finding such a talented violinist in his A level class.

'Pinch me, Molly,' Ella told her daughter after they got home. 'Is this really happening to those kids who had lost all hope?'

'There's always hope, Mum and I love you loads.'

Ryo and Harry Potter

Brentgold, 2000

Ryo Miyazaki arrived at Brentgold Comprehensive in perfect uniform, a brand new leather satchel strapped on his back and newly polished shoes. He had a well-equipped pencil case, a new notebook, a state of the art electronic translator and a copy of *Harry Potter and The Philosopher's Stone* in Japanese, the latter a present from his grandmother. Everyone knew it was *Harry Potter and the Philosopher's Stone,* although they couldn't read the title in Japanese, because it had the same pictures on the cover.

In form time, as he waited for the register to be called, he laid all these items out on his desk in a neat pattern and then concentrated hard on reading his book. His head was moving almost imperceptibly up and down

'He's going backwards and up and down,' Tanya Brown said to her best mate Tracy Williams.

'That's what they do in China, stupid.'

Ryo was a perfect student and nothing was going to deflect him from what he was doing. The other mere mortals in his form were in awe of this automaton, impressed by the way he quickly referred to his electronic translator when a word puzzled him. They had never seen such a machine – and neither had Ms Fonseca, the teacher who would be given the responsibility of persuading this boy to integrate with his fellow human beings.

The most admired possession of his was, without a doubt, his copy of *Harry Potter and the Philosopher's Stone* in Japanese; the fourth Harry Potter book *Harry Potter and the Goblet of Fire* was the latest fashion accessory to be held in the hands of any self-respecting teenager. Further investigation revealed that not everyone who sported the tome had read much beyond Chapter One of the first Harry Potter. However they had joined their friends to queue from midnight for the bookshops to open on July 8th and could talk the talk after listening to their more literary classmates who had actually finished reading all the books. Perhaps some would get around to reading them all eventually. Hats off to J. K. Rowling for firing the imagination of a generation!

Ryo, with his eyes forward at all times, seemed unaware of the effect he was having on his peers. Or was he? After a few 'withdrawal' EAL lessons, which seemed to be working, Ella was coming to the conclusion that the Dalek act was a defence mechanism. He was a frightened little boy, short for his age, thirteen, and eager to please his teachers and be accepted by his peers. Hence the exemplary behaviour and his Harry Potter book.

A day came when Ryo announced that he had finished reading the Japanese version of *Harry Potter and the Philosopher's Stone* and please could he read it in English with some help. Now, *there* was a challenge for Ella Fonseca. 223 pages of unabridged English, packed full of classical allusions and very English humour.

Naturally, the English Department had ordered two sets of the first book to be used as a set reader in Years 7 and 8. The opportunity of cashing in on the media hype to get reluctant readers on the path to literacy was too good to miss.

How, thought Ella, could this book possibly be made accessible to EAL pupils? She decided she'd have to volunteer to take on a MAPS project. Ryo, though not fluent in English, was very much a MAP, a Most Able Pupil and, as every teacher knows, there is no better teacher of a youngster than another youngster. She sent out a circular on yellow paper, rolled up and tied with a thin red ribbon.

Hogwarts School of Witchcraft and Wizardry(Circa 1000 A.D.)

Headmaster: Professor Albus Dumbledore

Postal Address: Ask the Owls

July 14th 2000

Dear Potter Potty People at Hendon School,

Have you escaped from Muggleworld yet again and drunk your fill from "The Goblet of Fire"? And do you think J.K. Rowling's fourth Harry Potter book should have won the Carnegie Medal instead of Aidan Chamber's "Postcards from No Man's Land"? (must be good.)

Or do you still have to find out how You - Know - Who managed to scare poor old Frank Bryce to death, or what happened at the Quidditch World Cup - or even just what that Goblet of Fire is?

Wherever you are in Muggleworld or the World of Wizardry, get on the Hogwarts Express at Platform 9 and 3 quarters (sorry Apple Macs don't type fractions) and come along to Room E8 at 3:30 on Wednesday July 19th (TWO DAYS BEFORE THE HOLIDAYS - YES !!!) and help to plan a/some FUN project(s) for next term when you'll be in YEAR 9. This would be quite a good time to get involved before you have to think about your Owl -Levels in Years 10 and 11.

Some ideas so far:

- Animation of a scene - Don Breach knows an expert he can contact.

-Your own tabloid edition of "The Daily Prophet" with News articles, ads.(..self-stirring collapsible cauldrons e.g.) Sports coverage(Quidditch?), cartoons, letters to the Editor, recipes (Every Flavour Beans maybe?) and spells (Petrificus Totalus for instance?), puzzles (..the 7 differently -shaped bottles?) Interviews with characters (e.g, Hagrid) an obituary - who's going to die? ++ much, much more. (Can we get in touch with someone in the REAL newspaper world - for help with printing perhaps?)

-Laminated posters and collages illustrating characters and scenes - there is so much scope for this.

Most important YOUR IDEAS - Please come and share them.

Your Muggleworld correspondent,

Come - and -find -out -Who.   P.T.O. >>>>

HOLIDAY COMPETITION

Who, what or where are these in any of the four Harry Potter books?-(Someone's put a muddling spell,

WHO?

WHIDEG   - cheaper than a stamp _____

YRENAL SHEELDAS CINK alias RIS SLOCHINA ED YSIMM-GRINNPOOPT
                                    - hasn't slept for 400 years

RINEHOME RAGGERN - character based on J.K. Rowling herself

LUDDEY SLURDEY - no knickerbockers are big enough for him

CUBBAKEK HET PIGFOPHIRF - can fly - surprisingly

RIS LOPPERRY PETACIDATED - MOOPERD - someone finished the job.

NOR SLEEWAY

CARDO FOAMLY

WHAT?

ETHCOLOCA GORFS _____ _____

ILISITYINVIB ALOCK -handy when you're in trouble

WORG OYRU NOW STRAW TIK - why? - one might ask

PHOSPHORLIES' NOSTE - has the Midas touch

HET STRONGI THA - shouts, "Hufflepuff!"

PUCAT SCARDION - a password

POXTECE SNAPROUT - essential spell for survival

BIMSUN WOT UNTHOADS - top quality - Harry had one until it was broken.

GRUNTSTARFIONIA - highly dangerous. forbidden but lots of fun.

NOT - GOUNTE - FEEFOT - just the thing for horrible cousins

WHERE?

GONADI YELLA - not exactly Brent Cross

HET KALEY DRAULNOC - not what it sounds like

FRYGINDORF WROTE - home to a ghost?

SHUFLOIR DAN STOLB - a bookshop

TEH BORFDENDI STROFE - where you can find centaurs and unicorns

DONKEYSHUE - can find every flavour beans here

VIPERT VERDI - not a happy or exciting place to be

HET DIDLER SHUEO - very scarey

AND IF YOU'RE MOONERISM SPAD TRY THESE

The Pally Drophet: Cagman and Brouch: The Foblet of Gire: Padam Womfrey: Bringotts Gank:
Sklast ended Brewt:

   and in 2 clicks of a mouse you can be transported to Hogwarts -

         www.bloomsbury.com/harrypotter

I would like to write something for 'The Daily Prophet'

Name_____ Form_____ Date_____

136

Ella had advertised the project as a Harry Potter project for the new Year 9s, rather than a MAPS project, because exclusivity to the school's perception of the most intelligent 10% of children stuck in her throat.

Predictably young Ryo was the first to hand in his perfect sheet, BEFORE the holidays, but was wrestling with the concept of 'picking the winner from a sorting hat'. First come, first served was more in his line, especially as he had been first; Ella decided to give a giant bar of chocolate as a special prize for the first one in. Nobody minded, although somebody suggested it wouldn't be fair if Ryo's name was also put in the hat.

The fifteen other enthusiasts bar two, were from the MAPS group so perhaps the school vetting system was 80% accurate. Ella was pleased they turned out to be a multinational group by origin: English, Ethiopian, Ghanaian, Hong Kong Chinese, Indian, Iranian, Irish, Israeli, Japanese, Malawian, Malaysian, Pakistani, Scots and Zambian, with some mixed origins here and there. This supported Miss Fonseca's pet theory that migration and the widening of the gene pool must ultimately lead to an improved and harmonious world so she was content. Luckily there were 8 boys and 8 girls which took care of the gender balance.

'Miss, have you finished Goblet?'

'Yes, I spent all day Sunday reading it, but my favourite's still Chamber.'

'But mine's still Philosopher, Miss.'

'Don't you hate Dudley Dursley, Miss?'

'Who's Dudley Dursley?' a young pretend fan dared to say.

'Duh? Have you even read the first one Dude?'

'Yea, course I have. I just forgot.'

Ms Fonseca added that she was sure everyone in the group would have finished reading all four books over the holidays or they wouldn't be real fans, would they?

'No Miss. Can we have a cartoon competition to see who can draw their favourite character?'

'Great idea, Sophie, and the best ones can be published in our very own Brentgold '*The Daily Prophet*'. What do you all think?'

'I'd do Nearly Headless Nick.'

'Mine's Fluffy the three-headed dog.'

'We could write recipes for Every Flavour Beans...'

'Yea, vomit flavour...'

'Or bogey flavour... '

'Eeuch...!'

'What about making up spells?'

'Or advertising magic wands, like the Nimbus 2000?'

'Or grow your own warts kit?'

'Yuk.'

Finally, Ryo relaxed as he was swept along by the enthusiasm of his age mates and even volunteered his own suggestion.

'I think we can write down the rules for Quidditch.'

'Good idea Ryo,' Joshua the unelected but natural leader of the group said. Ryo was accepted.

The welcome summer break arrived along with its sighs of relief and very long lies for a few days, before the Fonseca family packed for a hot holiday in Crete with two other families. Molly, in between swims, eating and nights out, was going to try to read the first Harry Potter, she said. She'd been busy keeping up with GCSE preparation being a practical, hardworking sixteen year old but she was mildly interested in what all the fuss was about. Even her dad had enjoyed 'Philosopher'. And it must be good, she reckoned, if they were planning to make a film of it.

'I don't get it Mum. I can't be bothered with all this magic crap.'

'Oh well, you either love Harry Potter or hate him, it seems. It's not as if you don't like reading.'

'I'm going to finish my *Beth*. I want to read about something that really might happen.'

'Oh really, you reckon Colin Frith might sweep you off your feet?'

'You know what I mean. I'm just not a fan of fantasy.'

'Well now fancy that,' her mother said with a wry but indulgent smile. Molly had watched Pretty Woman, Dirty Dancing and the TV version of Pride and Prejudice at least a dozen times each. She'd also read *Beth* a couple of times; it was another rags to riches story with a happy ending.

So, in between swims, meals and excursions, Ella spent time re reading *Philosopher* and having fun planning her little MAPS project, mainly from Ryo's point of view as she knew the others would fly on their own.

September came and so did a new, enthusiastic, deputy head, a woman called Louisa Fenton. She'd been in America and had seen the 'amazing' technology in the schools which had yet to reach London. She was also keen on stretching gifted pupils and showed an interest in Ella's Harry Potter Project.

'Have a look at this, Ella. If you think it might be of interest, I'll get some funding for your MAPS.' Mrs Fenton handed Ella an envelope with details of a trip for 10 to 19 year olds to experience a journalist's day and have a look around West Ferry printers in the Isle of Dogs

'This sounds brilliant. Thank you, Mrs Fenton.'

'Louisa, please.'

A long year of breaking into new technology had begun at Brentgold Comprehensive. Ella and her MAPS were controversially in the centre of it as there was some resistance to the change – and the cost.

The NET or Newspaper Education Trust sounded exciting so the New Year 9 MAPS couldn't wait to go. Voluntary contributions for travel were collected and the school would cough up funds for the rest. The English department had been approached as both Harry Potter and Year 9 Media Studies for SATs were part of their syllabus.

'Nothing but a junket,' Harvey Sugar had carped, hanging on to his money. The cash had therefore been unearthed from a Year 9 special projects' fund. The Year Head was none too pleased until Ella promised to get the MAPS to involve the others in their forms as far as possible.

Wednesdays after school were the times to get ready to become real life journalists through a crash course prepared by NET in conjunction with those who had prepared the syllabus for Year 9 Media Studies. They would soon be armed with the jargon and some of the skills. The lack of experience with modern computer equipment was going to be a handicap. There was one boy, Amit, who had all the stuff at home and knew exactly what to do with it. Luckily he was a Harry Potter fan; he was appointed chief advisor.

'This is NOT a junket; it's going to be tough,' Ella muttered under her breath.

Sixteen Harry Potter fans and two teachers set off from Brentgold Centre Tube Station at 07:10 hours instead of 07:00 hours. Only one student, Kazimba, was late. As the son of an ambassador, he was also the richest. The others were furious as the word from NET was that there were five hours to deadline and they would need every second. Kaz had the good grace to be disarmingly apologetic.

'I had to stop to get some newspapers like you asked, Miss.' In his arms he had a Sun, Daily Mail, Daily Express and Times. 'My dad bought them.'

The others quickly picked up a Metro from the pile outside the station and some said they had a free local paper in their bags.

Nobody had been on the Docklands Light Railway so that was adventure number one.

'It's like we're travelling through the air without a driver, Miss.'

'I've never sat right at the front of a train.'

'What happens if anything goes wrong?' But of course, it didn't.

Number two adventure was the walk through the strange modern blocks around the water's edge in The Isle of Dogs to reach West Ferry Printers. This was a far cry from the terraces, semis and detached houses in leafy North London.

'People seem to be living in big boxes,' Vandna observed. 'I can't see where they put their cars.'

'Underground car parks,' bright spark Eliot informed everyone.

140

'How weird are these statues?'

'They're not statues; they're old cranes, stupid.'

'Well, they're quite beautiful all painted black – just like a modern statue,' Ella piped up in defence of the little girl who had been so rudely crushed. Some MAPS could be arrogant.

'Wow! Is that where we're going?' A huge building, with gigantic newspaper titles beaming forth had appeared on the horizon as the group trudged beyond a tall block. 'It's huge!'

'It *is* the biggest printers in Europe and as you can see, several of our biggest newspapers are printed here,' Ella pontificated, glad to be able to tell these Smart Alecks something they might not know. 'If you want to print your own *Daily Prophet,* this is the place to learn how.'

'You'd think they'd save some electricity on those neon signs in the daylight,' Suzy, the group's little eco-warrior, volunteered.

Enthusiasm not dampened by that criticism, the young journalists began running to the glossy main entrance, their two teachers scurrying to keep up.

'Sorry guys,' an officious doorman was telling the front runners, 'but you need a press pass to get in this door. You have to go to the left and round the back.'

Tucked away to the left and round the back was a door where a camera man was taking photographs of everyone.

'We'll be printing your *NET journalist* badges in a minute, when you've decided on Editors and Sub Editors. Hurry up. There's no time to waste.'

'Group meeting in five minutes,' Sarah-in-charge-of-the-day announced. 'We're running a little late.'

'Your fault Kaz,' someone muttered.

Right we have ten computers, one scanner, one digital camera, one printer and one photocopier. All 16 of you will be expected to produce your own front page on Microsoft Publisher, to include Masthead or Title, strap line or puff, a lead story with headline picture and caption, a secondary lead, your own photo and by-line, a display ad and a table of contents.

'Wha a a t?'

'I presume you're all familiar with Microsoft Publisher…'

'Er… no o.'

'Some of us are,' Amit shouted out. 'I can troubleshoot.'

'Good!'

'Don't forget what, where, when, who and why for your lead story?'

'You can help each other in pairs or work alone but you must be finished by 11:15 hours. Any questions?'

'Where do we find our stories?'

'Today's papers or breaking news on the internet; there's no TV here.' Sarah's brisk manner had sharpened up the young journalists and they were launched. 'You'll have to take turns with the equipment. If you can't have a computer, have your photograph taken or write up your story by hand, ready to type, or look for a story in one of these internet printouts or the newspapers you've brought along. Go, go go.'

Luckily, Ella was able to share a computer with Ryo 'to provide EAL access,' as the jargon went, and he had chosen his lead story from The Metro which was about square melons and included a picture. It wasn't exactly world news but it was quirky and would do.

Task one for Ryo was to choose a name: he typed in DAILY PROFIT in Old English Text capitals.

'Shouldn't that be ph rather than f?' Ella asked.

'No miss. It will be financial newspaper not magician paper. Square melons in story cost 10,000 yen each. That's about £50, I think.' Ryo said, succeeding in missing out all the definite and indefinite articles in true far eastern style.

'I thought the story was a joke.'

'No, miss. Japanese farmer grew melons in glass boxes so they are easy to put in fridges.'

'Fine. You write the story but don't forget 'a' and 'the' where you need them. And answer the what, who, where, when and why questions.'

'Hokay Miss.'

'Sarah,' precocious Eliot yelled out, '

'I found a great ad for Professor Snape's potion lab with self-stirring wands.'

'Really?'

'Yea, you can get it at Toys R Us. Can I use it? There's a picture too.'

'Go for it.'

'Can I do Xbox?'

'Who's found out about something that has happened today or yesterday?

'Can I write about Mary and Jodie, even though it's old news?' Vandna asked,

'Yes, that's an important story – and we can discuss it later.'

'Can I say what I think about Mary having to die to save Jodie?'

'What *do* you think?'

'The surgeons had to separate them or they'd have both died.'

'Yea,' Eliot butted in, 'but it would have been a natural death. This way Mary was murdered.'

'But without the operation, Jodie would have died – and that's like murder,' Vanda replied.

'Write it Vandna, but think of both sides.'

'Right, Miss.'

The MAPs junior journalists were buzzing. When they had reported on a current event from the daily newspapers and were given the freedom to use any story up to a month old, they flew.

Tewdros, an Ethiopian Orthodox Christian, wrote a piece on the final burial of Haile Selassie, 25 years after his suspected assassination, a subject close to his heart.

Kazimba, son of a Malawi diplomat, covered the lost tribe on the islands of Chisi and Thongwe on Malawi's Lake Chilwa. Of the 2000 inhabitants, many of whom had never visited the mainland, most lived in houses built on reed rafts in mobile stilted fishing villages. Here,

Kaz was proud to report, there was no conflict, only love and unity and that was how it should stay.

Eliot chose to slam the USA for the huge number of birth defects caused by Agent Orange in Vietnam. The dioxin poisoning was affecting the 3rd generation of Vietnamese children and Bill Clinton, on a first visit to Vietnam of an American president, was promising more research. Too late, was Eliot's observation.

Siobhan liked the story of Michael Douglas marrying Catherine Zeta Jones, Akosua, herself an athlete, featured Cathy Freeman, Aboriginal gold medallist, carrying the Olympic flame at the 2000 games in Sydney, Wen Ting delighted everyone with The Lion Dance and Dotting of the Eye competition in Hong Kong and Amit was fascinated by the formation of the new state of Jharkand in India on November 15th, 2000. Other stories included the police foiling the theft of £350 million worth of diamonds from The Millennium Dome, Chancellor Gordon Brown offering concessions to the striking lorry drivers who had crippled the country, demanding a cut in fuel duties and the widespread flooding in England and Wales after days of heavy rainfall.

'Miss,' mused Ruchi.

'Ye..e..s.'

'We'd probably not have bothered with all this stuff if we didn't have to write about it. D'you know that?'

'Well, then it's been a good project.'

'It's wicked.'

'Is that good or bad?'

'It's bad meaning good of course. Don't you know that?' The three adults in the room grinned silently at each other.

Eventually, a lead story and a second story had been completed by all except Ryo, whose EAL status was his excuse, and Amit, who had spent his time rushing around helping his less computer literate classmates.

It was time for a tour of the building to find out how newspapers were actually printed before coming back to finish off putting in picture ads, by-lines and photographs of the journalists which had already been taken by this wonderful new-fangled thing called a digital camera.

Giant rolls of paper which would stretch eight miles from Westferry to Trafalgar Square, enormous digital printers and extra high-speed conveyor belts churning out newspapers had the desired effect. The youthful journalists were awestruck, and then fired with enthusiasm.

Back at their desks, they were rushing to download pictures and checking their articles, cutting words here and adding words there, until they had a finished mini newspaper they could print off and take home to show their families and keep as a reminder of a special, exciting day.

An exciting moment was to be the announcement of the best front page which would be displayed on the NET website, for three whole days, for the world to see. Very few people had had such a privilege. It was Joseph, a popular member of the group. The fact that he was a pupil from the Hearing Impaired Unit was of no relevance; he had produced the best page and everyone agreed.

Ryo was delighted with the A3 colour print of his page. No language errors had been allowed to get through and his picture of square melons was easily the quirkiest.

The happy bunch tumbled home on the DLR and the Northern Line, full of plans for their own version of *'The Daily Prophet'*, à la *'Harry Potter and The Philosopher's Stone'*. It was Friday, November 17th, 2000.

It was one thing to produce a newspaper in a modern office equipped with computers that work, large colour printers, easy access to the internet, a digital camera and people who know how they all work. It was quite another in Brentgold Comprehensive which had very few facilities.

Ella's report, a whole year later began like this: *There were times when I thought this project would never end. So many documents have been produced, so much has happened and so much has disappeared. I used to think that washing machines ate socks but they are nothing compared to computers which devour floppy discs like biscuits and wipe clean hard discs as efficiently as the fussiest of mums.*

When the team of reporters started to plan this edition of 'The Daily Prophet' in 2000, there was no Microsoft Publisher, no colour printer, no scanner and no digital camera in school...

Despite this, the enthusiasm of the Daily Prophet journalists spurred the school on. Someone just needed to say, 'Wouldn't it be great if we had a colour printer?' and hey presto a big box arrived with one colour printer and this was soon followed by the installation of Microsoft Publisher, then a scanner and finally a digital camera, for the entire school to share. However, grappling for control was a problem because the journalists had been saving their articles and pictures on computers which had to be shared with many others, so as often as not, the 'network' chewed up half of the copy.

Flagging spirits almost killed the project but two exciting things happened. Unbelievably, Harry Melling in 8R at Brentgold was going to play the dreaded Dudley Dursley in the Harry Potter movie. He was promptly interviewed for the Year 9 version of *The Daily Prophet*. The second was the local *Brentgold Times* running a series of articles on Ryo reading *Harry Potter* in Japanese and English, the Year 9 *Daily Prophet* project and Harry Melling, the local boy who got the part as a baddie in the film.

Even those Potter Potty People who were beginning to feel they'd got too old for Harry Potter and his antics decided to stick it out, despite the many frustrations. There was a deadline. Get the newspaper out by the time the film was released on November 16th. They'd be making history and Ryo, beside himself with excitement, was going to be part of the whole thing.

Harry Melling, not particularly fat, had to eat lots of chocolate, not that he seemed to mind; toffee crisp was his favourite. Unfortunately, when he tubbied up he had to put up with a bit of ribbing from his more empty-headed classmates, who didn't believe he was actually going to be in a film. They were going to have to eat their words before too long, but by that time Harry's earnings meant he could afford a fee paying school.

The first edition of *The Daily Prophet* for Brentwood School was finally released on November 14th, two days before the release of the film version of *Harry Potter and the Philosopher's Stone;* it was a strange mixture of magic world and Muggle word and of Microsoft publisher and old-fashioned cut and paste and photocopy. Just a few more upgrades in the IT equipment and expertise would have improved the result, but it was still an achievement the Potter fans of Year 9 of 2001 could be justifiably proud of.

Above the masthead The Daily Prophet was The Hogwarts School Coat of Arms with its motto *Drago Dormiens Nunquam Titillandus.* An article on page three explained that every Potter fan knows this means *Never tickle a sleeping dragon* or perhaps *Let sleeping dragons lie* and that the symbols for the four houses at Hogwarts are Gryffindor, a lion, Hufflepuff, a badger, Ravenclaw, an eagle and Slytherin, a serpent. In other words, if you don't know this yet, reader of The Daily Prophet, you are a numpty. More readers for J.K. Rowling.

A letter to the Editor questioned the American use of Sorcerer's stone instead of Philosopher's stone, to which the editor replied that this was ignorance on the part of the Americans who felt that philosophers were boring old dudes and sorcerers were exciting wizards. He said they didn't know there was a real philosopher's stone which turns metals into gold and brings immortality, and J.K. Rowling is a lot smarter than the Americans think.

Ella, Ms Fonseca, still overseeing the project, let that go, despite it perhaps not fostering goodwill across the pond. Besides it was true.

Ryo's diagrams and rules for Quidditch and his advertisements for Nimbus Two Thousand broomsticks, red quaffles and golden snitches took up a double spread and caused a good deal of consternation for the less imaginative non Potter fans who couldn't work out how to play.

'That's just stupid,' some boy said. 'Nobody can fly.'

'But … Oh, never, mind!' Eliot just knew he'd never win over the anti-Harry people – 'with NO imagination,' as he put it.

There were ads for 'Bertie Botts Every Flavour Beans', 'Grow Your Own Warts Kits', 'Flourish and Blotts' bookshop, 'The Leaky Cauldron' pub and 'Self-stirring Collapsible Cauldrons'. Even the sceptics managed a smile or two.

There was a 'Meet the teachers' page, introducing Albus Dumbledore, the headmaster and a long list of very odd teachers.

But it was a character in the 'Meet the Ghosts at Hogwarts' page which caused most hilarity. Sir Nicholas de Mimsy-Porpington, whose head had almost but not quite been chopped off. His alias 'Nearly Headless Nick' became the nickname, pardon the pun, for a rather stern and not always popular deputy head at Brentgold, whose name was Nick Papadopoulos.

The project was complete and thanks were given to everyone involved, all the reporters, especially Vandna for her extra hard work and Amit for his technical help, Matt Nixon for his advice and press coverage, Ms Rogers for IT help, Sarah at NET for making us work so hard and our star, Harry Melling, for giving us the interview. Remember us at Brentgold Comprehensive when you are famous, he was told.

On November 4th, the Brentgold team of reporters didn't make the first world premier of the new film in Leicester Square but by November 16th they had made certain they were near the top of the queue at their nearest cinema. Even some of the unbelievers condescended to go along. By the time they realised that Harry Melling was indeed a star, he had refused to speak to them.

By July 2002, it was time for a confident and bilingual Ryo Miyazaki to go home to Kyoto. His father's business contract in London was over. He left with a promise to read all of the Harry Potter books in English one day, but first he would read them in Japanese. He (or perhaps his mother) bought a beautiful gold bracelet for his teacher, Ms Fonseca, which she has always treasured.

It's highly unlikely that he gave much thought to his old school or teachers or that he realised how much he was part of the history of the dragging of one school into the age of digital printing. Without Ryo, this would have happened anyway, but perhaps not quite so quickly.

Zohra

January 2002

Zohra Massoud was handsome. She seemed too tall and statuesque for her Year 8 class at Brentgold and almost too big for the table and chair she had to sit at. Her high cheekbones, fine nose, cupid-bow mouth and enormous eyes gave her an aristocratic look; in some exotic time and place she might have been a princess. Her parents had brought her, her older brother Zemar and five younger sisters to London from Kabul. It was the beginning of the January term at Brentgold in 2002.

Four months earlier, the world had been rocked by the September 11th attacks on America; everyone could remember exactly where they were when that news broke. However, buried under the Harry Potter fever at school, was the fact that on October 7th, 2001, USA and UK had invaded Afghanistan and, with the help of the Afghan United Front, had launched Operation Freedom as part of the Global War on Terror.

Not everyone was convinced that freedom would be the outcome of foreign intervention. Mr Massoud declared he was an anti-Taliban activist whose life was already constantly in danger so he had set off for London with his wife and family because they wanted their daughters to have 'schooling'. He added that the destabilising effect of the so called 'War on Terror' was very dangerous.

Ella and Mrs Block, the school pupil welfare officer, were given this brief summary of the Massoud family background while interviewing Mr and Mrs Massoud who had applied for the casual entry of their son and daughter to Brentgold Comprehensive, as they were living within the catchment area. Little did Ella know she would find out a great deal more at a later date.

Mr Jawed Massoud was a tall, square-shouldered man with angular features and greying temples; his dark suit was shabbily shiny but he had a proud stance. Mrs Badria Massoud was a large comfortable, maternal woman, dressed in a western style maxi dress; around her shoulders she hugged a warm pashmina to fend off the January chill. Ella thought perhaps she might need to cover her head with it at times.

'My brother has given us a home in the top half of his shop and I have work in the shop. It is not my profession but we must have food,' Mr Massoud said.

'We came to England for the family to be safe. That is all.'

'I understand, Mrs Massoud,' Ella said. 'Do your children speak good English too, like yourselves?'

Mrs Massoud smiled proudly. 'I was a teacher in my young days so I always made sure the children studied every day, even when it was against the Taliban rule. You will find Zemar and Zohra good pupils.'

'I'm sure we will. Now, shall we ask them to join us?'

'But, please, before they come in,' their father added, 'we do not know what to do about religion. We are moderate Muslims and do not want the children to be indoctrinated.'

'We never indoctrinate pupils at Brentgold. We have pupils from all religions in the school, so we help them to learn a little about all the world religions, without asking them to worship any of them. We leave worship to the families. We also explain why people who have no religion can still be good people. Our aim is to teach the pupils to respect the beliefs of others.'

'Will you be in the classes for religion and can you explain this to our children?'

'We will try to make sure that they understand.'

Standard personal questions revealed that the brother and sister had a good level of spoken English and when questioned about their reading, they were able to name *Little Women* and *Treasure Island* on their list, which also included *Romeo and Juliet, Jurassic Park, Animal Farm, Star Wars* and even Jacqueline Wilson's *'The Story of Tracy Beaker'*.

'My goodness, you *are* well read. I'm sure many of your new classmates have not read some of those books.'

'We wanted them to read stories from England and America so

151

they can fit in here.' Mrs Massoud added.

'Right,' said Ella, checking that everything in the form was filled in. 'Country of Origin: Afghanistan: Religion: Sunni Moslem: Mother tongue: Tajiki/Dari. Address: Telephone number: That all seems fine and we have a place in Year 8 for Zohra and in Year 9 for Zemar, starting on Monday. Here are their school passports which tell you about uniform and equipment. If they could spend a day with us in the EAL Department, they can start lessons on Tuesday.'

'I have a selection of school blazers and ties if you would like to try them,' Mrs Block interjected. 'Just until you find time to get organised,' she added quickly as she detected a definite proud lift of Mr Massoud's shoulders.

'Why can't we start on Monday?' Zohra asked.

'We'd like to arrange your timetables, find student mentors to help you, and inform all the teachers that you are coming. You have missed a term's work and will need to catch up. Don't worry, you will soon catch up.'

When Monday morning came, the two Massouds had collected quite a large entourage of Afghan children who had been attending Brentgold for some time. There had been a wedding at the weekend so community links had been established.

'Miss,' Fatima from Year 8 piped up, 'Zohra's like my cousin sister. Can she come in my form, pleeee-ase, Miss?'

'That's up to your Year Head. It depends how many there are in the form.'

'Only 27, Miss. That Chloe girl went to Manchester.'

Zohra did get into Fatima's form and Zemar was placed in a Year 9 form with another boy from Afghanistan. Things were falling into place.

Ella decided to provide some EAL support for Zohra in the RE lessons, not because she needed much language support, but because she remembered her parents' concerns about possible indoctrination. And she was intrigued as she'd never had a chance to help out in RE.

Zohra was sitting beside a very small Irish girl, looking regal and slightly bored. The lesson was aimed at getting the pupils to put themselves on a scale of how religious they were, with the emphasis on all religions and non-religious beliefs having equal status as far as the lesson was concerned.

Young Miss Hadadi, having prepared a lesson especially for Zohra and perhaps Ella, drew a thick line diagonally across the whiteboard, with a cross at the top right corner labelled **fanatically religious** and another cross at the bottom left corner of the board labelled **atheist**. Half way along the line a cross was marked **agnostic**. The class were invited to put their hands up if they wanted to put a cross where they felt they fitted. No one responded. The teacher suggested that one's beliefs are often very private so that was fine.

'But what does atheist mean, or agnostic or fanatically?'

Lesson one for a teacher: never assume that the pupils know something.

After explanations, the class were invited to draw their own line and put a secret cross on it. Most felt able to do this but some hesitated.

Then the class were asked to discuss their decision with a partner and explain why they chose their particular spot on the line.

The discussions were hugely enlightening. Attitudes were revealed and those which smacked of intolerance were gently dismissed as negative and not helpful. The young minds soon cottoned on to what was expected of them.

'I'm definitely atheist. My dad says people who watch Songs of Praise must be really sad.'

'But have you ever watched Songs of Praise? They don't look sad.'

Not that kind of sad, Miss; no I've never seen it. It's when the football's on.'

'Is a humanist an atheist? I'm one of them.'

'How do you know? What does a humanist believe?'

'Well... my granny had a humanist funeral and she liked humans better than gods, she said.'

'I think I'm nearly very religious because the Hindu faith is more a way of life and I like going to The Temple. Have you *seen* that new Mandir in Neasden. It's so... oo... wicked.'

'Me too. I love the stories about Rama and Sita and Krishna and all that.'

'My mum says you're best not to take a chance that there's no Heaven and Hell so you'd better get yerself to Mass and say your prayers.'

'Which church do you go to?'

'Our Lady, ye know, the Catholic church.'

'I'm closer to religious than atheist, I think, but I'm not sure.' Charlie Lee added. 'Some people say Buddhism isn't a religion. Is it? Anyway, it makes people good so that's enough for me.'

Zohra was quiet. Eventually she was persuaded to speak.

'I think I'm religious but not very religious. Sometimes religion causes a lot of fighting and death and the same religion can be different to different people.'

'What's your religion?'

'Islam, but not the one that doesn't let girls go to school and makes women wear burkas. My uncle was assassinated for trying to save Afghanistan from that.'

The name 'Massoud' was ringing alarm bells for Miss Hadadi and Mrs Fonseca so the lesson was quickly moved on.

'So we can see that everyone has different beliefs but these shouldn't stop us from respecting each other's views. Would we agree?

'Yes Miss.'

'Let's see if we can come up with a list of things that everybody can believe in whatever their religion.'

'I know Miss. What about you mustn't kill people?'

'A good example. Now, everyone, write down at least ten things you think we'd all agree were good things to believe in.'

'Like rules, Miss?'

'It's the commandments, innit Miss?'

'Yes, in a way. We could call it a set of rules for everyone in the world.'

Zohra's comment dazzled both her teachers and her classmates.

'You mean we're creating a universal moral code to unite the world.'

'Exactly, Zohra, I couldn't have put it better myself,' Miss Hadadi replied with a mixture of gratitude and awe.

Mr and Mrs Massoud would have no need to worry about their daughter's susceptibility to indoctrination. She was mature beyond her years, no doubt nurtured by her family and influenced by recent events in Afghanistan.

The RE teacher and the EAL teacher both felt that the name Massoud had recently cropped up in the news but couldn't quite remember how.

Ella's colleague, Justine, in the EAL Department was spending time with Zemar in English lessons and reported similar intelligence and maturity. It was decided that beyond requests for help with homework, their new Afghan pupils would need little support.

However, Ella found some needy EAL pupils in Miss Hadadi's RE class to support, which pleased both teachers and meant Ella could keep an eye on Zohra so that she could report back during the next Parent-Teacher evening.

Zohra continued to flourish and soon became a popular member of the Year Group, getting involved in Drama, Music and sports, especially netball where, being tall, she was a star Goal Attack.

But Zohra and Zemar found it difficult to respect their parents' wishes regarding teenage get-togethers. They wanted a social life and were not prepared to stay at home when their peers were having fun.

Mrs Massoud came to school to see what could be done and wanted to see Mrs Fonseca. Ella could only suggest that she trust her daughter, if she really wouldn't listen, as she was a mature, sensible girl.

'I do know how you feel. My daughter Molly is eighteen now and I used to worry about her all the time. I suppose I still do but I trust her.'

155

This wasn't enough for Mrs Massoud and she wanted to be taken to see Mr Dixon, the Year Head.

'I'm sorry, Mrs Massoud,' he said. 'I'm not sure I can help apart from telling her to listen to you. Of course, I'll try to do that. Young people today care more about pleasing their peer group than their elders. Have you thought of asking her brother to influence her?'

'He is the same, wanting to go to parties but he is a boy.'

'Ask him to look after Zohra when they are out. Would that help?'

Mrs Massoud allowed her head to fall from side to side in that Asian shake-cum-nod which simply said, 'Maybe but I'm not sure it will work.'

Mr Dixon and Ella watched sadly as Mrs Massoud drew her pashmina up over her head and shuffled wearily away.

'Wait,' Ella shouted. 'I've thought of something. You live in Golders Green, don't you? When my Molly was fifteen they used to go to a disco there; they served only soft drinks and had lots of adult supervision. Only children under sixteen were allowed to go. Would you like me to find out if it's still going?'

'Maybe,' she said waving her head even more. 'Thank you.' Her shuffle homewards, however, still seemed dejected.

'It must be so hard for these parents to lose control. These kids are rejecting the old ways, left, right and centre,' Craig Dixon observed.

'We can only try and keep them safe,' Ella added. 'Do we know who their mates are? Are there any troublemakers? Let's see how the Junior School Disco goes. Have they got tickets?'

'I'll make sure they're offered them. Can I count on your help?'

'I suppose I can't say no, now. Which day is it?'

Mrs Fonseca was lumbered. She set off for home, reflecting on the past five years of her own Molly's teenage life. She had been tempted to say 'Don't let Zohra out' just as she had wanted to keep Molly inside, protected from the dangers of too much freedom out in the big bad teenage world where it was cool to 'have a spliff' and get up to 'what everybody does'. Whatever.

All was quiet at home with Rick out at work and Molly in her

156

room. She'd be sitting on the floor with her books and papers strewn everywhere making sense of her A-level studies. Safe and sound.

Ella's thoughts turned to Jawed and Badria Massoud who not only had 14 year old Zohra kicking her heels already but also Karima, who was 12, then Lara, Adela, Bano and 4 year old Fareiba. How would they cope? Who could blame them for feeling anxious? No matter how much they opposed the oppression of women by the Taliban, they were bound to be confused and scared by what seemed to be happening all around. The jump from burkas to 'see-level' skirts had to be colossal and the pull of teenage society had to feel too powerful to fight against.

Ella found out that the under sixteen discos were still running, but now went under the name of *The Black Tie Ball Society*. They had representatives in schools, ran coaches to and from venues and insisted on parents meeting their children at the door, or off the coach. The next venue, in Golders Green, was within walking distance of the Massouds' flat so Ella contacted some responsible Year 8s and 9s to form a safe group for Zemar and Zohra to join. The exams were over so she rang their home. Mrs Massoud answered.

'Hello. Mrs Massoud? This is Mrs Fonseca from Brentwood.'

'Oh yes. We are talking about you.'

'I have found a safe place for Zemar and Zorah to meet their friends.'

'I know. Some new friends have come to my house. One boy is from Kabul but he came to London five years ago. They are having tea now. They are nice. My husband will walk to the place and get them after.'

'And are you feeling happier now?'

'Yes, I think it will be ok.'

'Good. I hope they have a lovely time.' All we parents can do is hope for the best, Ella was thinking, but it wasn't the time to say that.

'Thank you, Mrs Fonseca. We'll see you at Parents' Evening.'

'Oh yes. That's next Tuesday. Bye.'

Molly's best friend Holly had a very English name but a Lebanese background and a very strict mum, Soraya. The youngsters had found the same alcohol free under- sixteen disco that Ella had recommended for Zemar and Zohra, with more bouncers than kids in Golders Green. Tickets were affordable so Ella would drive Molly and Holly to the door at eight and Holly's dad would pick them up at midnight. Soraya had to come too. Fine. Most parents dropped their kids off at a non-embarrassing distance away but Soraya just had to jump out too. The queue was particularly long that Saturday night so what did Holly's mum do? She marched up to the door and asked, 'Who's in charge here? The nearest adult was then marched down the queue where she loudly announced, 'This is my daughter Holly and that's her friend Molly. Now you make sure they are all right. Do you hear?'

'We can all hear,' the 'bouncer' said. Later on Holly and Molly reported that he was a moonlighting supply teacher. A big wink at Holly and Molly, when Soraya had left, had made them feel a little less humiliated.

There had been gate crashers at birthday parties, worries about skimpy skirts and practically non-existent tops and the inevitable stress at going out time.

'You are NOT going out looking like that,' Rick would say. 'Where's the rest of your dress? You look like a tart.'

'It's the fashion, Dad. You're so sad.'

'Mother! Aren't you going to back me up? Bloody pelmet.'

'I would if I thought it would make any difference,' Ella would say. 'Please put a jacket on at least, Moll.'

'Don't be silly,' Moll would hiss as she marched out of the front door, but not before Rick had called out, 'Don't forget to ring at midnight to say you're ok.'

'Now that's the daftest idea you've ever had, Rick.'

'Rubbish.'

But it was a crazy idea. Rick and Ella would be sleeping peacefully, in the knowledge that Molly and her three best friends would be taking a taxi together to sleep at Holly's house. They had been happy to promise to do that. Then, a dutiful Molly would ring from a noisy club and shout excitedly over the music, and sometimes squiffily, that she was having a 'wicked' time. That, of course, meant rattled nerves and another sleepless night.

'Please DON'T ring at midnight, Molly,' Ella said one day and watched Rick squirm but stay silent behind his *Sunday Times*.

Then there were the boyfriends, some more suitable than others; the clever ones knew how to talk golf with Rick – but those weren't the boys Molly was interested in. Luckily, Ella thought, she didn't seem to be too obsessed by any of them for long. The time would come soon enough.

Perhaps Ella would share some of her stories with Mrs Massoud, she thought. She only hoped that some of the other parents with more horrific stories wouldn't share those too. Ella was glad Molly had seemed to heed the warnings about pushers in the park and the friendly man with the dog and the cheap marijuana, wacky backy, weed or whatever he called it.

Ella, Rick and Molly seemed to have survived so far and Molly had decided she didn't think she could be called a chav because she felt she'd risen above that.

'Do you mean there was a danger?' Rick had demanded.

'Not really, but I know plenty of them. They're a pain in the neck.'

Neither Rick nor Ella pursued the matter even though they weren't exactly sure what a chav was until they looked it up on the internet.

Molly's 18th birthday was celebrated at a local football club social centre, with obligatory adults in one room, potentially rowdy eighteen year olds in another, a stingy barman rationing the measures, a couple of sturdy bouncers and a table of snacks which hardly got touched. The Karaoke was rubbish but fun, only one mobile phone got nicked, Rick's Caribbean mate almost wasn't allowed in and only one young guest couldn't remember where his auntie's house was so didn't know where he was sleeping. The party was therefore quite successful but Rick and Ella were relieved it was behind them.

'I thought I couldn't mix some of those chavs with my cousins, ye

159

know, Mum,' Molly confessed. 'But they were okay, weren't they?

'You a snob then?' was her mother's reply.

Now A-levels were over and it was time for the Brentgold sixth form prom, which, that year, was to be a buffet dinner dance at the Londesborough Room at Ally Pally aka Alexandra Palace, the peoples' palace. Molly, a beautiful eighteen year old in her parents' eyes, wanted, no needed, a special evening dress from the retail outlet street near Finsbury Park, which 'everybody' knew was the 'only' place to go. Who could resist a whole street of shops selling posh frocks? A mother buying a prom dress for an only daughter certainly couldn't so Ella and Molly had a wonderful day and had finally bought the very first dress Molly had tried on, but only after another twenty or so had been considered.

She was a vision in burgundy with a tiny waist and when the evening arrived some more visions in various colours with equally tiny waists and very smart penguins in snowy white shirts and bow ties piled into the back garden to have pictures taken by the trees before being swallowed up by a white stretch limousine which wowed the street before heading for Ally Pally.

'I think they could only afford one bottle of champagne and eight glasses,' Rick reported, having chatted to a penguin with a bottle. 'And that was cheap fizzy.'

'I heard the glasses were provided by the limo company,' Ella added. Laughing, the two shut the front door and settled down to watch *Judge John Deed* in peace.

No reports of chavish behaviour were received so it was assumed that there weren't too many chavs and chavettes at the ball or at least they had behaved themselves. Another hurdle had been crossed.

The year 8 parents' evening, in July, was the last of the academic session. On Ella's list of EAL pupils' parents were Mr and Mrs Massoud. She was happy to be able to report that Zohra was making excellent progress in her language acquisition which was helping her to access the lessons in other subjects and that she was popular with her teachers and classmates. Her colleague Justine had reported similar progress for Zemar at the year 9 parents' evening so Mr and Mrs Massoud were pleased and proud.

'How was the evening out in Golders Green?' Ella dared to ask.

'I think they enjoyed themselves. One of Zohra's friends came to sleep at our house and she and Zohra want to come for the school disco next week,' Mrs Massoud said. Mr Massoud stared down at the floor.

'Not Zemar?'

'He'd rather watch the football,' Mr Massoud said, perhaps proudly.

'Will you be there to watch out?' Mrs Massoud added.

'Yes, of course; I'll keep a special eye on her.'

'I will come to take her home,' her father said. 'I have a car now.'

'Good idea.'

Ella was glad it was the junior disco Mr Massoud was going to witness the end of; Brentgold Comp Senior Disco couldn't always avoid beer cans and snogging; not exactly reassuring for a protective Moslem father of a beautiful daughter.

Apart from a phone call to the local police to give the bum's rush to some shady characters lurking near the school in a car, the junior disco managed to take place without incident – apart from the usual headache music and screaming enthusiasm, designed to drive teachers to despair. There were odd conversations between songs like:

'Bootylicious man; that was wicked,' just after Destiny's Child sang *Jumpin Jumpin* and 'Britney's so bad,' after a rendition of the tweeny queen's *Baby One More Time* that they obviously enjoyed.

'Don't you like Britney then?'

'Yea. Bad means good, Miss … or good enough to … aw Miss, you don't wanna know …'

Ella thought she'd cottoned on when Enrique Iglesias's *Be with You* brought back delicious memories of his father Julio's *Crazy*. She recalled, though, that she must have been older than this lot. What was the world coming to?

'Who's this?' Ella dared to ask when a vaguely familiar sound was played. 'I quite like this.'

'Don't you know, Miss? It's Santana, *Smooth.*'

'Course I do. I used to dance to *Black Magic Woman*.'

'But you're old, Miss.'

'Not that old, pip-squeak.'

'What's a pip squeak?'

'You're too young. Look it up. And I liked *Killing Me Softly*, long before you were born.'

'No way. You bin trying to young down?'

'No idea. I'm just telling you the truth.'

'Hey, Miss int so horse and buggy. She digs hip music.'

'Is it?'

'And we knew dig and hip in the 60s too.'

'Cool.'

Zohra was having a great time dancing and chatting. She threw a 'Thanks, Miss,' at Ella. 'It's wicked here, the best. I just love *Destiny's Child'*.

The happy faces made up for the teachers' ringing eardrums; good clean fun in safe surroundings was the aim.

Zohra's dad whisked her off promptly after it was all over, without communicating with anyone. Ella imagined he wasn't too comfortable with this strange new London world he and his family had found themselves in.

End of term came with its sighs of relief and a much needed long lie or two. In the Fonseca home, along with many other homes, there was the nail-biting wait for A-level results and their crucial effect on university places. Would it be first choice, second choice or clearing? Elation or disappointment?

As it turned out for both Molly and Holly, it was second choice by a grade but not a disappointment because they both got to go the same city, though different colleges to study. Where could be nicer and more exciting than Brighton so the two rushed around making plans for the rest of their lives.

The Massoud family were doing the same; the children were all sticking to a daily routine of 'catch up' with reading, language development and whatever was on the school syllabus that they had missed. The parents were ambitious for their children and the children understood that it was for their own benefit.

Zohra's favourite place to study was the local public library; she used to enjoy the five minute walk there twice a day, past the shops in Golders Green road, and across the busy zebra crossing, thinking that one day she would able to afford these shoes or that dress. Her mother, not Zohra, told Ella and her colleagues about this.

It wasn't an email that brought the news. That had been the intention but most of the staff at Brentgold didn't have any connection to their work email from home. The deputy head teacher in charge of communications during the long summer break had not realised this. It was the mother of one of Zemar's friends, who lived in the same street.

'I suppose you're going to the funeral,' she had said.

'What funeral?'

'You mean the school didn't tell you. A year 8 girl from Brentgold, Zemar's sister, it was. She got knocked down by a bus.'

Ella dropped the keys she was about to open her front door with. 'Not Zohra. Oh no. It can't be.'

'Sorry I don't know her name. Lots of the Year 8s and 9s are going.'

Feeling sick, Ella finally got her front door open and rang the school; she got through to a new secretary who told her that everyone had been contacted and the funeral would be at the local crematorium at 2p.m.

'When?'

'Today.'

Ella slammed down the receiver and picked it up again and again but none of her colleagues picked up the phone. Rick was at work and Molly was visiting Brighton to arrange student accommodation, so

163

Ella sat on the bottom step of the staircase, unable to move. Why hadn't anyone told her?

By the time Ella had driven within half a mile of the crematorium there were streams of youngsters of every ethnicity trudging through the rain and wind in the same direction. There were few cars. Ella drove as far as she could within the graveyard, in the direction of the crowd which was probably about five hundred in strength. There was no sign of any other teachers so she parked, put up the hood of her jacket and plodded along with the flow.

'Oh, Mrs Fonseca, It's so awful. How could it happen?' It was only then that Ella was sure that it hadn't all been a terrible mistake. It was Fatima, Zohra's cousin sister and best friend.

The Moslem section of the graveyard was in a far corner away from the entrance. In the wind and driving rain it was a bleak sight. Bedraggled weeping teenagers, hugging each other in small groups and a quietly dignified family group laying flowers on a new grave completed the grief-stricken picture.

To make matters worse, Ella was bewildered and mortified because she was the sole representative of the school staff. What on earth had happened? There was no way of avoiding Mr and Mrs Massoud, so she passed on condolences on behalf of the school, explaining that there hadn't been enough time to tell everyone about the tragedy and that the school would pay their respects very soon.

'Can you believe,' Mr Massoud began, 'we came to London to keep our children safe? God can be very unkind.' The big man blinked hard while his wife wept openly, clinging on to his arm.

Back at school, remorse filled the atmosphere – and determination to improve email communications. There was no point in blaming anyone; Brentgold staff were almost but not quite computer connected and it was unfortunate that only one member of staff had been present at the funeral.

A group of teachers, among them Ella, were given the afternoon off to make a condolence visit. Mr and Mrs Massoud and all the family were hugely hospitable; everyone sat on floor cushions and

164

after sweet, spiced tea was served, Zohra's father addressed the group in perfect English in his deep voice.

'Unfortunately, my daughter ran across the road too quickly. She was rushing to study in the library. If you look out of our window, you can see it. The bus driver could not stop and my wife heard the horn and the brakes screaming. She did not think it could be our own daughter in the accident.'

'Allah has taken her,' Mrs Massoud said and cradled her head in her hands. The five remaining little girls fidgeted and squirmed but stayed quiet. Zemar clasped his teacup his faced revealing a struggle with bitterness.

'My son's name, Zemar, means lion. His uncle was a very famous man, a good man who first fought against the Russians until they left in 1989. Then he fought the Taliban but without the help of the Americans who broke their promise to help rebuild Afghanistan. Did you know that last year, in 2001, he warned the European parliament in Brussels that the Taliban in Pakistan, Saudi Arabia and Afghanistan would attack the West? And did you know that Ahmad Shah Massoud, known as the Lion of Afghanistan, was assassinated on September the 9th 2001.'

'That was two days before Al Qaeda attacked The Twin Towers,' Ayesha Hadadi, Zohra's RE teacher gasped. She and Ella looked at each other, remembering the day the name Massoud had rung bells.

'Indeed, and it was in their plan to kill my cousin brother. They thought the Americans might have defeated the Taliban if he helped them. He was very strong and a good man. He never made money through the opium poppy; instead he traded in emeralds and our blue stone, lapis lazuli.

'Who were 'they', who killed him?' Craig Dixon asked.

'They called themselves the soldiers of the light of Islam. For them a moderate Islamic Afghanistan was not enough. Unfortunately, people like them can be found in 21 countries.'

'That's frightening.'

'Ahmad Shah Massoud was Afghanistan's only hope. He once

165

said, *"As long as I control an area the size of my hat, I will defend it against the Taliban."* I am ashamed that when he died, I could not stay in Afghanistan. My family are too important to sacrifice to a long war which will be made worse, not better, by foreign soldiers fighting.

'And now,' Zohra's father went on, 'Allah has chosen to punish me by taking my oldest daughter in this god-forsaken country.'

'We are very sorry for your loss. The school too will miss Zohra. She was such a wonderful student and a well-loved friend,' Craig Dixon interrupted.

'My apologies. You are good people who cared for our daughter. I place no blame. It was her rush to get across the road. I forgive the bus driver and even share his pain. We will never forget but I know he too will not forget. Thank you for your visit. Now we need time to grieve.'

The dignified father had poured out his innermost thoughts but had taken control of the situation. The visitors were dismissed.

However, a few weeks later, in true Brentgold spirit, Zohra's year group arranged a beautiful and poignant remembrance service, packed full of meaningful readings, poems, songs, a rap and instrumental music. The afternoon ended with the planting of Zohra's tree in the memorial garden.

'There will now be a few minutes for us all to remember Zohra in silence, perhaps to pray, if we believe in prayer or if not just to ...'. Mr Dixon, Head of Year 8, proclaimed himself an atheist – but that day he was lost for words.

The children, of all beliefs, found those words and wrote them in Zohra's Remembrance book and spoke them on the video which they presented to her family.

Precious memories.

Winter Festivals

Love them or hate them, among the happiest of evenings at Brentgold Comprehensive were the annual celebrations of the Winter Festivals.

Bright national costume, music, dance, drama, poetry and readings representing the many faiths or secular beliefs found in the school were perfect ingredients for a rich, lively, colourful and inspiring experience for all concerned.

Ella Fonseca, in her capacity as Equal Opportunities Coordinator, was contentedly up to her neck in many such projects.

Typically the festivals included might have been Hanukah, Christmas, Eid ul-Ftra, Diwali, Guru Nanak's birthday, Bodhi Day, the day when Buddha found enlightenment, Hanamatsuri flower festival from Japanese Shinto, Haile Selassie's birthday in Rastafarianism or Yun Tan, the Taoist, or more often secular, Chinese New Year. The following year might have added celebrations of Samvatsari, the day (paradoxically September 11th) when Jainists forgive and ask for forgiveness, the birth, in 1817, of Baha'u'llah Baha, the founder of the Baha'i religion, No-Ruz, the Zoroastrian New Year, Al-Hijra, the first day of the Muslim New Year in 1427, World Humanism Day on June 21st and once a mention of Chrismukah in a family with a Christian mum and a Jewish dad.

The choice of items was down to the pupils and the emphasis was on an inclusive Brentgold where everyone was welcome and where their beliefs, whether religious or secular, would be respected – as long as these beliefs did not harm others. The aim was for the youngsters to feel part of a rich, diverse community on one hand, which need not detract from their home culture.

'What happens if you believe in all of them religions but only a little bit?' one young cherub asked Ella Fonseca one day. 'Are you just watered down nothing?'

'Not at all. It takes a lot of thought and courage to respect the beliefs of others. Perhaps when you think about it more, you might call yourself a Unitarian. Or you might find that your family religion accepts what you believe.'

'Or I might believe in only people.'

'Then maybe you'll be a humanist. But the most important thing is that you question it, you think about it and you decide for yourself. What do you think?'

'I'm still thinking, Miss.'

During those Winter Festivals, not only the pupils learned new things; the teachers and parents discovered a great deal about the lives, customs and core beliefs of the families of many of the children who were their own children's daily companions.

For example, the Zoroastrian world, they learned, is made up of 7 things: sky, water, earth, plants, cattle, humans and fire and the three core beliefs are in Humata, good thoughts, Hukhta, good words and Hvarashtra, good deeds. They may also have learned that there are 8 million spirits or gods in the Japanese Shinto religion and that it is very important to be extra clean to worship in Japan. Rastafarians, some might have been surprised to learn, are Christians who believe God revealed himself to them through avatars beginning with Moses, Elijah, Jesus and then Haile Selassie. Baha'ism, some did not know, promote world peace and harmony and have respect for all other religions which do no harm. Jainists believe that we all have a permanent soul and a temporary body and have respect for all living things and do not believe in violence. Some learned that on Guru Nanak's birthday, Sikh men do all the cooking and invite people of all ages, social standing and beliefs to a party to celebrate the notion of equality for all human beings.

Perhaps also it came as news to some that in Christianity, God loves everyone unconditionally and some may have grappled with the idea behind The Nativity Play the youngsters put on; the idea of Mary being a virgin and Jesus being the Son of God.

At any rate, it couldn't have been said that the children at Brentgold were lost in a bland secular wasteland, devoid of spirituality; or that they weren't taught how to think and question.

168

Schools in Britain are frequently taken to task for not including some form of daily worship, based on a religious theme, generally understood (but not always clearly stated) to be broadly Christian. This delicate pussyfooting around seems to be an attempt to impose a Christian ethic but avoid offending the different faith communities represented in many schools, especially in big cities.

The 1944 law states, 'Schools must provide daily collective worship for all registered pupils'.

Ella Fonseca, as EO coordinator, dismissed this as hypocritical claptrap. She decided to call the law's bluff, probably in a moment of less than good judgement. She devised a programme of assemblies based on various widely represented religions and enlisted the help of a Year Head to start off with the introductory one. As the 200 members of the Year Group came into the Main Assembly Hall they were told where to sit but not why. It took some time for a pattern to emerge.

'Can you sit at the back on the left, you at the front on the right (no, not the front row) and you in the middle that side and you in the middle this side?...Um... I think you should be at the front that side - and you're definitely at the back on the right... and you can sit on the front row.'

Once everyone was seated, the question was asked.

'Has anyone got any suggestions as to why we asked you to sit where you're sitting? Look around. Yes, Josh, what do you think?'

'You've separated the forms and the boys and the girls.'

'Yes, and...?'

'All the white people are at the back of the room.'

'Uh huh... yes, what else?'

'The Asians are in the middle and the Africans and Caribbeans are near the front.'

'Do you think you're sitting in the right place?'

'No, Miss. The different types of Asians are all mixed up if you want to separate everybody.'

'Okay, can you sort yourselves out, please?'

Some shuffling and seat swapping created a new pattern of Indians, Pakistanis, Hong Kong Chinese, Malaysian and Indonesian and Japanese, vaguely separated. A lone Nepali girl hesitated and sat on the end of a row.

'Are you happy now?'

'No, Miss,' was the loud communal cry.

'Why?'

'I wanted to sit with my friend.'

'And where's your friend?'

'At the front.'

'On the front row?'

'No, one row back.'

'You lot in the second row, Are you happy?'

'Yes Miss. But we're still mixed up. I'm from Angola and he's from Jamaica.'

'Does that matter?'

'No, Miss but I thought you wanted to segregate us.'

'That's a pretty unfriendly word isn't it 'segregate' and what we've done is unkind. What do you lot at the back feel like?'

'White.'

This managed to raise a nervous titter until Wendy up at the back chipped in. 'I don't feel comfortable all separated out. It's stupid.'

'Exactly! I knew you'd see how silly it is to judge people from outward appearances. And that's what we did.'

'Mrs Fonseca, why am I in the front row? Shouldn't I be at the back?'

(Eliot was Mrs Fonseca's only informed and rehearsed stooge.)

'What do you think everyone? Where should Eliot be?'

'He's white so he should be at the back, Miss.'

'True, but I know something about him that made me wonder where to put him so we put him on the front row.'

'I should be on the front row,' a red headed boy shouted out. 'I'm Jewish too.'

'But I'm not Jewish,' a fair to golden-skinned girl with an Afro

170

hairstyle called out.

'Where do you think you should be?'

'Well I'm white, black and brown because my granny was Afro Asian and my mum's white Irish.'

'Then, you are lucky because you have more than one culture.'

'Cool, Miss. I didn't think of it that way.'

Miss, Ahmed and I are both Indian but we've got different religions.

'Let's see how many religious differences we've got here?' Mrs Fonseca continued, working the crowd. 'How many people in this room would say they had a religion in their family?'

Around a third of the hands went up.

'Would anyone here say they had a Christian background?'

A sprinkling of hands from every corner of the room went up.

'Isn't that interesting? Christianity seems to be colour blind.'

'Who would consider themselves or their families followers of Hinduism?'

Half of the hands flew up in the middle of the room.

'And followers of Islam?'

The other half put up their hands.

'Judaism?'

A few hands went up at the back, one near the front and one on the front row.

'Buddhism?'

Three hands.

'Atheism?'

Ten or so hands.

'That's fine too. Have I missed out any beliefs?'

'Taoism, Miss.'

Shinto.'

'Jainism.'

'Sikhism.'

'Baha'ism.'

'Miss, I don't believe in nothing. I believe in people.'

171

'What does that mean, Year 9?'

'Could she be a humanist?'

'What do you think?'

'She is, Miss.'

'So, Year 9, we are all different but is there anyone here who would not respect the beliefs of anyone else in this room?'

Not a single hand went up. They knew what was expected of them.

'So we're all different, all equal and all special! So whoever you are and whatever you believe, be proud.'

There was a happy cheer to end the assembly before they were let out to regroup across the cultures. Kids have an uncanny knack of transcending cultural differences.

'Good assembly Miss.'

'Thanks.'

'Best assembly yet, Miss.'

'I'm glad you liked it.'

And they were gone - to absorb the message, perhaps, and create their own sub culture, tying all their common threads together.

The team of teachers could only hope that in the inevitable face of bigotry, these youngsters would be able to hold their heads up high. Their dearest wish was that world was changing quickly enough for them to avoid such prejudice or if not that they would have the courage to stand up to it.

EO coordinator, Mrs Fonseca, decided she could push the boat out a little bit further. Responding to feedback including requests from pupils she thought, 'Why not have short contributions, readings, poems, songs or sketches, representing as many religions as possible in more school assemblies?'

The project forged ahead on a wave of enthusiasm, the Christian parable of the Good Samaritan who helped a stranger, an Islamic story about a woodcutter who always kept his axe sharp so he could always do his best work and a favourite Hindu fable about a snake who lost

172

his hiss.

The favourite was a Vietnamese Buddhist story, *Long Chopsticks Heaven or Hell?* In Hell, people starved as they tried to feed themselves with metre long chopsticks while in Heaven people thrived when they fed each other. It was a simple story with an enduring message that the pupils loved to act out.

Liang Zhuang – Leo

'Looang Zooang, King Kang, Toilet Man.' Dwayne chanted as he, Kyle and Jordan were rappin' n dancin' along the school corridor behind a strapping, enormous Chinese boy who was paying absolutely no attention to them.

'Nah, that ain't right; it be King *Kong*, innit?'

'Oh Yeah. Loo ong Zoo ong, King Kong, toilet mong.'

'Mingin King Kong Leeong,' Jordan added poetically, not to be left out.

'You, you and you! My room. Now!' This was mild-mannered Ms Fonseca at her feistiest.

'I call that verbal abuse,' Ella said quietly behind the closed door. 'What's Leo ever done to you? Don't forget he's come to a new country and hasn't learned the language yet.'

'Aw, Miss, we's only joking.'

'If I counted the number of times I've heard that before and after a fight, I'd need a lot more than my fingers and toes.'

'Leo, man. He don't care. We ain't never seen him riled.'

'That don't mean - uh – doesn't mean he won't and I pity you lot if he does lose his temper. Look at the size of him.'

'You be right. He humongous – but he think he too good for us so he won't do nothing.'

'What makes you think he thinks he's too good for you? He's probably scared and doesn't know how to make friends because he doesn't know enough English.'

'He's a snob, Miss. We tried to speak – even Hong Kong Kam did. We just think if he get mad he'll speak to us.'

'Well,' whispered Ms Fonseca,' let me tell you a secret.'

'Whazzat Miss?'

'Leo's a karate black belt; I saw his certificate and a picture so I don't want to hear you've been abusing him again and one of you is in the hospital. Right?'

'Okay, no more, Miss.' The three boys looked at each other

anxiously which pleased Ella.

'It weren't dissin' just foolin'.'

'But why Toilet man?' Ella asked. 'King Kong, I get but…'

'Cos he built like a brick sh… .'

'Enough! I get it. I don't want to hear of any more bullying or trying to annoy him. Is that clear?'

'That's brick shit house Miss,' Jordan added rolling his cupped hand and swinging his hips.

'I know,' Ella hissed closing her eyes.

'Shuh up, Jordan!'

'You laughin' Miz Fonseca?'

'I'm *not* laughing.' And she didn't until they were well out of earshot. The three boys were harmless but Ella reminded herself to get Leo to back her up over her strategic white fib.

A few weeks previously at the beginning of term Leo had joined Year 9 from mainland China - a Mandarin speaker with practically no spoken English.

'I've tried to get him out of French so he can have extra EAL but rules are rules.' Ella complained. 'He has to do two Modern Foreign Languages. How daft is that? Why can't they say Mandarin and English are his two?' Ella was annoyed. What was the point of forcing Leo to learn French before he had acquired the English he needed to survive? She suspected that Language status for the school had attracted extra funding so all pupils regardless had to study two out of a list of European foreign languages. As usual it was about money and the ideas of people on high who knew damn all about youngsters and their needs.

Ella Fonseca was growing fonder by the day of her giant teddy bear of a pupil who was probably the most anxious to please teenager she had ever come across. An only child, his only focus was on success in the eyes of his wealthy Chinese parents. Right now the expectation was success in British GCSE exams. When he had arrived, the Head had shown a special interest.

'We'll need William Wu again, if the new fellow has *no* English.'

175

William Wu, also Mandarin speaking, was a highly intelligent, successful student, verging on the geeky if Ella was to be honest.

'William will love that. Now that he's in Lower Sixth he wants to be a mentor at Homework Club. I'll see him this afternoon.' Ella was fond of her star student, who hadn't really needed her support for long and had soon outshone his peers. As predicted, William was the first and keenest volunteer reading mentor to arrive at Homework Club.

'Great results, William,' Ella said and added, although she knew very well what they were, 'What was it you got?'

'9 A*s Mrs Fonseca – but I only got an A in English Language.'

'Well then, that's just not good enough, William.' After the chuckles Ella continued. 'You'll have to help me out.'

'Your wish is my command,' he replied with an old-fashioned chivalrous bow. Where had this boy learned his manners?

'First of all, how do you pronounce this?'

On a form were some incomplete details of the new boy Justine had interviewed: Name: Liang Zhuang: Country of Origin: China Language(s): Mandarin / Hanyu-Pinyin

'Ooh,' said William. 'Maybe he's from my province. It's Leeang Zooang, by the way. I can guess his ethnicity might be Han Chinese and if he says one of his languages is Hanyu-Pinyin, he's probably pretty educated. When can I meet him?'

'Wendy Ng should be bringing him here now. They put him in her form.'

'Maybe that would be okay but Mandarin talking to Cantonese is a bit like a chicken talking to a duck. Not everyone speaks both.'

'But you do – and you're the only one in school.'

'Looks like I'm encumbered,' William said, making a rare mistake in colloquial usage of language; of course, the meaning, though formal, was absolutely correct. That was William. 'I'm happy to help. I've read up quite a lot about my A level courses already. There's nothing too onerous.'

'Thank you, Mr Pompous,' Ella teased, smiling fondly. 'Ah, here they are.'

Liang Zhuang, at six foot something and rugby broad, was certainly a big boy for Year 9. He had a large round face and huge hands and feet, unlike the other smaller Chinese students at Brentgold. Wendy looked like his baby sister. His smile was also wide but there was a diffidence there, bordering on terror. Wendy must have told him that Mrs Fonseca was his teacher because he held out his hand to Ella who overcame her surprise in time to shake it without seeming to hesitate impolitely.

'Welcome to Brentgold. I'm Mrs Fonseca.' After a quick translation by William he replied hesitantly, 'Thank you.' It was going to be a tough journey.

'William will ask you questions today, Liang.'

Liang nodded but perhaps not with much comprehension.

'Wendy, have you been speaking to Liang?'

'Yes, Miss. We can understand some words and he knows little, little English but only writing. That's how he learned in Shanghai, no speaking, only writing.'

'Thanks Wendy. That's really helpful. Can you be his buddy for a while? Make sure he gets here every morning after registration so we can help him with survival English. William here speaks Mandarin so he'll come at lunch time or after school.'

'Can I come too?' Wendy asked eagerly.

'Thanks Wendy, of course you can. William, I'll leave you to get Liang's form filled in.'

The two boys chattered happily and after some time William spoke.

'Mrs Fonseca.' He was too grown up and formal for 'Miiisss'. 'Zhuang wants you to know that Zhuang is his given name or *ming*, like an English first name but if that is too hard, his mother gave him a *shuming*, Leo.'

'What's a shooming?'

'It's a study name that teachers can give but his mother gave him it.'

'Hello Leo. What is the name Liang?'

177

'Famiry,' Leo tried.

'That's the surname,' William explained, 'but it comes first. It's called the *xing* but you don't need to know that.'

'Fine,' the teacher replied, feeling her intelligence had been questioned. Feeling feisty she added briskly, '*Ming* is the first name, *xing* is the family name and shooming is your nickname that teachers give you. That's easy.' She was tempted to add the cheeky 'I knew that' like teenagers did when they clearly *didn't* know that. William hadn't realised that he had patronised his teacher so he continued.

'As I thought, I can write on his form Han Chinese as his ethnicity, no religion of course,' (Of course, thought Ella?), 'and his level of education is good in Mandarin and written English but he can't understand a word people are saying but he *will* soon. He's not really a beginner. Oh and his date of birth is 10th October, 1989.

'So he *is* only fourteen. He's so tall.'

'Also, his father is a pilot but he is not living in London right now but he will come to visit.'

'Why does he want to learn English at Brentgold?'

It took some time before some translated answers came back.

'He and his mother are living nearby with his uncle and family. His father wants him to learn spoken English because he might do International Business. He and his mother will move to a small flat soon because he wants to study hard.

'I see. We're going to have to be busy then. I think I'll start with a 'getting to know you conversation' tomorrow morning. Thanks William, you can go now. I'm going to ask him to watch a video and make him speak English with me before his mother comes at 4:30.'

In fifteen minutes, the 'false beginner' in oral English language acquisition was able to meet, greet, introduce himself and ask for someone's name.

It occurred to Ella that '*A journey of a thousand miles must begin with a single step*' was rather an appropriate Lao Tzu quote for Liang Zhuang alias Leo. The most important progress Ella felt was that he had begun to relax and smile a little.

178

Barry Latimer accompanied Leo's mother to Homework Club which wasn't one of his usual Head's duties and he was showing some deference towards the woman and asking a lot of questions about how Ella would be helping Leo with his English. Mrs Fonseca managed to thank Mrs Zhuang for the *shuming* Leo for her son and demonstrate through role play that he was already learning quickly. The mother bowed politely and the head teacher almost sighed aloud with relief. After Leo and his mother had left, Barry Latimer told Ella that he had been given an enormous cheque for the school, almost as large as the one from William Wu's parents.

'That puts a different perspective on the concept of "voluntary contributions". I wonder why they didn't choose private schools for them.'

'Wrong ideology, I suppose,' Barry Latimer suggested, beaming contentedly.

Leo turned out to be one of those students in the EFL or EAL world known as 'false beginners' who have a massive amount of passive knowledge which hasn't been activated. Sometimes it just takes a few buttons like an intense period of listening and being forced to speak to bring all this knowledge to the surface, ready to put to use. Ella pushed the buttons and on a one to one basis the two were chatting and laughing as he rattled up through the stages of language acquisition.

He shone in Maths, Science and Geography almost immediately and before too long he was able to grasp most of what went on in his History, English and even *French* lessons. Ella had lost the battle to get her Leo out of French.

But he didn't engage with Shakespeare's *Romeo and Juliet*.

'This is not the English I learned.' The 'English he had learned' was meant for 'modern business purposes' he informed Ella who had been trying unsuccessfully to teach him some conversational English so that he could make some friends. This was proving to be a challenge. Shakespearean English, he felt, was not useful for business interactions.

'Shakespeare isn't very easy for me either Leo; it's the English of 400 years ago so let's try this,' Ella said showing him a graphic version of *Romeo and Juliet* with speech bubbles and cartoon figures. Next day he came to school saying that he knew the story; he'd been told it in Mandarin when he was a child. 'My mother tells me educated English people study Shakespeare so I am now happy to try.'

'Excellent. Your class are going to watch the film with Leonardo DiCaprio and Claire Danes so you'll be able to understand it.'

'I did see that film. I did not know it was Shakespeare.' Leo's spoken English was painstakingly accurate and rather formal, perhaps because in Shanghai he had been carefully taught in the written form.

In Hong Kong it was a different story. Pupils straight from Hong Kong spoke fluently in a garbled fashion. It was no surprise to their British teachers that they had been taught in Cantonese using English medium textbooks. Students had a good understanding of concepts but when it came to describing things the English words were spoken using Cantonese sentence structure resulting in incomprehensible disaster. Justine and Ella agreed that undoing those ingrained mistakes was probably the EAL teacher's worst nightmare.

Hong Kong Kam, as he was called, was in Leo's English class. He was one of three brothers called Kam; Kam One, Year 9, Kam Two, Year 8 and Little Kam, Year 7. Kam One's name was Kam Wan, which explained the One bit as his *ming*. Cantonese and Mandarin shared the concept of *mings* but they struggled to communicate.

'I no rikee this bruddy clap too, Leo,' Ella overheard Kam say one day when some passage of Shakespeare's lyrical iambic pentameter was being discussed.

'I am trying because it is important.'

'Hokay - still bruddy clap.' Kam was beginning to tire of trying to befriend this mountain of a boy who didn't speak his kind of Chinese. Ducks and chickens sprang to mind.

Another day the street wise guys in the class were trying to teach Leo every swear word and insult in the urban dictionary when he stopped them in their tracks.

'My English teacher in Shanghai gave me a list of those words. He says I do not need them.'

'You need them on the street, man, or they'd think you're stuck up.'

'That's not important.' From then on, Leo was detached from the unwelcome bad influences.

Kam was heard to mutter, 'Ass ho – he definitry snob – bruddy clappy chap.' He was making sure he wasn't going to be alienated from the boys who had accepted Hong Kong Kam as one of them.

Liang Zhuang gravitated towards William Wu, at break times and socially outside school, and within a year, he had pulled himself up by the bootstraps, guaranteeing his place in the top sets in the GCSE subjects he had chosen. EAL support for Leo had developed from oral conversation practice to proof reading essays which were as good as many of his first language classmates. Ella was proud of him and he showed her respect and something as close to warmth as he could muster.

Leo's mother was a large, well dressed handsome woman who was ambitious for her son. She telephoned the school regularly to check up on her son's progress.

'We expect our son to attend Shanghai University but he must have a good level of British Education if he is going to join his father's business circles,' she announced one day. 'We are very grateful for the help you are giving him.'

'Will Leo's father be coming to school for a Parents' Evening soon?' Ella asked and immediately regretted asking in case it appeared like she was prying – which she was. It would have interesting to meet this mysterious pilot with 'business circles' to move in.

'He is a very busy man, Mrs Fonseca, but perhaps one day he will come to his only son's school.' There might have been a wistful tone in her voice.

It wasn't too long before Leo was coping without language support. Perhaps he was bullied a little by the chavs but he ignored them and kept his distance. Perhaps his sheer size was intimidating enough; they may not have wanted to anger the giant. Leo was delighted to learn that everyone thought he had a karate black belt; it was one of the few occasions when he indulged in a good old belly laugh.

By August 2005, there were two remarkable sets of results at Brentgold Comprehensive School. William Wu had 5 A-levels at grade A under his belt and Liang Zhuang had 6 A*s and 2As but a B in English Literature. He also had an early A grade in A-level Mandarin. Ella Fonseca didn't ever feel she could take much credit for those successes; but she did feel privileged to have met those two outstanding pupils.

Leo's mother expressed her gratitude by presenting Ella with a very pretty brooch with a pearl and two diamonds in a boat-shaped gold setting. After all her only son was her own Little Emperor imposed on her by China's one child policy. William Wu was another only son who had been equally cherished. Ella felt inexplicably bereft when, after a formal handshake and thank you, the two boys disappeared from Brentgold Comprehensive and London, probably into the higher echelons of Chinese society somewhere. Perhaps they were plotting China's takeover of the West on the road to world supremacy.

'Easy come, easy go, eh Justine. Another two bite the dust. I wonder if they ever remember us,' Ella asked her close colleague Justine.

'I doubt it. Do you think about your old teachers? '

'Sometimes – there's one teacher I won't forget.'

Ella Fonseca, born Mackay, clearly remembered her old Dominie at Balnahuig Primary School predicting China's rise. How had Ewan Cameron known that in the 1950s?

She had a strange request for Rick. 'I've got this urge to go back to Balnahuig and sit on that stone overlooking the sea at sunrise. Can we go up there soon?'

'Do you remember when I asked you to marry me and come to Zambia?'

'Yes, I wasn't too sure.'

'You said you had to find out if your soul was in the soil of the land of your birth and then you said it was a joke – but it wasn't, was it?'

'Maybe I didn't really understand what I meant back then but now... I feel the land and the sea have a voice. When everything else changes, they seem to be watching and they seem to stay the same.'

'But they don't stay the same.'

'In some quiet places they do, like Balnahuig, and I need to go back there for some answers. The sea might have changed but I'm sure that old rock will still be there. I hope so, anyway.'

'Fine,' said Rick to keep the peace. 'we can go at the start of the summer holidays.' There had always been something a bit fey about his Scots wife.

She didn't reveal her anxiety that her whole mind and body were constantly feeling exhausted. She was afraid.

Hada and Abdulkadir - Myths and Misconceptions:

Sometimes children come along who tug especially hard at the heartstrings; they often have refugee status. Thirteen year old Hada and her younger brother Abdulkadir were two such thin little wide eyed children. Not only did they have no English, they had never been to school or if they had, they hadn't learned much.

They were Ella's first two pupils after the summer break and her nostalgic, soul-searching, restorative trip to that giant boulder overlooking the ocean which she was very relieved was still there. It had survived builders and developers – her own grade A listed rock. All around her might be changing rapidly but there was permanence about that solid rock.

Fade out the bad and the sad
Where have you come from my lovelies
your ebony skin so shiny
and your eyes so bright but so sad?
What on earth could have been so bad?

What in your world was the trouble
that brought you to freeze in this cold?
Distressed, haunted eyes – never glad.
What tragedy turned them so sad?

Your new, white, school shirts are perfect
but not your second-hand blazers.
Your papers say, '*No mum or dad.*'
I guess that's why your eyes are so sad.

Two silent children, hand in hand,
not ready to join in the fray.
Those smouldering eyes still so sad
I so long to make them look glad

184

Schooling, it says, *'Non-existent.'*
Level of English: *'Beginner.'*
Where are the sounds that tune in 'glad'
and fade out the 'bad' and the 'sad'?
A tentative, 'What is your name?'
is answered with questioning stares.
Silence, no words; certainly no 'glad'
hovers in a hushed mist of 'bad'.

'I Hada, he Abdul,' she says.
I smile and at last they smile too.
Is this a switch to light up 'glad'
and turn off the darkness of 'bad'?

'She sister, I brother,' he cries,
his smile lighting up his new world.
'I teacher,' I say, feeling bad
I missed out *'am your'* – but I'm glad.

And sometimes, only a poem can convey how those heartstrings
are pulled. And sometimes such children blow the common myths
and misconceptions to pieces.

Myth number one: all children learn second languages quickly and
easily. That statement assumes so much about a child's background.
Myth number two: once children can speak a little of a language they
have acquired it.

Hada and Abdulkadir had a long hard struggle ahead of them; they
had no knowledge of the written form of their own language and had
barely grasped the numbers one to ten, far less the concepts of
addition, subtraction, multiplication and division. Mrs Fonseca had
come across two, authentic tabulae rasae and was relishing the
challenge of building up the language skills and filling in the huge
gaps in the general knowledge and basic skills of these two, adorable
children.

The painstaking daily task began with the phonetics of the English alphabet with pictures, some of which meant little to Hada and Abdul. A for apple, B for ball and C for cat were fine but I for Ink, J for Jam and K for King needed some explaining. Listen, speak, read and write was the order of skills acquisition; at 11 and 12 years old writing was completely new to them. Hada and Abdulkadir needed to learn how to hold a pencil before they could begin to form letters, joining dots to form shapes over and over again.

'What is this?'
'It's a ruler.'
'What can you do with a ruler?'
'You can draw a line with a ruler?'

That little lesson was more than a language lesson. The two youngsters had never used a ruler before - or a rubber, scissors, glue stick or pencil sharpener. A protractor, a set of compasses and the basic science laboratory equipment had to wait until the most basic equipment had been mastered. It was heart-warming to watch the other pupils and their teachers helping and sharing in Hada and Abdul's childlike wonder at discovering yet another new thing in their strange new world. In the Somalia they had left behind only 20% of the population had acquired basic literacy, numeracy and life skills.

'These two seem to be doing well in lessons,' Barry Latimer observed.

'They're certainly full of enthusiasm,' Mrs Fonseca replied.

'Let's hope they keep off the khat or it'll all be a waste of time,' said John Russell, cynical Year Head.

'We have to have hope, John,' Ella said, 'Otherwise what's the point? Right now they're terrific.'

The sister and brother were forging ahead; teachers gave them differentiated homework at their own level to test what they should be expected to have learnt. All was well.

Then two things happened which might have threatened their progress, if it hadn't been for a third event.

186

Justine Samuels, a vital link to other schools and the borough, had been part of the local borough's EAL Section 11 project and as Brentgold Comprehensive was moving to Grant Maintained Status, they were expected to employ their own Language Support Teachers.

Just before this happened, Ella Fonseca had fallen ill. The increasing exhaustion and mysterious abdominal pains turned out to be growing cysts which her G.P. had insensitively told her sounded suspiciously like ovarian cancer; she was whipped into hospital for their investigation and removal and there was a wait before the diagnosis could be confirmed.

There had been rumblings of another kind over Justine's future at Brentgold but everything had come to a head while Ella had been recovering. Justine had decided to pull out of the EAL project.

Justine's hospital visit had brought news of her leaving Brentgold by Easter but she assured Ella that there was nothing to worry about as everyone was rallying around supporting the neediest EAL pupils.

'It's high time they started taking responsibility for EAL pupils in their classes. They keep expecting us to be everywhere at the same time. This will be just the reality check they need,' Justine pontificated, 'so don't you dare rush back until you're completely better. Is there any news about the biopsy yet?'

'Next week. Goodness knows why these things take so long. I haven't been able to sleep a wink.' Ella was scared, exhausted and worried about Rick, whose job was a killer and Molly, who was coming up to her finals for her Science degree, which was in Cancer Biology, which had made her horribly aware of the consequences of her mum's illness. It was a tense time.

Barry Latimer sent a get well card with a note saying the school had advertised for a second teacher to help Ella when she had recovered from her operation. Ella wondered how he could be sure about the outcome. He threw in, what she already knew, that the project was now to be named EMAG instead of Section 11. Ethnic Minority Achievement Grant, Ella conceded, sounded better than The Section 11 Grant but while she was looking mortality straight in the face, she didn't much care. He asked her to ring if she wanted to have some say in the short-listing of candidates. She did ring and next day was surprised to find her Head Teacher at her hospital bedside with a pile of completed application forms. He wanted her list by the following day.

'Are we looking for a coordinator?' Ella asked.

'I wasn't. I thought I was looking at her.'

'I'm still waiting for the all clear so perhaps this would be a good time to step aside from Equal Opportunities and avoid taking on EMAG coordination and maybe go down to four days a week.'

'Are you certain, Ella?'

'I think so but I'll consider it overnight. I'll give you my short list suggestions and my answer tomorrow.'

It was an easy decision for Ella. There were several candidates who seemed perfectly capable and experienced enough to take on responsibility and she was still feeling apprehensive about her health.

'We're looking for a coordinator, Mr Latimer. There are a few on the list who could start after Easter.'

'We'll arrange the interviews by telephone – the sooner the better.'

The day of Ella's test results arrived, just before Easter. Molly was at home cramming for her finals and Rick had taken some time off. The school had already appointed an EMAG coordinator.

Ella had been allowed home as long as she rested but all three were going to meet the consultant together to be given the results.

'Are you happy to have your husband and daughter with you, Mrs Fonseca?'

'Yes – but it's up to them.' This didn't sound too good.

'There's some good news and some bad news. The good news is that most of the growths were benign cysts on one ovary. There was one malignant cyst on the other ovary but there's good news about that too. We managed to get it all out and if you are still clear in a month you won't have to have any treatment.'

'Which treatment?' Molly had to ask.

'Perhaps chemotherapy but not radiotherapy although at the

188

moment I think it's unlikely that your mum will need anything.'

'Will I able to get back to work after the Easter break?' Ella asked.

'You need to rest for a week or two but I can't see why not. You're a teacher aren't you? What about part time? Could that be arranged?'

'I shouldn't think so until September – but I'm sure I can carry on until July.'

'We'll see,' Rick added. 'Right now, I'm taking you home to put your feet up.'

'Good idea Mr Fonseca. Meantime, Mrs Fonseca, I want to see you in a month so please make an appointment at the desk before you leave.'

'Thank you Doctor.'

Rather shakily, Ella walked to the car.

'You ok, Mum?'

'I feel fine – and it's time for you to get on with your studies but first let's have lunch at Jun Peking. I haven't felt this hungry in weeks.'

Later, with Rick back at work and Molly engrossed in her studies, Ella was paralysed with apprehension. There was still that month of anxiety before getting the all clear; there was so much to stay healthy for, so much to do and so many things to look forward to. Molly might need a granny for her children one day but she might not even see her graduate or get married. And she couldn't imagine Rick coping alone; he didn't even know which button to press on the washing machine. She curled up on the sofa to watch Countdown but exhaustion took over; when she woke up she had made up her mind to treat each new day as a gift. A touch of lipstick, rouge and eye make up every morning would help – and some of that Chanel Number 5 she normally kept for special occasions.

As Molly was about to set off for Brighton and her final term at University she said, 'I can't believe how well you look, Mum. I'm glad you're so cheerful.'

'I'm absolutely fine. I'll be back at work on Monday so go break a leg Molly Fonseca and make us proud.'

189

'Yes daughter,' Rick said, 'and don't forget, keep...'

'...your wits about you! Yes, dad, I will. When are you going to stop telling me that?'

'Never.'

Back at school, it was strange without Justine but the EAL pupils were being well looked after by Teaching Assistants and mainstream teachers. Homework Club was fraught however, as so many pupils needed help, especially Hada and Abdul who had been missing both Justine and Ella desperately. Very few people had had the time, patience and expertise to really help them.

The Sikh lady, Baljinder Chahal, who had been appointed, was just the right person. The name Baljinder means 'the one who looks after others' and that was what she did. She had patience and expertise and she made the time to get down to the level of early beginners; Hada and Abdulkadir loved the attention and Ella let go of the reins and felt the stress draining out of her.

Baljinder was comfortably middle-aged, funny, somewhat laid back but got the job done. Ella found herself reaching her new colleague's serenity level and feeling the happier for that.

Baljinder wanted to make a few changes, like using registration time for tutoring EAL pupils and bringing the EAL Department out from under the umbrella of Special Educational Needs.

'Being a speaker of another language doesn't mean you have a special educational need. That's an insult. It might happen that a child who is learning English might have a learning difficulty but if they are early beginners, we should wait to see if such a difficulty develops and then address it,' she maintained.

Mr Latimer was not convinced, despite EMAG directives agreeing with the changes; he needed Baljinder and Ella as form tutors and wanted funding for SEN and EMAG to be interchangeable. Baljinder didn't get her way. Justine hadn't got her way so this may have been part of the reason she left. Ella didn't mind the idea of being a form tutor and felt EMAG pupils ought not to be separated from their fellow form tutees. Baljinder and Ella agreed to differ and moved on

190

amicably.

The school had allowed Ella to have Fridays off. Equal Opportunities responsibilities were shared by the Year Heads and Form Tutors so Mrs Fonseca had some time of respite to get back to her EAL pupils. Baljinder had a growing number of needy pupils on her timetable and, as coordinator was expected to produce reams of statistics. Ella was given Hada and Abdulkadir to work with. Hada had quickly acquired the expected basic skills and her assessment form of descriptors, a hugely detailed and complex document, was filling up with ticks in listening, speaking, reading, writing and social skills.

Abdulkadir on the other hand was stuck. No amount of poring over NALDIC (The National Association for Language Development in the Curriculum) documents in search of advice was making any difference. He was happy, comfortable and being helped by other Somali speaking peers in Homework Club. Hada understood.

'Abdulkadir is like that. He can't change,' she said.

He had learned how to use all the equipment and could copy letters and numbers and answer spoken questions but when it came to reading or writing he had ground to a halt. He needed to be referred to SEN and a Somali interpreter had to be located.

The Brentgold SENCO (Special Educational Needs Coordinator) was an Irish woman called Bridie O'Connell who was proud to tell everyone she could chat the hind legs off a donkey. Sometimes she didn't know when to stop and if any member of the Brentgold staff needed an excuse for being late, they just had to report that they had been 'O'Connelled' and they were forgiven.

Poor little Abdulkadir was subjected to a barrage of, to him, incomprehensible questions before Ella rescued him.

'Bridie, I'm afraid he didn't understand a word of that.'

'Sorry, dear, I need to get the picture matching out don't I?'

'I'd say so.'

'I don't suppose we could try him on the CAT tests.'

'Perhaps the non-verbal one, Bridie, but he hasn't got enough language or education to cope with the verbal or quantitative tests.'

'I'll get on to the Borough about a Somali speaking Ed. Psych.'

Three weeks later, Aisha Hassan Hodge arrived to assist the Educational Psychologist, Mary Askwith, with an assessment of little Abdulkadir who was happily unaware that anything was amiss.

'I'm afraid he's having problems with words and concepts in Somali too,' Aisha explained. 'It's like he knew it five minutes ago and now he's forgotten.'

'Would you agree the best way forward is to slowly build up his English vocabulary and hope that he'll manage to achieve an acceptable reading age?' Ella asked.

'I'll see what we can do about getting a bilingual EAL assistant,' Bridie added. 'Could you do it, Aisha?'

'I'm interpreting freelance at the moment but I'd really love to work in a school; it would have to be part time.'

'Any help for Abdulkadir would be brilliant,' Ella added.

'Normally I'd agree that first language input would be good,' said Aisha, 'but in this case, Abdulkadir seems to know as much in English as he does in Somali. It's almost as if he wants to reject his own language.'

Mary Askwith joined in. 'It could be he hasn't got over whatever trauma has brought the family here, minus the parents. Do you think we could get his sister into the discussion? Aisha, see what you can find out. Bridie, can you get in touch with the Somali Community to see if they know anything more than we've been told. Ella, can you get a hold of the sister and bring her here – no time like the present?'

Aisha walked along the school corridors with Ella to locate Hada, who was at the far corner of a different school building, in Maths.

'The war out there was supposed to be over, I thought.'

'It's on-going I'm afraid, especially along the borders,' Aisha replied. 'By the time the news has finally got to one group that the war is over, they've already started another one. I'm ashamed to say I never want to go back to my country.'

'I was wondering,' Ella asked, 'about the name Hodge.'

'I married an Englishman. We met at university.'

'I married a Kenya Asian, a Goan; we met out there. We used to hear about skirmishes on the Somali border.'

'That's the thing. People hear about troubles and then forget about them; they don't think about the victims like little Abdulkadir and his sister.'

'I'm afraid that's true; now it's my turn to feel ashamed.'

'I wouldn't. You're not as bad as most.'

'Nine years in Africa was going to help me purge my third world guilt. How naïve was that?'

'But it wasn't your guilt. Why take the blame for what others did?'

Back in the SENCO office Hada was persuaded to talk in Somali for a bit with Aisha but this revealed little more than what the school had been told. Hada and Abdulkadir had witnessed the shooting of their parents and four other siblings during fighting between the government and rebels. Abdulkadir had run away into the bush and hadn't been found for days. When an old lady brought him to Hada he didn't speak for a long time. Then he tried to run away again but Hada followed him.

'How did you get to London?' asked Ella.

Aisha repeated the question and translated the answer:

'Some doctor and nurse people found us walking alone and put us in a lorry which took us to Nairobi. Then we stayed in a big building for many days before we went on the plane to London. We didn't know any of the other Somali people but they looked after us. Now we don't know what will happen. We have no passports and we live with a family that is not our own because our family is dead.'

'Can you ask her why she thinks Abdulkadir didn't speak?'

Aisha's translation was shocking: 'He told me some men wanted him to learn to shoot and he did not want to. Then one man said he was young and strong and if he didn't learn to shoot they would kill him and drink his blood. Then the old woman woke him in the night and took him back to me. I told him we would walk out of Somalia to

193

Kenya and then this lorry stopped and found us.'

'Do you believe that?' Bridie asked.

'It must have been in his imagination,' added Mary.

'Perhaps not,' was all that Aisha could bring herself to say. There was a chill in the air.

It was arranged that Aisha would come to Brentgold every Wednesday to liaise with Ella until it became apparent that it wasn't language that was inhibiting Abdulkadir. Hada was forging ahead and was close to reaching her proper reading age, while Abdul couldn't retain any information, in English or Somali.

Bridie had just the person to offer help. Ansuya Rana Dasa, of Nepali Royal descent was a highly qualified Special Needs teacher who had recently arrived with a complex box of tricks up her sleeve. Abdulkadir was a huge challenge for her. Meticulously, she weeded out various specific learning disorders in the autistic spectrum and visual or hearing impairment but didn't rule out post-traumatic stress disorder or anxiety despite his calm air of serenity.

'I worry that he's *always* so happy looking. I suspect he's repressing something. Whatever is happening in his mind, the result is he has moderate to severe global learning difficulties. I can work with that but it will be a slow process and he might not get very far.'

Ansuya worked with that, and didn't get very far but Abdulkadir didn't seem to mind. His classmates treated him as their baby brother until his big sister met him at the school gate so they could walk back to the family they called their own in the house they called home.

The summer holidays came with time for teachers, like Ella, Baljinder and Ansuya to socialise, time to find out that Ansuya was close enough to the Nepali Royal Family to have got a private phone call an hour after the massacre of the entire family and close enough to know about the curse of Kathmandu which had predicted the tragedy ten generations ago - and time to find out that she was married to a professor of a different caste which had led to her being ostracised by the royal family.

There was also time to find out about Baljinder's Sikh background and the husband who was still running a business in Nairobi while she put the children through school in England. Ella Fonseca's marriage to a Kenyan born Goan was also of interest. Happily the three husbands seemed to hit it off so friendships were formed.

When September came, there was a shock.

Hada and Abdulkadir had been sent back to Mogadishu. The threat was deemed to be over and an uncle and aunt had claimed them.

'One minute they seem to have just arrived and the next they have gone. It's the transience of all this I find so hard to handle,' Ella said to Baljinder and Ansuya as they examined the details of a new Year 7 pupil from Colombia.

Disappearing Children

From 1990 onwards

'Me Quasimodo,' said a small boy with mischievous eyes and his rain jacket on top of his bulky back pack. Ella and Baljinder had to laugh.

'Well, hello Quasimodo,' said Baljinder. 'And what is your other name?'

'I'ng Juan Pablo Silva. My uncle, he is Carlos the school caretaker,' the boy sang as only a Spanish speaker can. This was going to be a happy boy, unlikely to be traumatised and probably cherished in his family. Carlos had been talking about his sister and her husband coming to London with their family. The husband had a job in the Colombian Embassy and there were two little sisters at the nearby primary school. Mrs Silva was going to be a stay-at-home mum while she had English lessons in preparation for looking for a job.

'Where did you see Quasimodo, Juan Pablo?' asked Ella

'In Mexico - it was a Disney film in Spanish, not Eenglish.'

'Ah.'

'I think I need to learn more Eenglish – most in writing. My uncle he take me this room. And he say my form it is 7B in Room E9 because the tutor she is Miss Alvarez and she speak Spanish.'

'Excellent,' said Baljinder, happy that the organisation had been done. 'When, Juan Pablo Quasimodo, are you planning to learn more English?' She wanted to find out how much his uncle had told him about his pre-arranged timetable.

'Can I start now?'

'First you must go to Miss Alvarez for registration. When she tells you to, come back here to Room F10 for this morning and we'll see,' replied Ella who had been given the task of inducting him – an easier task than with most EAL pupils. Also this happy boy would not be disappearing in a hurry.

Her thoughts returned to her early years at Brentgold when she had first switched over half her timetable to EAL from Geography. There had been a boy called Dominique Lumumba from French speaking Africa. The memory of him still haunted her. The boy was slippery, never wanting to sit in one place to be registered or taught. His eyes had a glazed look and he was constantly looking over his shoulder as if there might be some danger behind.

At the time Ella remembered feeling there probably <u>had</u> been threats surrounding him in Zaire. She recalled when, in 1974, she and Rick had feared for their lives when driving along the Pedicle Road, across a narrow finger of Zaire pointing into Zambia. They had been taking the shortest route home to Mpika from a visit to the Copperbelt; the rumour was you could be shot for refusing to pay a fine for wearing the wrong hat or no hat if you were black, or simply for being brown or white. Women had a worse fate.

At Brentgold Dominique wasn't engaging with English but wanted to help out with French lessons. Ella had to admit defeat when he walked out of a one to one session for the third time; he had simply walked out of school and disappeared along the street before anyone could stop him. The following day he appeared outside the head teacher's office announcing that he would go to French lessons but no others. The Head escorted him to a French lesson with instructions for Mme. Delacroix to put him to good use helping the other pupils. He then called a meeting with Dominique's Year Head, Form Tutor and EAL teacher, Ella. Everyone agreed he was impossible to pin down. He did, however, turn out to be a competent bilingual assistant in French lessons. According to Mme Delacroix he was an intelligent boy who felt that English was one language too many to learn. Nothing was going to change his mind.

'Mme Delacroix, can you cope with him for the meantime? Register him carefully and we'll keep a record of his shenanigans. I'm afraid this whole thing is very disruptive.'

'He's not a problem in class as long as he can help with conversation with the juniors but I can't always have him in A-level classes. There's too much to cover.'

197

'I can try to interest him in the new Macintosh II,' Ella suggested. 'But we can't often get on to the internet and any instructions for the games are in English.'

Mme Delacroix had to bring him to the EAL Department and show him the computer. It worked like a dream. The boy was fascinated and would have spent all day watching the moving images and listening to the tunes on the hard drive. He simply watched the colours, shapes and speeds change until he at long last seemed calm. Ella risked asking a question in English.

'Do you like the computer?' The response was a shoulder shrug, French style pout, palms turned up and a noise which sounded like, 'Pfoof.'

'Pardon,' Ella replied in her best guttural French accent.

'Peut-être – un peu.'

Ella responded with 'Bien' and got on with teaching another child, making a point of ignoring Dominique. After a few minutes, Dominique crossed the room and sat at the table.

'Parlez vous Français?'

'Un peu – peut-être,' Ella replied echoing his pout and shrug. There was the ghost of a smile before he went back to the mesmerising influence of the colourful computer screen.

'Mais, nous sommes en Angleterre, n'est-ce pas?' Ella pointed out.

'Je suppose que oui. Mais je ne l'aime pas.'

'Quel dommage,' Ella risked, beginning to think she was running out of her limited repertoire of French.

'Pfoof,' was Dominique's reply before he went behind his wall again.

It was apparent to Ella that you win some and you lose some and in Dominique's case, she might never be able to communicate.

Next day, however, he was sitting on the floor outside the locked EAL room long before school was due to start.

'Good morning, Dominique,' Ella said breezily refusing to indulge him with a 'bonjour' or express any surprise at his presence. As she was unlocking the room he stood up.

198

'English, please.'

'Come in. Please sit down,' said the teacher and dipped into the box with cartoon pictures with speech bubbles showing two people introducing themselves to each other. It was worth sacrificing a bit of marking and preparation to grab the chance of harnessing this evasive character. He turned out to be a quick learner. After half an hour he stood up.

'I say hello, my name is Dominique and how are you Mme Delacroix, okay?'

'That's okay. See you later.' Instinct kept telling Ella to stay muted in her responses.

Dominique loped off down the corridor, still empty of pupils for a few more minutes. Ella wondered if he needed to avoid his peers and reach the sanctuary of Mme Delacroix and a language he understood.

During the morning break, Emilie Delacroix sought out Ella and asked her if she knew that Dominique had slept in the school all night.

'No – I don't believe it. Where?'

'It sounds like the sixth form centre wasn't locked so he slept on the soft seats and raided the fridge and the biscuit box.'

'And the loos aren't locked either of course. The next question is why?'

'He says when he got back to where he's been living there was nobody there and his key wouldn't work.'

'You'd think someone would have waited for him.'

'Who knows what happened?' the anxious Emilie continued. 'Eviction, arrest, deportation, whatever? Dominique reckons nobody in the world cares about him.'

'Poor kid. Where is he now?'

'I took him to the pupil office. Mrs Block gave him tea and she's been trying to phone his so called "guardian".'

Ella had a free lesson after break so she headed for the pupil office for answers to that question which Mme Delacroix couldn't give her.

'What happens to kids like him, Mrs Block?'

'Oh, Ella this is a mess. This guy doesn't seem to be known to *anyone. The contact phone has been cut off.'*

At this point Barry Latimer came rushing into the Pupil Services Office.

'I've just heard about our lodger. Sorry, I'm afraid we have to refer this fellow to The Notre Dame Refugee Centre. Keep him here and we'll get someone to collect him. Where's Emilie Delacroix? Get her here now. We don't want him panicking and running away. They will help him, even though they might not prevent him from being sent back home.'

To cut a long story short, later in the day Dominique Lumumba left Brentgold never to be seen again. Enquiries established he was being supported as an orphan minor asylum seeker at a refugee centre specialising in help for French speakers.

'What happened to that weird boy who only wanted to speak French, Miss?' a random sixth former asked.

'You mean Dominique. I sometimes wonder.'

Nobody else showed any interest.

'Ola, Mrs Fonseca. You okay?'

'Oh, sorry Juan Pablo, I was miles away. Now where shall we start? How many of these subject names do you know on your timetable?'

'Habla usted Espagñol Ms Fonseca?' the little boy asked.

'Un poquito - but you can teach me.'

Why didn't I think of asking Dominique to teach me French all these years ago? Ella thought. On reflection, there was still no chance he could have stayed on.

'I teach you Spanish and you teach me English, okay?'

'But I have to teach you English first so you can understand your lessons and do your homework.'

'Bueno.'

This induction was going to be an easy one. Before too long Juan Pablo would be fluent enough to go off and learn from his peers, the best teachers. With Ella he would carefully work through the detailed

200

tried and tested scheme of work to hopefully give him a grasp of the sound and structure of the English language starting with the use of 'a' and 'the', 'some' and 'any' with vocabulary lists and moving on to lessons on phonetics, nouns, pronouns, relative pronouns, adjectives, adverbs, comparatives and superlatives, tenses, mood, voice, word order, positive and negative statements, questions and orders, punctuation, direct and indirect speech, countable and uncountable nouns, prepositions, phrasal verbs and a myriad of minutiae like, for example mastering the b and v confusion, a hard task for a Spanish speaker.

Was it any wonder that second language learners often ended up writing more accurate English than their first language English peers who in many cases had to learn their language by osmosis with little reference to its structure? It came as no surprise to Ella that many of her students from a variety of educated backgrounds, having learned their own language in a strict grammatical way, made quick progress when they were launched into the mainstream curriculum.

Happily, in UK, the penny seemed to be dropping during the nineties and noughties and British children were once more being introduced to the building blocks of the English language which their educated grandparents were familiar with, though not always their parents or even, occasionally, their teachers.

Juan Pablo set off for his first Science lesson with a picture booklet with the English names of all the equipment he might find in a laboratory and a few survival phrases to help him along such as, 'Excuse me. I don't understand. Can you say that again?' and, 'How do you spell that?' His teacher Mrs Fonseca was quite confident that he would survive. He already had a few little friends who were competing for his attentions and the chance to show him around.

Ella had been given the afternoon off to go for what she hoped was a last check up at the hospital after her cancer care. As she was driving her little Ford ka out of the school, her mind was racing through her many years at Brentgold and sometimes flipped back to her youthful teaching days in Kenya and Zambia.

'Why are some kids so blessed and others ...so not blessed?'

There was Berrington in Zambia who perished on the battlefield for Zimbabwe's freedom before he could even get the results of the school exams, and Elizabeth 145 who believed so strongly that she was a victim of a Kenyan curse that she took her own life rather than face the threat of torture.

At Brentgold countless children had slipped in through the shadows of asylum seeking, struggled to grasp a new language and identity only to find it was all in vain and they had to return to God knows what in the place they had been too terrified to stay in. Only a few people knew much about their circumstances and it was never considered the place of the teachers to get involved so most of them didn't. Sometimes, however, they had to listen and listen and listen, while children unburdened themselves and always, this was emotionally hard. Ella hoped that some children got a little comfort from a positive learning environment and, wherever possible, a cheerful ambience.

As she sat in the long hospital queue, she thought of that Russian boy who loved boxing, what was his name? He left after a month; someone suggested he was connected to the Russian Mafia. Then there were the five little Angolans who were supposedly children of Embassy staff; they stayed a term before going back to Angola. Their motivation was so poor, they hardly learned anything. Then she thought of Hada and little Abdulkadir with his global learning difficulties. Had they survived the fighting in Mogadishu? Would Hada still be looking out for her brother? Ella would never find out.

There were the clever little rich ones who came, shone in EAL groups and moved on to expensive private schools their parents saying thank you very much for the English lessons but their son or daughter needed to be with the kind of children you find in a private school. One mother actually said that in front of some other Brentwood pupils, Ella recalled.

'Why didn't you smack her, Miss?' one of the group, Oliver, said. In a rare moment of indiscretion, Mrs Fonseca broke her silence. 'I

202

wish I had, Ollie.'

In a way, all school children come, learn something, or don't, and disappear into the world without a backward glance. That's usually absolutely right and proper but what about when you don't know where they've gone? Visions of the horrors of trafficking rear up and pictures of forced return to abject poverty, repression, persecution or the worst violence of war.

'Mrs Fonseca, the doctor will see you now. Sorry to keep you waiting.'

As Ella was driving home from the hospital she contemplated the news she had been given. Never more would she take life for granted. It was time to treat each new day as a bonus, be happy and hope the happiness rubbed off on others. She rubbed the tears off her cheek with her sleeve as she negotiated parking the car outside her home. Molly and Rick were at home but she hadn't wanted them anywhere near the hospital. Her tears were filling them both with dread.

'Any chance of a cup of tea?'

'Sure Mum. Are you all right?'

'I'm fine. He gave me the all clear and I don't need any more appointments. These are tears of joy.'

After more tears and hysterical laughter, a group hug and the best cup of tea ever made, Molly made an announcement.

'I've invited a friend for the weekend. His name's Mike, and I'm sure you'll like him... well I hope you do because I do.'

This time there was a mother and daughter hug but a dubious sideways glance from Dad.

Next morning, Juan Pablo couldn't wait to tell Ella what he had been doing in his Science, Maths and PE lessons the day before and was eager to learn more words connected to Geography, History and Food Technology which were the subjects he had spotted on the day's timetable. What a joy of a boy to teach Ella thought on her first special day after she had escaped from under the shadow of imminent mortality.

She spared a few thoughts for those fleeting visitors to Brentgold

Comprehensive, those disappearing children and hoped with all her heart that some if not all of them had found some stillness in some peaceful corner of the world.

Most of all, however, she was looking forward to meeting Molly's Mike. Hopes and dreams beginning at home were now firmly part of her new life philosophy.

"From the dust of my body, may trees grow
Let people learn a lesson from trees
They give food to the hungry
Water to the thirsty
Shelter to the tired and homeless
Let us learn to be selfless, grow more trees
And make the world a beautiful place."

(From a Himalayan women's folk song.)

A Promise on a Postcard

February 2005

'Reduce, reuse, recycle and be responsible - and save the planet,' was the theme of the 'Cultural Interaction Programme' in the large, round and rising auditorium which acted as the assembly room at St Xavier's School, Kathmandu, Nepal.

Ella felt hugely privileged to be there; her health now fully restored and with renewed energy she was delighted to have the opportunity to climb on her soapbox and pontificate on her favourite topic.

'*Think Global Act Local*' had been her cry in Brentgold classrooms and now in front of young eco-warriors and their adult advisors from three co-ed London Schools and three co-ed Kathmandu Schools, she was holding forth again.

Within the programme of exotic and colourful school pupil Nepali traditional dancing, a fashion show using outfits made from recycled items from the London pupils and technologically enhanced carefully planned presentations by a variety of teachers and Nepali dignitaries, Ella's little whiteboard spider diagram on how the efforts of individuals might collectively save the world risked being forgettable.

The idea for the presentation had arrived during a spell of insomnia around 3 a.m. in the tiny room shared by Ella and Baljinder in 'The grand old lady of Thamel', the Kathmandu Guest House, during a school trip to Nepal by Brentgold, another local comprehensive school Meadowgreen and Queen Ealeswith, a fee-paying but informal co-ed independent school.

The London pupils were staying with the families of pupils from Neptune Boarding High School in central Kathmandu, St Xavier's a Jesuit Catholic-funded extremely strict, efficient and well-equipped school and Shuvatara, a privately funded independent school in a beautiful hilly location just outside Kathmandu.

The two teachers were tossing and turning as quietly as possible until Ella slipped out of bed to the little wooden-arched window to look across the silent, dimly lit, domed and pagodaed horizon which was so different from London's.

Baljinder finally said, 'Something on your mind? I can hear your brain.'

'Sorry. I HAVE to write it down before I forget it.'

'What?'

'I've got an idea for a presentation.'

'Go ahead. I can't sleep anyway. I can't stop worrying about the kids.'

'They'll be fine with their families. I'm sure it was an overreaction sending the British Ambassador home.' But Ella wasn't so sure; according to the internet, the Maoist uprising was becoming dangerous. When the news hit the London press, there were going to be some panicky parents.

Unfortunately the teachers couldn't contact the Nepali host families as the internal land and mobile phone links had been suspended. The pupils were due to come to the Guest House at four p.m. the following day but that wasn't nearly soon enough. The idea was to let the parents hear the voices of their little darlings while the international connections between The Guest House and London were still open.

Planning this eco-presentation was a distraction.

'Come on then. Inspire me.'

'Right we need a big glass container and hundreds of postcards.'

'Mm?'

'The glass box is going to be a kind of time capsule.'

'Huh?'

'Then I'll give them one of my *Think Global Act Local* spiels on saving the planet a hundred and one tiny ways like saving plastic bags, planting a tree or switching the lights off and then I'll get everyone from the ministers to the teachers and the parents and pupils to make a promise to do one small thing and then write it on a postcard and sign it.'

'Haven't you noticed there isn't a plastic bag in sight here?'

'Sure. I'll tell them how much better KTM is at recycling than London and that London and KTM can learn from each other. Yeah?'

'Okay. Then ... yawn ...what?'

'They put the promise on a postcard in the box and we plan to open it after say ten, fifteen or twenty years and see who kept their promises.'

Baljinder sat up, suddenly wide awake. 'Hey, that might just work. And we'd have to come back to Kathmandu for the opening of the time capsule.'

'Of course. So tomorrow we need to find postcards and a container.'

'Right. Maybe we can sleep now.'

But there was little sleep. On reflection, the special warm welcome for the five pupils and six teachers, complete with golden ceremonial scarves and an armoured escort for the mini bus must have been a carefully planned security measure. The pupils had been excited to see goose-stepping soldiers and had enjoyed making cracks about 'The Ministry of Funny Walks'. Everything was different and exciting and they were totally unaware of the sinister side of the quasi state of emergency in Nepal.

Ansuya Rana Dasa, teacher at Brentgold and connected to the Nepali Monarchy, had assured the teachers that all would be well as her brother, a high ranking army official, would look after their security. She had got funding for this visit from the King Mahendra Trust for Nature Conservation and DFID, the Department for International Development so nothing was going to stop it. Certainly not the Maoists.

Sleep finally came but the alarm clock rang soon after and, spurred on by the cawing of what they now knew to be red-billed blue magpies, the distant tinkling of temple bells and chanting of priests, the two teachers were raring to go.

There was nothing they could do about their charges except trust the gentle, cultured families whose care they had placed them in.

However, they could work on their project for when all six schools and a group of environmentalists would be getting together to exchange views and reflect on the visit. Ansuya would be arriving from Delhi the day before, having had to address a conference on identifying dyslexic pupils in Indian schools.

This was the second day that the London youngsters had stayed with the families of the Nepali pupils and although the teachers had all the addresses, today was the day set aside for family trips out so it was going to be impossible to round them up.

It was decided that at least one teacher from each school would stay in the Guest House in case of problems. Any returning pupils would be asked to ring home immediately and then kept there. Yvette Windvane from Brentgold was happy to hang around with the Head of Meadowgreen, Paul Featherstone, Patsy White, also from Meadowgreen and Andrew Lesion representing Queen Ealeswith. It might be their only chance to relax.

Ella and Baljinder could set off round the streets of Kathmandu in search of postcards, something to act as a time capsule and three picture frames for three A3 posters on the environment, rolled up for their journey from London, one for each Nepali school.

They escaped from the relative quiet seclusion of the Guest House along a walled access road, tip-toeing past the silent taxis and cycle rickshaws, their drivers still slumbering in the early morning.

Soon they were in a quiet hurly burly of swishing long brushes and slowly meandering shopkeepers making their way to work. This was soon replaced by frantic honking rickshaws and the raised voices of enthusiastic haggling. Kathmandu attacks you with strong smells of spices, incense and espresso coffee, gaudy colours, fluttering flags, singing bowls, tinkling bells, impatiently hooting traffic and loud babbling voices. There seemed to be no tourists around. Had they been warned of imminent danger? Ella stood out like a sore thumb.

Within an hour the two teacher friends had acquired a travel book with amazing pictures of Everest, pashminas, silk purses, a rude terracotta figurine and some silver jewellery but no picture frames, postcards or time capsule.

'Ah, here we are,' Baljinder said as they squeezed their way into a tiny shop selling tourist tat and headed for some dusty, faded postcards. The rickety rack tilted as they grabbed handfuls of the once pretty picture postcards of temples, rickshaws, Nepalese wildlife and the snowy Himalayas. The elderly, bearded shopkeeper looked expectant.

'How much for the lot?' Baljinder, ever the haggler, began.

'Please ma'am I got more plenty in the back too. Nobody wants to buy. Blinking e mail killed postcards.'

'So you can give me a good price?'

'You get my grandson a nice school in England and you can have all for 200 rupees.'

'Fifty.'

'A hundred.'

'Done.'

'That's only 80p for all the postcards in his shop.'

'Shush, he thinks that's more than enough.'

After wandering around in vain in search of a time capsule, it was time for lunch. Breakfast at the busy outdoor courtyard Bahal Café back at the Kathmandu Guest House had been tea and run. The ladies were ready for momos and cappuccino. Momos are an exact cross between Indian samosas and Chinese dumplings; Ella felt they perfectly reflected the diversity of Nepalese culture. Like some temples: on Mondays Wednesdays and Fridays, a building is Buddhist, on Tuesdays Thursdays and Saturdays, Hindu. On Sundays the same building caters for both religions.

Refreshed they had just set off along Mandala Street when Baljinder set eyes on a tailor's shop with a floor to ceiling display of swatches of the brightest of colours carefully coded according to the spectrum. She was thinking about how much material she could fit in her suitcase, when Ella called out.

'There it is. Look, Baljinder.'

Ella's eyes were on a box stuffed full of an untidy mess of threads, needles, scissors, packets and remnants. A plump lady in an orange and lime green sari was sitting on it.

'Wait.'

When the lady finally moved, Ella pounced. The 'box' seat had an upholstered lid and a metal hasp and padlock. More to the point, although grubby, three sides were glass.

'My time capsule.' Ella couldn't contain her excitement – although it didn't look as if it was for sale.

'You wouldn't sell this seat, would you Sir?' she began. 'I really need it.'

Baljinder pulled her ingenuous friend to one side. 'Don't show how desperate you are. He'll rip you off big time. Leave it to me.' With that she left the shop.

After an aimless wander Baljinder felt it was time to go back. The greedy glint in the tailor's eyes had subsided so she began.

'We've seen something else but if you give us a good price, we'll take that old box off you.'

The deal was finalised at 1000 rupees. With a shrug, the man emptied the box into a giant hessian bag, dusted it with one of the remnants and handed it over.

'What about the padlock and key?' Ella said, thinking of locking a time capsule for ten years.

'10 rupees more.'

'Okay,' she said handing it over and putting the key and padlock in her handbag.

'What's so funny?' she said to Baljinder.

'You'll never learn, will you? I could have got that for 5 rupees or even nothing.'

Ella still looked shamefaced.

'Stop worrying. A thousand is a great price for Kathmandu. He'll be dining out for weeks on the story.'

'And I suppose it needs a good clean.'

They filled the 'time capsule' with all their purchases, the postcards taking up most space and started to carry it between them.

Immediately, a bevy of young boys surrounded them.

210

'Okay, one of you,' Baljinder cried indicating the tallest boy. 'Two rupees to KTM Guest House.'

'Thank you, Madam,' he said politely and hoisted the box on to his shoulder. Ella and Baljinder had to run to keep up with him while the other boys melted back into the crowd with a disappointed groan.

Back at the guest house Yvette had no news of the youngsters but wasn't going to worry until the 4 p.m. deadline. She and Patsy from Meadowgreen had rested themselves into boredom and needed to escape into town to soak up the atmosphere and change some more money into rupees. Paul announced he was popping round to The Pilgrim Bookshop and Andrew had long gone on a visit to some Nepali friends.

The receptionist quickly found someone to give the new box a proper clean but when she heard Ella's story of the time capsule, she looked bemused but smiled indulgently.

Ella spent some time in the computer room, firing off reassuring emails to Brentgold and husband Rick. Truthfully she could say that everyone was fine and they had seen no evidence of unrest in Nepal. Rick came back with a message citing an alarmist Daily Telegraph article about shootings in Kathmandu which was sure to be scaring the parents of the London children. At the end of the message he asked about the best way to cook rice in the microwave.

4 p.m. arrived. All the teachers were there, waiting in the lobby. Paul was padding up and down like a caged lion and Baljinder was sitting cross-legged shaking her foot up and down, up and down.

Patsy thought she heard some distant gunfire but the others dismissed the idea. It didn't bear thinking of.

5 p.m. came. Tea and biscuits came rather late but no children. The guest house staff could not have been kinder.

'It's usually outside the town that the trouble is. Please don't worry. These people are parents too. They will be as careful with your children as they are with their own.'

6 p.m. arrived and Paul began to feel desperate for a beer; this he wouldn't allow himself while on duty. So they waited some more,

tried the local phones once more, tried the mobile phones once more. Still silence.

At 6:45 a bedraggled little group could be seen making their way towards them.

'It's Barney and his family – oh and Dal Maya and hers!' Patsy ran towards them while Paul wiped his brow and visibly sighed. That was Meadowgreen safe.

'Where have you been?'

'Oh, we've had a great day! We went shopping and visited a paper factory and had a great big meal with curry and rice and....'

'Thank goodness you're here. We were so scared,' Patsy gushed.

'Why?' None of them had been aware of the panic.

Paul took over. 'The world news hasn't been the best. Before you do anything else, the hotel will allow you to use the international line to phone home. Do it now.'

'We've been fine Sir,' Barney said. 'You needn't have worried.'

'Go tell your parents that. You too Dal Maya. Go.'

At 7 p.m. it was dark when Oliver from Queen Ealeswith sauntered in with his family. They were equally unaware of the consternation but Oliver was soon on the phone to his dad who had indeed read The Daily Telegraph and was very relieved to hear his son's voice.

Baljinder, Ella and Yvette from Brentgold still had their two girls, Diana and Lilly to worry about. Every minute was feeling like an hour. Eventually they arrived with a big group of Nepali youngsters and several sets of parents.

'Miss, Miss, we've had a lovely time!' Lilly gushed. 'They took us to a matinee show at The National Dance Theatre. You should have seen it. We got to go on stage.'

Their teachers couldn't bear to show how worried they'd been but made sure the girls rang home, giving them the reason why.

'I don't think my parents had read the papers,' Diana said.

'Good,' said Ella. For once that was a blessing.

The guest house staff had produced soft drinks for the growing number of parents and youngsters. They were now beginning to wave

212

some menus, expectantly.

Ella noticed the hotel manager having a quiet word with one of the fathers who turned out to be one of Kathmandu's wealthiest businessmen.

'Listen everyone,' the hotel manager began, 'we are very sorry that the London teachers have been so worried. To make up for this, we'd like everyone to enjoy some dinner here at the Kathmandu Guest House.

'Can I suggest the youngsters and anyone not very hungry and non-alcoholic could have a hot dog or hamburger and soft drink at the Café Pamello? Teachers, we have a nice menu with wine in the restaurant.' This was one thoughtful hotel manager.

At this generous father's expense, the youngsters and some parents snacked in the café and, along with tasty curry and rice, Paul got his beer while the other adults enjoyed a welcome glass of wine. A jolly night followed but only after Paul had insisted on keeping the London youngsters at the guest house, much to their annoyance and the disappointment of their new Nepali friends.

'Just for tonight, to see if everything is all right,' was Paul's promise.

It took a few moans and groans and promises by Nepali youngsters to bring toothbrushes and a change of clothes the next morning before the plan was accepted.

Everyone slept the sleep of the exhausted and by morning, peace was reigning so the trip to the zoo was back on. (Truthfully, according to the Nepalis, it had never been cancelled.) The Nepali youngsters had made their way to the guest house by 8 a.m. with packed canvas bags. The minibus to transport everyone to the King Mahendra Central Zoo arrived soon after.

The Zoo project was the responsibility of Neptune School and a group of ten pupils were sporting new overalls boldly printed with 'Conservationist'. They were proud to say they had had many meetings to discuss how best to conserve nature in Nepal. The Royal Family donated money to the zoo, without which it would be difficult to feed and look after the animals, they told the Londoners. There were also many projects throughout Nepal to save endangered species, such as snow leopards, tigers, wild elephants, red panda, musk deer and Himalayan black bear.

'Our main aim,' announced a small boy whose 'conservationist' apron came down to his ankles, 'is to disseminate the message of the 4 R's – reduce, reuse, recycle and be responsible.' He went on to explain how elephant 'excrement' was being converted into fuel and the London visitors were escorted to a smelly corner of the zoo to witness this.

After everyone had had a picture taken with the friendly elephant, representatives from St Xavier's and Shuvatara arrived and a meeting was held during which Baljinder presented each school with a framed eco-poster. Neptune's Head teacher then presented Baljinder with a few samples of a large consignment of canvas bags which could replace the dreadful plastic bags The West were creating, which not only wasted fossil fuels but also created a massive litter problem.

Each side graciously accepted the gifts, with a nod a smile but no comment. This was followed by a lunch consisting of sandwiches, fruit and soft drinks designed to cater for youthful London palates. It didn't take long for the hosts to discover that these particular teenagers and adults were dying to taste Nepalese cuisine.

The Principal of Neptune School, Mr Katwal, addressed everyone from the six schools.

'Now we will take our visitors to our beautiful place of palaces, Kathmandu Durbar Square, which has been made into a UNESCO World Heritage Centre. There you will see Kasthamandap, a wooden temple made entirely from wood; some say from a single tree. This pavilion gave Kathmandu its name. Tomorrow we will visit the ancient city of Bhaktapur which also has a famous Durbar Square. Another day you will do what every visitor to Nepal must do. We will show you which direction to circumambulate the famous Boudhanath Stupa and teach you the Buddhist Mani mantra *Om mani padme hum'*. I'm afraid this cannot be translated easily because it contains a

214

very deep and wide meaning but it may relieve suffering or bring peace to the individual who chants it.

'Miss,' Ella whispered. 'What's circumnum – whatsit?'

'Walk round. Sh.'

'Today we will pass the Kumari Ghar. Nepali students, can you tell me who lives there?'

Sir, our living goddess lives there,' a Neptune girl, Kusum, replied. 'She is called the Kumari. In the real world she is called Preeti Shakya and when she was four in 2001 your date, and 2007 Nepali date, she was made Kumari, the Virgin Goddess, when the old Kumari, Amita Shakya, began to menstruate. She is now seven or eight years old and we believe she is the embodiment of the goddess Taleju and she is worshipped by the King and all the people. Perhaps she will be carried across Durbar Square today but if she is not, you must not take photographs while she is looking out of her window. It is not allowed.'

'Thank you, Kusum. That was a good answer. We hope that our Kumari will take a short trip out today. Then you can take photos, as many as you like.'

'*Poor child,'* was Ella's reaction.

'Then,' the Principal went on, 'if there is time we can visit some other Hindu and Buddhist Temples. And finally, as Durbar Square is not too far from Thamel we will take you on foot to KGH to meet up with your families, children. Teachers, you can rest before another busy day tomorrow.'

Then and there the London visitors were bundled into a bus with two teachers and two students from Neptune while the others from St Xavier's and Shuvatara went their own way.

On the walk from the bus towards Durbar Square, one busy aroma-filled narrow street lined with rows and piles of baskets full of brightly coloured spices, rices, vegetables and fruits led into an even narrower but strangely deserted cobbled alley where prayer flags fluttered, temple bells tinkled and the atmosphere was clogged with incense. There had been few tourists since King Gyanendra had dismissed the

215

government at the beginning of February, the Nepalis told the Londoners.

A step into Durbar Square was like a step into a forest of temples, shrines and palaces, the hub of a city and a nation like none other. It was enchanting. Spirituality oozed out of the pores of the ancient buildings and there was serenity about the people as they moved around.

'Miss, how many temples are there?' Diana gasped.

'Fifty, sixty, a hundred? I don't know,' Ella said. 'See if you can find out.'

By the time the group had 'circumambulated' a small Buddhist stupa and almost mastered '*Om mani padme hum*', Mr Kadaria, a teacher from Neptune School, was looking at his watch.

'Today our living goddess will be taken out to meet the god Changu Narayan at the gate of the Taleju Temple. We'll have to hurry if we want to see her.

'I thought Changu Narayan was a temple,' Barney from Meadowgreen said.

'You are right but he is also a god and he has many temples. Our Royal Kumari will meet him today'

'Is he a living god?' Lilly asked

'No, he is a statue.'

Ella noticed how easily the London youngsters respected and accepted the alien beliefs of this strange country whose people had so graciously and kindly offered them hospitality.

They got to the large brick palace with ornately carved window frames which acted as the Kumari Che, home of the little girl goddess, just as a long white cloth was being laid on the ground between the door and an elaborate golden palanquin. The Kumari's feet must not touch the ground. Tiny three or four year old Kumaris are carried to their chariot but this Kumari, at eight years old, stepped slowly to her chariot before being whisked away by eight strong men to where another white cloth was spread out near the Taleju Temple, a short distance away.

216

She emerged, dressed in red from head to foot, with a tall headdress, a huge golden necklace and a third eye painted on her forehead. The child stood still while a priest washed her feet and waved some incense around. She then took a seat and solemnly watched as the statue of the deity had its feet washed and a procession of people came to sprinkle water on both her own feet and those of Changu Narayan. Offerings of garlands of marigolds and food were left on the steps of the temple and candles were lit. It was a solemn act of worship which was over in minutes. Kumari Preeti then clambered into her chariot without a smile while crowds jostled each other in their attempt to get a picture of her. Oliver from Queen Ealeswith managed to get one which he agreed to share with the others.

'There are many stories about why our Kumari never smiles,' Kusum explained, 'but the truth is, she is not allowed to in public.'

'What about her family?'

'She'll go back to them when she's twelve or so and then live a normal life. There is one sad thing, though. Some say if she marries, her husband will die young.'

'Do you believe that?' Barney asked. He had been overwhelmed by the beauty of this child.

'Not really. Many Kumaris have married and had children with no problems.'

'Maybe I'll come back after ten years then,' he joked and got the right response.

After the spectacle the group wandered around the temples with Kusum and Karuna asking their new London friends to guess which temples were Hindu and which Buddhist. The visitors learned that the square pagodas were mainly Buddhist while the beehive temples were Hindu but each temple could be both. The Kumari was worshipped by Hindus and Buddhists alike.

Karuna told them about the World Peace Pagoda in Pokhara, Nepal, which had been built as a place for people of all creeds and nationalities to pray for world harmony. Everyone agreed this was a

217

wonderful idea.

'What about the three eyes?'

'The third eye is the eye of wisdom or enlightenment and is recognised by both Hindus and Buddhists,' Mr Kadaria explained.

'Is the tika on the forehead a third eye?' Lilly asked.

'Exactly.'

There was just enough time to meditate on this thought while sitting on temple steps enjoying the view of the snowy Himalayas beyond the pagodas and temples.

'Did you find out how many temples there are Lilly?'

'Nobody seems to know, Miss.'

Back at the Guest House, there was time for thick, milky masala tea, nimkis and tomato achar, (like triangular Nepali 'doritos' and pickle), before the families arrived to whisk the London youngsters away giving their teachers time to finally relax before another busy day.

The bus arrived at 8 a.m. as Shuvatara Day and Residential School, in scenic Lamatar, was a bit of a drive into the hills. Leaving the smells and sounds of bustling Kathmandu behind, the travellers arrived in a land of many valley side terraces, rice drying in the sun, home-made paper hanging out to dry, roadside potters, woodcarvers and weavers with their dyed yarns strewn over wooden racks.

Women and children carried enormous, back-breaking bundles of wood, hay, rice and leafy gingko or saag (spinach) in heavy baskets with forehead straps; one lucky baby was the basket load. Goats and cattle wandered freely. Buffalos tilled the land.

In the distance the snowy Himalayas hid Everest.

They had been promised a tour of the school, some lunch and a trip into the countryside to see some sister primary schools which were supported by the staff and students at the relatively wealthy Shuvatara Residential and Day School.

It was a beautiful school with beautiful views; the pupils wore red uniform and all seemed to have enormous smiles.

The London pupils witnessed discipline and hard work and were

218

impressed by classrooms tiered like lecture halls, the colourful art work and nuggets of philosophy displayed on every available bit of wall - like this one:

Time is precious

To know the value of one year ask the student who has failed in the examination.

To know the value of one month ask the mother who has delivered a premature baby.

To know the value of one day, ask the editor of the weekly newspaper.

To know the value of one hour ask the lovers who are waiting to meet.

To know the value of one minute ask the person who has missed the train.

To know the value of one second ask the person who has survived the accident.

To know the value of one millisecond ask the athlete who came second in the Olympic Games.

BOOKS AND FRIENDS SHOULD BE FEW BUT GOOD.

Done by Sweta Shresta, Shuvatara School, Nepal.

A focal point in the central courtyard of the school was a vivid shrine displaying predominantly Hindu and Buddhist symbols but also symbols for all the major world religions. Pupils had placed elaborately illustrated poems, prayers or messages, near the offerings of food on the shrine which was festooned with flowers and surrounded by candles.

'We come here for quiet reflection when we need to,' Nhooja, one of the senior boys told the London visitors. 'It is a private thing.'

A quick tour of the swimming pool and even the unused skating rink confirmed how well-funded this school was. There was even time to inspect the dormitories where the longest imaginable washing line of socks stretched like a row of prayer flags drying in the sunshine.

After a lunch of rice and dhal, a banana and a mug of sweet tea, it was time to visit some local village schools whose poverty stood out in stark contrast with affluent Shuvatara. The Shuvatara students were encouraged to help out where they could.

Ella was moved.

The first of the many little shacks dotted around the area turned out to be the sparsest imaginable set up you could call a school. It was closed because Teacher had to get the harvest in. She was a pupil's mum who had a smattering of English and a distressing lack of equipment or books.

The building had one classroom and a lockable, walk in windowless cupboard which served as both office and storage room. In the classroom were two long wooden benches, a table and chair near a blackboard, newly painted for the London visitors, and some bricks and planks acting as makeshift benches. Three illustrated but shabby posters of The Alphabet, The Numbers 1 to 100 and an outdated World Map adorned the crumbling walls.

Nhooja from Shuvatara opened the rickety drawer under the teacher's table and laid out one dog-eared exercise book and one each of a pencil, rubber and ruler.

'These are for demonstration purposes as they are too precious to use,' he told Ella. 'They are happy to believe that one day they will have the luxury of their own exercise books and pencils.

'How do they practise writing?'

'When it's not raining they bring their own stick to write in the sand outside. Look, we have put extra bags of sand and a rake for them. And we were very lucky to be given a kind donation of many boxes of white and coloured chalks.'

It would have been crass to say these were probably cast offs from a school which had moved on to white or electronic boards.

Along the road, school was open as presumably Teacher didn't have to get a harvest in. It was break time and there was a skipping game in progress with plenty of running around and childish laughter. A game of ping pong, with a difference, was in full swing. The table was a single stone slab, not quite rectangular but securely held up by a brick-built pedestal. The 'net' was a line of bricks, the wooden 'bats' were roughly carved into shape and the balls, Nhooja told his visitors, were made of cloth stuffed with hay and firmly stitched. There wasn't much bounce but if your ball missed the table or got stuck on the bricks you lost a point. If you managed to hit the table on your opponent's side you gained a point. Simple. The game seemed to generate lots of hilarity so who needed expensive equipment?

Again Ella had to blink back her tears. These children had nothing that money could buy but they had something better; the ability to have fun.

Suggestions of the need for easy texts with stories in a Nepalese setting with audio versions were bandied around. This seemed obvious until you considered the lack of electricity and the cost of batteries. Some small cassette players, audio tapes and books had once been provided but these had mysteriously disappeared.

For the moment, it was up to the richer school to carry resources to and from these little schools. One day, it was hoped, things would be better.

Significantly, Ella felt, the chosen learning medium was English. In the case of the little schools with their willing but unqualified teachers this wasn't going to be NQE; unless something could be done, it would be NNE (Not Nearly English). In reality, Nepali was the more common and more practical medium.

Back at palatial Shuvatara an elaborate programme of song and dance had been arranged for the entertainment of the Londoners. Lilly from Brentgold was overwhelmed; when Shuvatara heard she was spending her birthday away from home, they treated her to an unforgettable celebration complete with a huge 'Happy Birthday Lilly' banner on stage, making sure that endless photographs were taken.

Not to be outdone, the following day, Neptune School produced a huge pink birthday cake decorated with strawberries and burst a balloon full of confetti above Lilly's head.

Barney, from Meadowgreen, announced it was his birthday too in a day or two.

Ella remembers chatting to the pupils in the Neptune classrooms. Perhaps they weren't as privileged as Shuvatara pupils or as impoverished as the little rural primary school children but they were bubbly, curious, delightful and very interested in Big Ben. Of course everyone wanted to visit London.

Once more an excellent programme of song, dance and drama had been prepared.

Next day brought a step back into medieval times and into the eerie silence of early morning. The Himalayas sparkled in the sunshine on the not too distant horizon. A bus ride had taken the Londoners and their hosts to the ornamental main city gate to Bhaktapur beyond which no motor vehicles are allowed. Foreigners need tickets to enter this ancient city.

Mr Om Thapa, a teacher from St Xavier's, was in charge of the tour; he explained that Bakhtapur in Sanskrit means 'Town of the Devotees' and the city was once the capital of Nepal.

'We will observe,' Om continued, 'the traditional Nepali way of life, some wood carving and other arts and crafts, the drying of rice and other foodstuffs and visit an open market before we visit the famous World Heritage Durbar Square of Bakhtapur. As our UK partnership project is on the 4 Rs: Reduce, Reuse, Recycle and be Responsible, please notice that nothing is wasted in our culture.

Traditionally we have always tried to keep our environment safe and clean. For example we never return soapy water from washing our clothes to the river and if we have a container, it is always used again. Just recently, there has been a national ban on plastic bags as they have been the cause of ugly litter and a danger to animals. Please enjoy your visit but remember to be respectful of your surroundings in this sacred place.'

Suitably subdued, the youngsters joined the tour of the working city. Instead of yelling, 'Look, somebody's having a bath in the open air!' in their usual uninhibited manner, they quietly observed. Steps leading down to sunken courtyards with communal taps and ornately carved stone water sluices provided places to do the laundry have a wash or collect water for cooking in a metal or clay pot. Huge brightly coloured saris were hung out to dry next to hugely wide oddly shaped white garments.

'These are panchas which men wear like a kind of skirt,' Om explained.

'Oh like Ghandi's nappy?' Oliver asked.

'No that's different. That's a dhoti. And please don't ever say a Nepali man is wearing a dhoti because he would not like that.'

'Sorry, Sir,' Oliver said, anxious that he'd been disrespectful.

A small girl in a mini sari approached Ella with leaflets in her hands and a hessian sack of brightly coloured bags slung over her shoulder. The leaflets read,

'Please do not make beggars of our children.

Buy the things they have made.'

'Purse, jewel bag, thing for mobile phone I make myself,' the girl said clearly but hesitantly. She indicated that the material of her sari was the same as that of the bags and mobile phone covers. Ella bought two of everything and probably paid her more than the going rate but didn't care. It could never be too much, she felt.

'Dahe, Dahe,' called a man on a bicycle weighed down by a shoulder yoke from which hung dozens of flat clay bowls full of what

223

looked like white custard.

'You must try this. It's sort of sweet, delicious yogurt and honey; you eat it with a wooden ice cream spoon,' Avasha from Shuvatara said.

Everyone agreed it was delicious; even more so as they stood not too far from a stupa festooned with marigolds while a snake charmer's flute raised a snake from a basket placed outside a computer shop whose sign read: 'Education is the only window from where we can see the world'.

Of course, in the spirit of the project, the clay pots were returned to the vendor to be reused. It was explained that the snake charmer's flute was called a pungi.

Pottery square was the next stage of the whistle stop tour which was speeding up as time was running out.

'We must leave for Nagarkot quite soon,' Father Lawrence said. 'We have just enough time for a quick look at the Durbar Square. We don't want to miss lunch or sunset over The Himalayas.'

The group picked their way through a field of clay pots spread across the ground while out of the corner of their eyes they could see Nepali ladies throwing rice in the air from huge baskets before sprinkling it out to dry in the sun.

If any place could be more spiritual than Kathmandu Durbar Square, Bhaktapur Durbar Square was. It seemed more spacious which they were told was because many buildings had been destroyed in the earthquakes of 1833 and 1934. Father Lawrence marched his visitors swiftly to the magnificent Lion Gate and then straight to The Golden Gate which is said to be the most beautifully carved and embellished gate in the whole world.

'Look at that roof. What a chunk of gold! Is it real?' asked Barney.

'You bet. That guy with the uniform and the red and white crash helmet is a military policeman guarding it,' Father Lawrence said.

'That's amazing,' said Lilly as all the Londoners, including Dal Maya of Nepalese origin, gazed incredulously at the intricate gold carvings of elephants, monsters, gods, goddesses and other symbols

224

all set off by bright red brickwork.

'This gate leads into the courtyard of the Palace of Fifty Five windows which was built by King Yaksha Malla in 1427 AD,' Father Lawrence continued. 'There is a balcony which has fifty five windows, some say carved from a single piece of wood.'

Awestruck yet again, the group were left to wander and reflect as they chose, but only for thirty minutes. There was a lifetime of detail to be found out about the many storeyed square pagodas and beehive-shaped temples but that would have to wait. Sunset over The Himalayas would wait for no one.

They left the relative tranquillity of the traffic free city and piled into St Xavier's school bus for the one hour journey to Club Himalaya in Nagarkot.

The journey was slow but never tedious through terraced valley sides, often slowed down or stopped by goats or cows by the roadside. One farm house stored hay on its flat roof; others perched precariously on the valley sides, defying gravity.

Behind was a panoramic view of the greenest part of Kathmandu Valley. In front could be seen the drier, dustier higher land above the valley and the road became rougher. Occasionally The Himalayas popped into view and then disappeared again as the road wound round another bend.

The driver just missed another leaping goat and came to a halt, tired.

'Shall we have a look at a traditional village distillery? I think Rohit needs a rest; but no raksi for you, driver,' said Father Lawrence.

A village woman had recently distilled a large pot of raksi so the adults were allowed to taste some. She expertly poured some into tiny clay pots from a high height from a copper pot with a long spout.

'It tastes like Japanese sake,' said Patsy.

'That's not surprising. It's actually rice wine.'

'It tastes better with food,' Father Lawrence added.

'I think it's smooth. Lovely,' said Paul. Of course he had to buy a bottle and some of the others felt it was only polite to do the same.

'Be careful. It's strong stuff,' the priest warned.

'It stinks anyway,' said Lilly, wrinkling her nose much to everyone's amusement.

The driver said he never touched the stuff and please could they get going as the road was steep from now on. Up and up and round and round they went, now past tall, spindly trees until they reached the sign to Nagarkot, a sprawling village made up of roadside shacks, flat roofed blocks and more imposing buildings perched on hilltops. It felt high as they looked around and definitely chillier.

As they rolled up to Club Himalaya, it was clear that they would be enjoying a night of luxury. This began with tea and cakes, mainly for the London youngsters who were disappointed that funds had not stretched to bringing their new Nepali friends for the trip. What they hadn't realised was that this was a last minute extra with a huge discount, arranged by Father Lawrence who was friends with the owner. Unfortunately, neither teachers nor pupils could take advantage of the spa and swimming pool as nobody had packed a swimsuit. Baljinder, however, wanted a haircut.

After tea, everyone rushed up to the wide roof terrace for a once in a lifetime experience for most. It was a bright afternoon and the sun was dipping towards the land and soon began spreading its shades of crimson and gold across the Himalayan horizon. Cameras were clicking, groups huddled together and friendships were forged as the sunset kept changing into yet more dramatic shapes. Someone was missing.

'Where's Baljinder?' Ella cried, bitterly disappointed for her friend. Just as the last little spot of orange was lingering on the now dark mountain range, Baljinder rushed out, barefoot.

'Oh no, I've missed it; I decided to have a pedicure.'

'You'll have to make do with the sunrise now,' Paul laughed. 'Don't worry; they say that's even more spectacular than the sunset. Just don't sleep in!'

'The hotel will never let you sleep in. We are providing you with bed tea at 5 a.m. before you rise and wash up,' the hotel manager said.

Ella, the not quite English teacher, managed to keep her mouth shut about the difference between having a wash and washing up.

After dinner, some live Nepali music and 'having a go' on traditional Nepali musical instruments the planned early night for the youngsters didn't happen. The London pupils and teachers had a go on the sarangi, a wonky fiddle that was played like a cello and sounds like the human voice and the madal drum but they left the flute, horn and pipe, whose names they couldn't remember, to the experts.

There was still time after the pupils had retired for the adults to test the quality of the raksi on the big open wood fire before enjoying a fiery nightcap and some deep conversation. These are the evenings when inspiration comes and plans are made.

Next morning 'bed tea' arrived promptly and all the hotel guests, wrapped in blankets, were on their balconies facing the mountains. Sleepy 'good mornings' floated across from balcony to balcony.

The smell of wood burning hovered in the atmosphere as little spirals of smoke from widely spread out dwellings dotted around the valley below indicated that breakfast was being cooked.

It was disappointingly cloudy and there was a danger that the sunrise over the snow-capped Himalayas was going to refuse to come on stage.

The sleepy unwashed audience waited and waited, and waited. It was almost time to 'wash up' and 'bed tea' had been drunk. Suddenly a tiny orange ball peeped out from behind a cloud then disappeared. Then slowly the cloud seemed to evaporate and the white snow glistened and changed to all shades of red, orange and yellow. Mother Nature had decided to entertain her guests.

'Look, there's Everest,' Andrew shouted. Ella wished someone was close enough to point out exactly which one it was. Her 'oh yes' was unconvincing. Her roommate Baljinder was equally uncertain.

The sheer splendid grandeur was indescribable and Ella could only say. 'Life's all about making memories and this one is truly unforgettable.'

'Wow.'

227

'Hey, look at that.'

Gasps of admiration echoed from the spectators but within minutes the clouds had drawn a curtain across the sun drenched mountains. The show was over and after a wait in vain for an encore the spectators shuffled off, still pulling blankets around them.

After breakfast at 7 a.m. and departure from Nagarkot at 8 a.m. it was back to Kathmandu by 9 a.m. for a short rest and then a trip by rickshaw to the British Embassy for a British Council lunchtime reception, followed by a visit to Boudha village to visit Boudhanath a giant stupa, home to 120,000 Tibetan refugees and a workshop where Buddhist monks raised money to help the rising number of orphans in Nepal.

The British Embassy is less than half a mile from Kathmandu Guest House and by midday five brightly decorated cycle rickshaws and their young drivers were waiting for their double passengers. It was decided that one teacher and one pupil would travel in each, to curb some of the excesses of recklessness that rickshaw boys are notorious for.

Each rickshaw was gaudier than the next, tricycles with collapsible hoods like prams and seating for two thin people or one fat person on a cushion between the two back wheels, except for one.

'How come,' asked Oliver, 'I got the rusty trike with the umbrella tied on with an elastic band?'

Painted on the back of one were the eyebrows with the third eye, on another a colourful wheel of life. All five were decorated with paper flowers; a couple were lucky enough to have garlands of fresh marigolds. All the young drivers wore identical pink and blue cotton Nepalese hats like a uniform and each vehicle had a prayer wheel and a bell fixed to the handlebars.

'Take mine. I'm the fastest,' Ella and Lilly's fellow said.

'But I want the safest,' said Ella.

'Aw, Miss Fonseca,' wailed Lilly as they clambered on.

Once everyone was settled, it became apparent that the five rickshaw wallahs were up for a race. This resulted in an exciting ride for all; Ella loved it but was grateful that five sets of parents weren't witnessing their offspring weaving and rattling in and out of the chaotic traffic of Kathmandu at top speed in such flimsy contraptions.

It was a surreal relief to tumble out of the rickety rickshaws and crowded noisy streets into the oasis of the calm seclusion of the grounds of The British Council with its manicured lawns, shrubs and neat flower beds. A long table with a pristine white cloth was laid out with plates of sandwiches and tumblers of orange squash. An elaborate flower arrangement was placed exactly in the middle. A middle-aged lady in a flowery dress, smart court shoes and pearls completed the very British picture.

The Principals of St Xavier's, Neptune and Shuvatara schools were present, much more smartly dressed than their UK visitors who hadn't packed for such a formal occasion. Flushed and ruffled after their hair-raising journey, the Londoners seemed even scruffier than usual. Paul Featherstone, in a fashionably creased cream linen jacket looked just reasonable after opting to arrive by proper taxi.

'Welcome to the British Embassy,' said the smart lady whose name was Mildred. 'I'm afraid the Ambassador has had to make trip to London but we have representatives from both DFID and The British Council who will talk about The Global School Partnership after lunch. Please help yourselves. It's buffet style I'm afraid but there are fresh brown and white bread sandwiches.

'No momos today,' Baljinder whispered to Diana who had been indulging her new passion for the dumplings at every opportunity. The others appreciated the joke.

'How are you supposed to hold your drink and eat your food at the same time?' Barney complained. 'I'm not so keen on these standing about dos.' He swallowed his drink and plonked the glass back on the table.

The DFID rep, a pale, chinless man around forty, held up his hand and coughed loudly. He then launched into an oration above the heads of most present, certainly the pupils, on the global dimensions, accessibility and equitable sustainability of the GSP (Global Schools

Project) currently in operation.

'What's he on about, Miss?' Oliver asked Ella.

'Let's just say he hopes you pupils are learning from each other when it comes to saving the environment and that the project will carry on for years to come.'

In fact, Ella wasn't sure the DFID man himself understood the concept he was trying to get across.

The young British Council rep introduced himself as Sam and dived in with enthusiasm, admitting he needed to learn more and began by asking the London pupils what they had seen and done in Nepal, which was related to saving the environment.

'Well, sir,' Oliver began. 'We watched how elephant poo is recycled at the zoo. And Nepal doesn't have all the packaging stuff like we have at McDonalds in London.'

'Yea,' interrupted Lilly. 'And we ate yogurt from a clay pot we gave back for washing; we use a plastic pot in London which makes litter.'

The young lad had achieved more with a short question than the other fellow had in twenty minutes of speechifying. Building on that, he left them to consider what they could do to make the world a better place.

Ella was impressed and told Sam so. Had he ever thought of teaching as a career she asked him and he confessed he taught English to Nepalis.

Mr DFID had melted away to somewhere he was more comfortable, probably an office, and after some lively banter between Sam and the five London youngsters, teachers and pupils clambered into the St Xavier's school bus to be whisked off to Boudha, 6 km away.

The steep climb up the many steps past stands and kiosks selling singing bowls, prayer flags, wheels, rings, bells and all things Buddhist in Nepal, digested the lunch and lightened the purses of the UK visitors. Ella's canvas bag now held one silver and one brass singing bowl, some prayer flags and a silver ring in two parts engraved with *om mani padme hum*; an instruction leaflet read, 'please turn this ring in a clockwise direction'. She was a little puzzled. Wouldn't it depend on how you were looking at your hand?

The white washed stupa, with its Buddha eyes painted on three sides was festooned with prayer flags stretching out from a central, golden spire. Its ornate magnificence dominated the horizon for miles around and close up was even more breathtaking than the wonders of Kathmandu and Bhaktapur Durbar Squares. The London teenagers were silenced. As they entered the temple, they copied the visitors who spun the prayer wheels on the wall and walked slowly in a clockwise direction around the cool, darkened, incense filled room. Accompanied by their teachers, they paused while Nepalese and Tibetan visitors placed offerings of food and flowers on a candlelit shrine. Were they remembering deceased loved ones or praying for the safety of their families in these troubled times? Ella prayed for Rick and Molly who were so far away, back in London, possibly worried about her safety.

All around the Boudhanath are little alleys with all kinds of restaurants and shops. The visitors were guided to premises where Tibetan monks were hard at work creating unbelievably intricate works of art with the tiniest of brushes imaginable. Copies of completed works of all kinds were on sale for huge amounts of money. The proceeds would go towards a new charity which was fighting for the growing number of orphans in Nepal whose dire plight was described on wall displays and in leaflets.

After a good deal of thought, most of the UK visitors, adult and teenage, dug in their wallets and bought something. Ella forked out for a picture of The Wheel of Life which was rolled up in a sturdy scroll holder. Fortunately there was a detailed description of the complex symbolism; she thought perhaps the concept of the wheel representing the endless cycle of life, death, suffering and reincarnation might be the only one she could grasp.

After Nagarkot, rickshaw racing, The British Embassy, Boudhanath and the Tibetan art there was so much food for thought churning around in everyone's head that sleep didn't come easily.

Ella was no exception. Next day was to be the day of The Cultural Interaction Programme at St Xavier's School where she'd have to be ready with pens, postcards and her 'time capsule' for the 'Promise on a Postcard' for the environment project. Would she be able to inspire them? Would it work or would it be a flop? Would the school have a large white board, board pens and spare pens for people to write their promises? She tossed and turned but managed not to wake Baljinder and finally succumbed to exhaustion.

In this vast assembly hall of St Xavier's School, the dignitaries had welcomed everyone, the students had danced in dazzling costumes and strutted in funky outfits created from recycled materials, each school, The Zoo and an eminent Nepali Environmentalist had reported on how they had, or planned to use the FOUR R s to save the planet.

It was Ella's turn to try to inspire the large audience, without dazzling costume, overhead projector or computer power point presentation, armed only with a whiteboard, coloured pens, vast amounts of adrenalin and the vital assistance of Baljinder and some St Xavier's pupils handing out postcards and pens – and centre stage the glass Time Capsule.

Could she scintillate? She wrote HOW CAN WE MAKE OUR PLANET A BETTER PLACE? in the middle of the board and took a deep breath. She put a circle round it, drew a line in a north easterly direction and before she could answer her own question a spontaneous reply came from a small boy: 'Save the tiger and all the endangered species.'

'Good answer.' She wrote SAVE at the end of the line. What else can we save? Six more lines for TREES, WATER, ELECTRICITY, PLASTIC BOTTLES, GLASS ACHAR BOTTLES and BEAUTIFUL BUILDINGS; there was no more room for the many answers that came gushing out.

The orchestration continued. She wrote STOP to the bottom left and elicited a dozen more answers: CAR POLLUTION, FOOD WASTAGE, WAR, PLASTIC BAGS, EATING MEAT, GLOBAL

WARMING and DEFORESTATION found space.

She wrote DEVELOP bottom right and got: SOLAR POWER, FORESTS, PAPERLESS BUSINESS, WATER POWER, WIND POWER, CLEAN PETROL and WAYS TO TELL EVERYONE HOW TO SAVE THE WORLD – before space ran out.

Finally she wrote RECYCLE in the top right section of the board and immediately got ELEPHANT POO, a laugh, then PAPER, MILK BOTTLE TOPS, CLAY POTS, CLOTHES, GRASS CUTTINGS, TEA BAGS and lots more.

These youngsters were eco-warriors, aware and enthusiastic. London had learned from Kathmandu and vice versa and there was no question that they were together and equal in the fight against the destruction of the earth's resources.

All that was left was to explain the concepts of THINK GLOBAL ACT LOCAL as being how an individual can do one small thing to help the global cause, and of a TIME CAPSULE staying locked for a number of years before it is opened and examined.

'Now I am going to ask you to think deeply and write down a promise to do one thing that you really believe you can do, to save the earth. Write it on your postcard, sign and date it, and come down here and place it in the TIME CAPSULE. Before you start, can I have an example of a promise?

'I promise to adopt a vulture from Kathmandu Zoo,' teacher Andrew Lesion pledged, 'and Queen Ealeswith will raise funds to look after it. We'll call it Ealeswith.'

'I promise to pick up litter whenever I see it – and tell people to stop dropping it,' said Kusum from Neptune.

'I'm going to switch off the tap when I'm brushing my teeth,' said Diana and got some peculiar looks from her new Nepali friends.

There was a long silence into which Ella's heart sank. Had the whole thing bombed? Then, miraculously people began to drift down to the box with their postcards until eventually there was a deluge and a queue had to form.

'Thank you,' said Ella when almost everyone had returned to their seats. 'Father Lawrence can decide when the box can be opened and we can see how many promises were kept.'

The applause seemed thunderous. Mission accomplished; for the moment; until the capsule is opened in years to come and some promises have been broken or need to be changed as the world has changed. New ways to produce or save energy might have been found and our efforts deemed futile or, with luck, our promises may have saved some good things for the next generation. Who knows?

After the programme, a simple lunch of rice and lentils was followed by a tour of working classrooms. London students observed what they later described as old style learning where teachers talked and pupils listened and wrote. One London youngster felt that St Xavier's was for education, not for enjoyment. In another classroom they were surprised to still see chalk, talk and massive text books and were impressed by the strict discipline. Oliver was pleased to notice that the guys weren't perfect; he had noticed some copying behind the teacher's back in a Maths test.

The following day was kept free for shopping or any other activity and in the evening there would be a traditional Nepali feast with song and dance entertainment at the best restaurant in Kathmandu.

The teachers were persuaded to waste some more aviation fuel and take the best mountain flight in the world as advertised by Buddha Air so that they could say, 'I did not climb Everest but touched it with my heart.' The younger generation were more conscientious eco-warriors and spent their last day with their host families, conserving energy.

Parents, teachers and pupils got together for an evening of delicious food eaten while sitting on cushions on the floor. Exotic and exciting professional dancing to live music added to the atmosphere. At the end of the meal Barney was overjoyed when a huge birthday cake arrived in his honour. Happy Birthday had to be sung in English and Nepali and the evening ended joyfully with all generations, including baby brothers and sisters singing and dancing together to a current favourite pop tune *'Resham Firiri'* which the London kids kept singing all the way back to London.

Back in London the youngsters wondered why their families had been worried about them.

Half term was over so it was back to school after a day's rest with so many tales to tell.

But there was a job to do so it was back to reality with a bump.

10D, The Rainbow Form

2002-2006

The EAL department was the sanctuary where pupils actually wanted to learn and delighted their teachers with their warm enthusiasm. Beyond that was real life.

This was the nightmare of a military operation which accompanied the coming out of 'special measures' which was a euphemism for 'bog standard going downhill and in need of a kick up the proverbial'.

Morning registration had to be done in absolute silence while students were involved in a silent reading task – not something that comes naturally to lively teenagers. There was zero tolerance of a host of minor demeanours including, not properly knotted ties, homework diaries unsigned daily by parents, lack of a pen, pencil or ruler, not wearing proper black shoes or lateness by even a minute.

'Late detention 3:30 in the Main Hall Lee,' Form Tutor Mrs Fonseca snapped in a vain attempt to seem intimidating, 'and it can double up as a uniform detention for no tie and no blazer. Count yourself lucky.'

'Can't do it Miss.'

'Really?'

'My father's picking me up and driving me to the doctor.'

'I'll ring him then to see if the appointment can be changed.'

'It's okay Miss I'll do the detention.' He grins, not really minding that he hasn't got away with it. After four years of his form tutor Mrs Fonseca, he knew she was fair, though not very good at being fierce. Mrs Fonseca also knew that Lee's father, unlike some parents, was supportive of school discipline and would never pander to his son by driving him around. And Lee knew she knew that.

Form 10D of Forms B R N T G L D (who needs vowels?) had been at the bottom of the pecking order since Year 7 – or so it seemed to their constant ally, Form Tutor Mrs Fonseca. 200 pupils in a year group (210 with a squash) were divided up into 7 forms making groups of 30 under the pastoral care of a form tutor. Form B usually

236

got the pick of the bunch and D was the form which often had the also-rans.

D also had the split bands. The year groups at Brentgold were split into two bands of four smaller teaching 'sets'. The smallest groups tended to be the bottom sets, the plan being that more difficult or intellectually challenged children would get more support teachers and teaching assistants and have fewer pupils for the mainstream teacher to handle. 7 forms into 8 sets doesn't go so half of D were in Band 1 and the other half in Band 2, leading to double the organisation of timetables and more complicated classroom dynamics.

Ella Fonseca for her sins was tutor of 7D, with co-tutors at times, for the four years up to the end of her career.

Unlucky Form D had had more than its fair share of challenging pupils but a core of well-rounded, well-behaved, hard-working stars. Despite being driven crazy at times, Ella loved them and had stuck with them. Occasionally, there was a slip of the tongue such as, 'Thanks Mum, I mean Miss, sorry,' to which Ms Fonseca's reply, with a smile, was usually, 'I like it when you forget I'm not your mum.'

But not every pupil in Form D was from a happy place.

There was Billy who might charge into Form and kick his chair across the room or throw his bag at the wall. ADHD, Attention Deficit Hyperactivity Disorder, was the diagnosis and Ritalin was the medication. The withdrawal symptoms were traumatic for him.

'Have you been to see Mrs Block, Billy?' Ella would ask.

'Oh Miss, I forgot again.'

'Don't worry. Go now quickly.' Billy could just about get through the day with a morning pill and a 3 o'clock one. On bad days his teachers failed to see the sweet side of his nature.

Luke had an angelic face, big blue eyes and an unruly mop of long, fair hair. Mum was a distracted artist and Dad an absent-minded professor of philosophy and any structure in little Luke's life was his own ragged version. He was never quite on time or properly dressed and his homework was not quite finished or he hadn't quite remembered all his books and equipment.

'I was nearly organised today Miss,' he would say.

'But if you'd only nearly caught the bus you wouldn't be here, would you, Luke.'

'And I only just caught it, Miss,' he'd say and laugh.

By the time Ella had called in his parents for a chat about his lack of organisation, Mum had left to 'find herself' and Dad was distraught. He did manage to bring himself, his scruffy corduroy jacket, his anxious expression and his son into school before registration. He left with 'to do' and 'to bring' lists for Luke amid unconvincing promises that everything would be perfect from then on, leaving his son with a relieved but exhausted look on his face.

'Look Luke,' He loved this little joke. 'Who's the best person to get you sorted?'

'Me, Miss.' If CRB checks and health and safety had allowed it, the teacher would have hugged the little boy.

Tracy was something else. Her school skirts were at what Ella called 'see level' barely covering her tomorrow's washing and if she wore tights, they usually had ladders or holes. This dress code was not allowed but when the Head of Year sent her home to change, she went AWOL to the Shopping Centre and got nicked for shoplifting. When Tracy's mother was told that the skirt wasn't 'school uniform' she said too bad it was 'the fashion' and she couldn't afford to buy her another one. Some reasonably fashionable and relatively modest black trousers were found for Tracy, which Ella discovered her stuffing in her locker at the end of the day. As she set off in the mini skirt which had been neatly stored in her locker all day she hissed, 'I'm not wearing these minging things in the street. What do you think I am?'

'I wouldn't know, Tracy,' was all Ella could think of saying.

Dwayne had a big brother with a relationship with the police and illegal substances. Judging by his big smile, he was always happy to come to morning form time. Ella wondered if it was one place that he felt secure. However, he was known to have a short fuse if discipline was too strict in his view, or he felt misunderstood. Form Tutor's copies of incident reports regarding Dwayne often found their way into her staff room tray but by the time she was discussing those with him, he had calmed down and was very remorseful.

'I done the crime so I'll do the time Miss,' he'd say about the inevitable detention.

'Good but shut your eyes and count up to ten before you kick off next time, okay?'

'Okay, Miss, but not every teacher's cool, innit?'

'But *you* have to try to be cool.'

'Thanks Miss. Later.' And he'd rush off, pulling his tea cosy over his curls and unwrapping another Mars bar to feed his plump face, now that school was over.

Dwayne's mate Karl, also from the Caribbean, was more sullen and disturbingly quiet. He just didn't do anything except write his name on a piece of paper because he'd forgotten the relevant exercise book. Ella kept all of his Form Time Personal and Social Education stuff, such as it was, in a folder which she had allowed him to decorate with graffiti which she had to admit was beautiful. He did eventually begin to take some pride in his PSE work after a huge amount of encouragement. His mum was very supportive but there was no sign of his dad.

Suzy hated school and struggled with her puppy fat and every other person in this world.

'I'm starting a diet tomorrow,' she'd say as she scoffed a bag of crisps.

'About time,' a rude boy would shout.

'Shuh up,' would be her reply in dulcet tones – not. 'I hate him.' But Suzy responded to being made form monitor and made a good job of putting up 'Thought for the Week' or 'Word for the Day' on the Form Room notice board.

'Miss, we haven't changed the word yet. And I've got a good thought.'

'Here, stick this word up.'

239

'*Immediately.* Yea that's a good word, Miss. What do you think of 'If you think you can or you think you can't, it's true'?

'Brilliant, print it out and pin it up. What would I do without you Suzy?'

'Not a lot probably, Miss.' This girl would be fine given a favourable wind.

Dennis was a skinny little fellow with a caring family but he was a prime target for bullies. They will find that weakness and play on it. By the time the bullies had been discovered, after Dennis had been persuaded that the school policy of 'telling' someone was safe enough to follow, he had lost his packed lunch, his lunch money, his bus pass, his pencil case and his memory stick. At least he had had the good sense not to bring a mobile phone into school. He 'named and shamed' but only got his memory stick and pencil case with half its contents back. Ella was relieved that the bullies weren't in Form D but disgusted they were in the same year group. When Dennis came to school with a black eye for 'telling' the culprits were easy to catch and suspend. He'd given one of them a split lip in defence.

'I told Mr Porch, Miss and I smacked one in the mouth. They won't come near me again.'

'I hope not Dennis but make sure you tell if anyone tries.'

These six, Billy, Luke, Tracy, Dwayne, Karl, Suzy and Dennis, though vulnerable, lasted through Ella's four years before she retired. She hoped they would make it to adulthood unscathed

Some others came and went for various reasons. Anuradha, a star, was whisked off to the Swaminarayan School in Neasden for her parents' perception of her own safety. In some respects Ella could understand why, though it is disappointing when rich parents keep removing their children from local schools. If a school has a majority of well-rounded and motivated youngsters, this pulls all of the youngsters up. If the balance is the other way, it is harder to fight the downward pull.

David, unfortunately, was too much for Brentgold to handle. He bunked off, stole, disrupted lessons and was constantly fighting. He

240

joined D in Year 8 to replace Grégoire, a disappearing refugee from Rwanda, who had come for a few weeks but had hardly got past the silent, listening stage before he just didn't turn up one day. He in turn had replaced Sophie, a 'looked after' child, whose mother had died suddenly and whose aunt and uncle had taken her away to Manchester.

David turned out to have a drug and alcohol problem which had occasionally led to his arrest. At twelve years old this was tragic.

'Look I bet you ain't got wrist bracelets like mine.' He was proud of his handcuff bruises. Straight after form time, Ella took him to sit outside the head teacher's office.

'Sit there, David and don't move. I need to speak to Mr Latimer. Mrs Court, can you make sure David doesn't move. Thank you.' For once, David seemed subdued so Ella managed a private word.

'I'm sorry, Mr Latimer, but I don't feel Brentgold is the right place for David.'

'I agree and so do all his teachers and he certainly doesn't want to be here.'

'What about his parents?'

'I think they've been expecting this. There's a referral centre they've been considering but they thought they'd try Brentgold first. He's been round most of the schools in the borough. They've been struggling. As you know, he's adopted and it hasn't worked out. Bring him in before he absconds and I'll ring his mother.'

'I don't want my mother,' David screamed when he realised who Mr Latimer was about to phone. 'I only like my father.'

'But your father's at work.'

'I don't care. She hits me and he stops her,' David shouted pacing up and down the office.

'All right. Sit down and I'll ring your dad.'

'And you can tell her to get out too.'

'Pardon?' Barry Latimer said when he realised he meant Ella.

'I don't want any bloody women bossing me around!'

'I'd better go,' Ella said.

'Not before this ill-mannered boy apologises. David? Your tutor has been trying to help you and this is how you treat her.'

'Fuck off. I don't want anybody's fucking help and I don't want this fucking school.'

'You're right, Mrs Fonseca. Brentgold is not the right place for David.'

'Stupid cow got something right then.'

Barry came to the door with Ella with a supportive shake of his head. 'Don't worry about him. It's not your fault; he's going to be a hard nut for anybody to crack.'

'You win some, you lose some,' Ella said shakily.

'Think of his poor mother.'

'I'm wondering if she has a lot to answer for.'

That was perhaps the lowest point of Ella's career and the lingering memory of this bitter little thug disturbed her. She thought of the bruises she assumed had been inflicted by fighting and wondered how many had been caused by his mother.

It took a listening ear from Rick and a happy phone call from student Molly in Brighton to lighten Ella's mood. It was time to be happy for the others in the form.

She recalled the first term of 7D. The Year Team had planned a Winter Festivals Performance for the parents who would no longer be a captive audience by the time their children had moved into Year 8 and hit the teenage stage where they no longer wanted them around.

Forms B R N T G L and D were each expected to depict a festival of their choice. B chose Chinese New Year and improvised, for the nth time, the story of Heaven and Hell and the long chopsticks – where people would starve with long chopsticks in a Hell where people didn't help each other, unlike in Heaven where they did help each other.

R, N, T, G and L chose from Diwali, Eid, Hanukah, Bodhi Day and Kwanzaa Day while D chose Christmas. They decided on an adapted dramatisation of 'How the Grinch stole Christmas' by Dr Zeus.

Co-tutor Judy suggested the book and Ella adapted it to a script with a part for everyone in the form with lots of narrators: Whooligans of Whoville, Cindy Lou Who and her Dad, children wrapping presents, people of Whoville feasting and dancing, A Nasty Grinch in Green, a Good Grinch dressed as Santa and Max and Fido as Rudolph and another reindeer. D being at the end, 'Christmas' had the last word which they made a meal of, with a Christmas Tree, presents, Santa Claus and his reindeer winding their way through the audience ending up on stage with all 28 of 7D singing *We wish you a Merry Christmas* at the top of their voices. Their play had been a bit too long and somewhat complicated but D had loved it as did the audience. Ella's hope was that everyone had gone home with a bigger heart and the message that Christmas was more than just presents.

Ella wondered if David would have been inspired or whether he would have totally ruined the fun. Perhaps it was a good thing he hadn't been there. Ten years later, Ella was to learn, with pride, that Ollie, the little actor who played The Grinch was now a TV star. How gratifying is that?

As the four years went by, the Rainbow Form drove their teachers mad but at times made them proud, which made it all worthwhile. Ella kept asking during testing moments, 'What would I do if this was my own child?' It seemed to be a pretty good yardstick to go by.

Totting up the PSE projects, daily form activities and school trips over the years came up with an impressive list including the teachers' pet hate, condoms on cucumbers in sex education. It wasn't surprising that strong bonds were formed. From videoed improvisations of scenarios illustrating different relationships with family, friends, teachers, people in authority, bosses or the public to awareness raising of the dangers of drugs, alcohol, smoking, sex or prejudice, life was pretty well covered and the young minds were coaxed in the right direction. They were encouraged to be proud of their heritage and give and expect respect from everyone in the diverse school community, to believe that each person is special in his or her own way. On the classroom wall Ella made sure there was a permanent thought: '*What unites us is stronger than what divides us.'* She would get on her high horse from time to time and say how strongly she believed this.

The thanks she got was when pupils used their own initiative to raise money for earthquake victims or filled Christmas shoeboxes for orphans or helped out at Homework Club or offered to scrub off the graffiti, a delinquent member of the Year Group sprayed the school walls with. Gratification came from good exam results as well as sporting, musical, artistic and drama successes for some. For others success was something smaller but equally important like raising a reading or spelling age or simply getting organised.

The real heroes for Ella were the ones in the middle who neither had special educational needs and extra help nor were deemed gifted and in need of extra stretching. These boys and girls were on time, in uniform, homework done, polite, helpful, uncomplicated, fun and not boring. Not everybody noticed them and they were left to get on with it. D had many of them. If they minded the attention that had to be given to the difficult characters, they didn't complain.

The real fun in The Rainbow Form started with a random suggestion to have everyone describe his or her family tree in Form Assembly. The first one to stand up was Frederica McKenzie who looked a bit Indian but with sandy blonde hair and green eyes.

'Well, wait for it… My dad's mum has an Indian mum and a Scots dad and my mum's mum is Irish Italian but I can't remember how. My mum's dad is Syrian and Nigerian and her mum, oh yea like I said, Irish Italian … Um… oh yea, my dad's dad has a bit of English … Yeeeeeah… and a bit of Scots; that's the McKenzie bit. Is that it?'

'Miss, what does that make Frederica?'

'Ask her.'

'Me. … Oh… and we're Buddhists these days.'

'Are you joking?'

'No. My dad says if we're Buddhists we've covered it all.'

'Miss, Miss can I be next?'

'Go on then, Miresh.'

'Indian, Indian, Indian, Indian, Hindu. … That's it.'

'That's boring, man. Where in India?'

'I dunno, I was born in Neasden, innit.'

'In't you been to India?'

'We might go next year.'

'Thank you Miresh. Well done. We'll ask you the same question when you get back. I take it your family tree isn't boring then Altaaf.'

'No Miss. My mum and dad met in Nairobi, which means cold place in Masai, in Kenya. My grandparents on my mum's side were from Pakistan and on my dad's side they were from Hydrabad in India. My mum says her ancestors came to India from Persia. They were all Moslems but our family are not big on religion. We're sexular.'

'That's secular... with a c.'

'Sorry Miss... secular. That means I don't have to learn the Koran off by heart.'

'Thank you Altaaf. That was interesting. Does anyone have any questions?'

'You Jammy Dodger,' Mohammed piped up. 'I get to do Koran for 2 hours every day and Saturday and Sunday too.'

'Why did your grandparents go to Kenya?'

'One grandad was building the railway and the other one was a shopkeeper.'

'Me now, Miss.'

'We'll have a girl first, Mohammed, then you. Yes... Tracy.'

'I'm, you know, all London, you know, except one granny.'

'Where's she from?'

'She's from, like, um Essex.'

'Oh, that's not too far away.'

'No, Miss... .'

'Can you tell us more about your family?'

'My other granny is in retail.'

'Oh yes. Where?'

'Woolworths in Finchley... . I can't think what else, Miss.'

'That's fine. Good. Now, Mohammed.

'I used to be a refugee but not now. Should I tell that Miss?'

'If you want to, that's fine – but if anyone in the class doesn't want to share things about their family, that's fine too.'

'Anyway, I was born in Somalia and so was my mum and all her family. My dad speaks Arabic because he's from the Yemen and his mother was born in Ethiopia – so you see guys get around in Africa too, you know.'

'And how long have you been in London?'

'Ages Miss. That's why my English is well good.'

'Very. I mean it's very good.'

'Thanks Miss – very well good.'

'He's well funny in'ee Miss?'

'Very funny… if you say so. All right Karl, before your arm drops off,'

'I never met my grandad because he was a black American G I over here in the war and then they all had to go back and my great grandparents, the English ones, kicked my granny out because the baby, my dad, was gonna be a bit black, like. That was so wrong, right?'

'So wrong.'

'Then my dad married my mum. She's Irish and white and my dad's Catholic so it's all good, right?'

'Right.'

'And now me and my brother are a bit black and my cousins aren't but nobody minds.'

'Can I ask a question, Miss? Karl, how come your cousins are white?'

'Cos my granny married my new grandad and he ain't black… And they had two more kids, my auntie and uncle and their kids are my cousins. Get it?'

'Yea… I think so.'

'Well done Karl. Thank you for sharing that with us.'

'There's more Miss… but maybe that's enough.'

'Rosa. What about you?'

'It's long, Miss but I'll try. I had to ask my Brazil granny; she's here on her holidays. She's Brazilian... surprise... and my grandad who died was from Angola in Africa and he spoke Portuguese too. Did you know I speak Portuguese?'

'No, but that's interesting.'

'Then my mum, she's like really, I mean really really pretty; her dad was French and her mum was kind of Indian like Mauritian. That's my maternal grandparents... yea, that's right.'

'Yes.'

'And me and my sister and little brother were all born here so we're British and my mum says we're lucky because we're trilingual. We speak, English, French and Portuguese.'

'How come you landed in London?' Chi Wai asked.

'My dad got a job here so my mum came too and then we got born.'

'Thank you Rosa. Now, I think you have an interesting background too Chi Wai. The surname Takahashi tells me that.'

'That's right, Miss. My mum's Chinese and she gave me my first name and my dad's Japanese. I think the combination is pretty unusual these days but my father says it's always good to widen the gene pool.'

'Have you met your grandparents?' Karl asked.

'A little bit. They're cool but they're far away and we don't see them often.'

'I wish I'd met my G I Joe grandad.'

Miss, me now....

And so it went on. Suzy was given the task of listing all the countries mentioned in the family trees and the list kept growing: India, Syria, Nigeria, Italy, Ireland, England, Scotland, Pakistan, Persia, Somalia, The Yemen, Ethiopia, USA, Jamaica, Trinidad, Afghanistan, China, Japan, Brazil, Angola, France, Mauritius, Malaysia, Indonesia, Lebanon, Uganda and Zambia.

'Miss we forgot Malawi,'

'Oh yes.'

247

'And Essex.'

'I think England covers that. Right your next task is to put all these countries in alphabetical order and after that you can stick a pin on the big world map for each one.'

'But Miss, what about you?'

Ella McKay Fonseca had been waiting for that so she was vaguely prepared.

'Well for the past few generations both sides of my family were farmers way in the far north of Scotland and they were all born within a few miles of each other. I often wonder if far back there might have been Vikings or Normans in the family. I'm going to try to find out when I retire. My name was Mackay before I got married and my ancestors might have come from Ireland. Some of the extended family went to Canada, America, New Zealand or Australia and now have big families there. Four of my dad's uncles married in New Zealand and had lots of sons so if you meet a Mackay in New Zealand, it might be my relative. I think one great great uncle married a Cherokee princess in USA so the story goes. One auntie went to India and another to Africa but they came back again.'

'Miss you're well weird. How come you know all this?

'My granny used to talk about it.'

'What about your mum and dad, Miss?'

'Well, my dad married my mum who was from a farm 2 miles along the road, the girl next door I suppose, and my brother is still on the farm where we were born. My sister married a Yorkshire man but they live in Scotland now.

I'm the one who has widened the gene pool as you say, Chi Wai. When I went to Kenya, I met another teacher whose parents came over from Goa, which was once Portuguese India, and Catholic, Karl. He looks Indian but might be a bit Portuguese, as you say. We went to teach in Zambia where we got married. That's why I can greet Chilufya with "Mwapoleni Mukwai" every day. We have a daughter and she has an English boyfriend who has a Welsh grandma.'

'We can add USA and Canada now to the list, Miss, and Australia and New Zealand.'

'Yes.'

What about Yorkshire?'

'No, that's a *county* in the *country* of England,' Most Able Pupil Jonathan pointed out.'

'Miss, he swore.'

'No he didn't. You misunderstood. He wouldn't anyway.'

'Bet he would.'

'We haven't got Wales.'

'Neither has my daughter yet so let's leave it out for now. Anyway, there's enough to write a book on Form D here.'

'Are you gonna write a book about us?'

'Will we be in it?'

'Do you know what? I just might one day and yes, you will be in it, well bits of you and you'll have different names.'

'Wicked.'

As the pupils filed out of the classroom Ella overheard, 'I bet she'll never write that book.'

The Gin and Tonics

Francesca in Year 7 looked great in her red wig. She was going to play Isabella Mackay, aged 8 and 12, Ella Mackay aged 22 and Ella Fonseca in her 50s. Quite a task but she was one of the Gin and Tonics who had been making officially retired Ella Fonseca feel better on a Friday afternoon.

The G and T s are the Gifted and Talenteds of Year 7 at Brentgold Comprehensive. Ella doesn't really approve of too much fuss being made of extra clever youngsters. Her own daughter Molly had been a MAP (a Most Able Pupil) and hated it with an embarrassed passion. The MAPs had been renamed G and T s over the years but there was still that mixture of pride and mortification plus the threat of being bullied attached to the idea.

In this case, Ella was loving the group, which met in the music room at the far corner of the school after the other pupils had all gone home. She was often surprised that they were willing to stay behind. They had read her book (yes, that book the Rainbow Form thought would never be written) or at least they'd read the bits which were interesting for 12 year olds and missed out the chapters which were more for adults.

Now they were about to go on stage with 'Fusion' a play adapted from the novel, a musical interpretation of Ella's school experiences in Scotland, Kenya and Brentgold Comprehensive. The G and T s helped to write the play and were certainly the inspiration behind it,

Ella, however, wanted to include anyone in Year 7 who wanted a part. The cast needed one red head but there wasn't a single red head in the 210 pupils. It also needed a variety of rural Scots-looking kids, Kenyan African-looking village kids, actors to play Rosa Parks, Martin Luther King and Barack Obama and kids to represent Brentgold Comprehensive in all its glorious diversity. There was no real problem there. Some of the Scots bairns were Polish, Albanian or similar, Rosa Parks was Nigerian as was Martin Luther King and

Barack Obama was Somali; the Kenyan African youngsters were a mixture of Caribbean and African and just about all of the world's ethnic groups and their combinations were represented in the musical finale representing Brentgold International Evening.

The small reading project had grown and grown. Carl Murray, the Year head, had 'covered' Ella's session one Friday, as if he didn't have more than enough to do and Martin Harvey, whose music room had been hijacked, had been witnessing the enthusiasm of the G and T s and been drawn into some of the musical and technological aspects of the performance which an elderly Ella was clearly not 100% comfortable with.

The tickets for *'Fusion' a musical celebration of happy cultural integration* had been sold. Tonight was the night and the opening backdrop was of projected images of Scottish landscapes flickering to the haunting strains of Steve McDonald's *Sons of Somerled* which faded to leave a mountain scene behind a school playground. This was all mysteriously happening as buttons were pressed on an incredibly small hand device.

"A big boy is bullying a little girl and Isabella MacKay, played by Francesca, comes to her rescue before Mr Cameron, the Head and only teacher (the Dominie) calls them into school.

Francesca in her magnificent long red, curly wig is asking Alfie, a small boy playing Mr Cameron in a gown, mortar board and eye patch, a DIFFICULT question.

'Why am I the only one in my family with red hair and why is everyone here different?'

'That's a hard question to answer Isabella.'

'But can you try? Please, Mr Cameron…'

You tube scenes of an ancient battle are projected accompanied by the pulsating tones of *Per Mare per Terras – Sons of Somerled,*

When the volume drops and Alfie launches into his confident explanation of Viking migration - and the audience seem spellbound, Ella relaxes.

From her viewpoint in the wings it seems as if all is going to run smoothly. For a little while it does. She soon finds the inspiration for the following short story:

Where's Boom Boom Pow?

'Where's Boom Boom Pow?'
'Mr Ogden took them to the dining hall out of the way, Miss.'
'Why?'
'They had a fight... argument.'
There's no time to ask why; they're the street dance group who've missed their vital cue. The 12 year old female lead's soulful solo about the end of racial apartheid (the nuances of which may have escaped her co-stars) ends with, 'It must have been the darkness of the shadow of a dream ...' and it appears she might be right.
'Curtains!'
(This gives us time to think.) Mr Murray, Head of Year, though exhausted after a zoo trip, has had his steely grip on script and actors but has been forced to desert his post to deal with the fracas. It turns out it had something to do with a slipped waistline on hipster jeans and vertical challenge.
'Right we'll have 'Hakuna Matata' on 'You Tube'. That'll keep them busy.
'The Ghosts of Culloden' are erroneously wailing out instead of the jolly 'Jambo Sana' with scenic images of Kenya. It's definitely not 'Hakuna Matata' (Swahili for no worries). I resist the temptation to use a 'word' as I consider my young audience.
'Right we'll have the African sharing song. Where are they?'
'They don't know the code for the staff toilet and they put their costume changes in there!
Another word springs to mind but stays firmly unuttered but we finally set up scene though all notes and lyrics have vanished into thin air in the excitement – along with more than half of the scene's performers. I blow hard on a whistle and clap loudly offstage. (The drummer isn't around. Was he in Boom Boom Pow too?). Even the

reliable stars have muffed their words – and when they finally remember them their mouths are full of large soor plooms (cued for the end of the scene.). This makes it difficult to speak far less project!

Curtains again (thank goodness) and we have the clarity and gravitas of Rosa Parks, Martin Luther King and Barack Obama to see us through the next few minutes. Oh yes, it's fine; they even remember to jiggle on the bus - though Obama is clearly overcome by the shock of being in front of an audience.

The all singing, dancing and technology performance is now back on track and there's a timely google image of Rosa Parks on a bus. Thank you Mr Harvey, who's ensconced in front of a keyboard (but no monitor) rubber-necking around curtains (which keep opening and closing like a fiddler's elbow) at a hugely enlarged and skewed image on a screen which has had to be pushed back as far as possible to allow dancing on stage. Once again, in my rose-tinted imagination, a screen had lowered smoothly from a recess above the stage to become suspended conveniently above the stage. Hmm.

'Boom Boom Pow are ready, Miss!'

'Turn around where possible!' my internal sat nav screams. 'Reconfigure!'

Mr Murray has returned to his post. Right, I can go and open that toilet but there's no time to go and get a female teacher to stand guard. If I was still a teacher here, I'd know these new things about Hendon School, and build in a plan B, but I'm supposed to be retired.

Boom Boom Pow have performed – spectacularly I believe - despite a lollipop (oh horrors!) in one mouth. I didn't see their entrance (or I would have retrieved the offending lolly) or the leaping performance. Another Prima Donna had a costume problem. How many changes do they NEED?

'Miss, I have to go now; it's my brother's birthday.'

I wonder why he's telling me this now but I end up hissing, 'Go then!'

The superhuman Mr Harvey has leapt for the grand piano and is pumping out accompaniment for 'The Greatest Love of All' as Ruchi a

253

pretty little girl and a driving force behind the project, fulfils her dream on stage – singing solo for the first verse – after which cast and audience it is hoped will join in with enthusiasm. They do.

The conscientious stage management team get into the swing of things. The next scene is set in seconds and a correctly sized, unskewed image of Brentgold School is projected. How did Superharvey manage that?

Only a few more mistakes to go and all can be left behind in a gleeful Cha Cha Slide and we can call it a day! No such luck.

'But there's still another scene.'

Darn it, they've remembered – so curtains are closed again, a new scene set and the action continues. I'm glad because there are some significant serious messages to get across. By this stage I'm wondering if anyone has noticed - or if anyone in the audience has <u>not</u> lost the will to live.

Next time (if there is another performance) we end with Cha Cha slide. Definitely.

Meantime, the audience are experiencing a 'best' moment as a smiling cherub in stage management has read his script and has peeped through the curtains and directed an order in Superharv's direction.

'I want to teach the world to sing', he whispers very audibly – but with one thing or the other, like a full timetable, a trip to the zoo and an unexpected date change, Mr Harvey hasn't had time to perfect that song. Not to worry, the small, captive audience have been charmed. In the confusion, to which was added an unexpected three hour clear up of the behind-stage debris from 'Guys and Dolls' which unearthed four months out of date coursework and a schoolbag packed with books, I've forgotten this hasn't been rehearsed so ...

We limp through a re run of 'The Greatest Love' and then there's a thank you to the director (yours truly) which I should have predicted but didn't; I manage to mumble a few words of thanks and generate a cheer of appreciation. I see it's a bottle of red wine. Perhaps they reckon I'll need it.

Ella later entered this little story in a 1000 word competition and won a bent bottle of 'iffy' red wine as second prize. What was it about red wine?

More importantly, Ella had got her way about giving all the Year sevens regardless of creed, colour or ability a chance to take part in her little play whose message was, 'We're all different, all equal, all special and whatever we are we need each other'. How could it have been otherwise?

The story of Ella the Not Quite English Teacher could have ended there. She had risen to the challenge of proving her inspirational Rainbow Form D wrong by going to writing school and typing non-stop over three months until her story had tumbled out – and with the help of the little play, she hoped the message had got across.

But Ella still teaches New to English adults one evening a week and spends most of her time writing. She doesn't call herself a Not Quite Writer although she suspects some people might. Novels one and two have been published and when novel three 'The Not Quite English Teacher' goes to print, she'll finally have told the tale of running away from tiny, cosy, rural, monocultural Balnahuig village into the melee of the multicultural world.

Meantime Rick and Ella are in their own cosy corner of the world.

Rick needs only good weather and a golf course.

Molly and Mike, now married, are showing clear signs of wanting to escape to the country to bring up the brood they are planning. This would have to be this side of the broadband divide; after all, they say, we are in a global village these days.

Ella remembers all the other pupils she hasn't yet written about and all the trips that haven't been reported on, like the day trip to Bakhtivedanta, George Harrison's gift to the Hare Krishna movement, where the monks fed 120 Year 7s and the Year 7s donated their pocket money in thanks, or the return visit from the three Kathmandu schools where they got the fountains at Somerset House specially switched on in out of season April for the visitors from the Himalayas.

She also gets a kick out of all these successful ex Brentgold pupils who keep cropping up in films, TV programmes and pop bands.

'I'm sure I know that guy, Rick,' she yells at Casualty on the TV screen.

'Never.'

But she's right. She remembers where she has seen him. His picture is on that mug 10D gave her. 'It's Ollie. Look.'

'Oh yea, so it is,' Rick says, smiling incredulously as he peers at the mug, almost as excited as his wife.

'And there's Antony … and Michael … and Amber… and Harry! I wonder how many more Brentgoldians are going to be famous. I can't wait for the Gin and Tonics to grow up.'

She remembers telling everyone that D, her Rainbow Form, was the best form in the school except the world didn't know that. Now it knows.

At times her mind reaches back across the millennia beyond the mythical Tower of Babel to when the "whole earth was of one language" before God questioned proud Nimrod's tower, the stairway to Heaven, and "scattered the people upon the face of the earth and confused their languages."

Then her mind stretches forward towards an evolution that transcends those differences in language; in the 21st century it seems as if some form of English, be it Globish or Not Quite English might be a powerful aid to achieving that harmony. Ella thinks of all those students of English from all those countries and all the different kinds of NQE that they use with each other and wonders if English belongs to England any more, or if it ever has.

But most of all, Ella hopes that any grandchildren that she and Rick are lucky enough to have won't be living too far away – and wonders if there might be a new little redhead. You never can tell what the genes are going to do.

***

Glossary

Chapter 1

Noo, fit wye nae?	Now, why not?
Fa says	Who says?
Thrawn-ness	Stubbornness

Chapter 2

They're all Jock Tampson's bairns so all equal	They are all God's children

Chapter 3

Cornkisters	songs sung by farm workers as they sat on chests (kists) of corn
Skalk (n)	a tot of whisky drunk at breakfast time
Fa thraoo	fall through, slip up and stop using a 'posh' accent
Stammy gaster (v)	flabbergast
Clamjamfry (v)	plaster with mud
Clishmaclaver (n)	noisy chat
Feuch!	Ugh
Yokit (adj.)	yoked, stuck into a job
Baffies	bedroom slippers

Chapter 4

Ah'm nae deein	I'm not doing
Moo	mouth
Siller	money (silver) as wages
Coory doon	cuddle down
Puddock	frog
Ye ken	you know

Chapter 8

Insegnante di inglese	Italian for English Teacher
Sinistra	left wing
Con mio zio	with my uncle
Shampanskoe sotsialisticheskogo	champagne socialist – a rich person who claims to be on the side of the poor

Limousine liberal/ gauche caviar   as above

Acknowledgements

I am very grateful to the following fellow writers for their advice and encouragement:

All who tutored or encouraged me at *Swanwick Writers' Summer School Greenacre Writers Finish That Novel* group: Lindsay Bamfield, Helen Barbour, Gema Belamonte, Rosie Canning, Bettina von Cossel, Christine Freeman, Lianne Kolirin and Raj Persaud and *Greenacre writer* Linda Louisa Dell

Watford Writers Audrey McCracken, John Ward, Susan Bennett, Helen Nicell, Rob Summers, Brian Bold, Sue Petit, Jackie Green, Mary Crowner, Margaret Vaughn, Phil Cooper, Trevor Spinage, Peter Young, Rae Argent, Liz Simpson, Steph King, Rosemary Morris, Angela Hunter, Chris Glover, Vicky Parr, Norma Luetchford, Stephens Clifford and Cadwell, Boo (Sioux) Bradshaw, Natasha Kavanagh, Mari Anne, and too many others to remember (apologies). I'm sure some will be famous soon.

My sister Margaret Woodward and *The Elgin Writers*

Bertha, Mary, Susan and Julia from the Kenton group

My thoughts are with Ron whose wife Lynn Philips (of Watford detective stories' fame) passed away in 2011.

Thanks also to my husband Gerry for his patience.

But the most important people to acknowledge are the colleagues and students over forty years of teaching in Kenya, Zambia and London. It would take many books to record all the memories. There are too many colleagues at Hendon School to thank here but you know who you are. The inspiration which finally kick started the project that ended up with *Fusion, The Cosmopolites* and now *The Not Quite English Teacher* was The Rainbow Form 10 D's farewell to me (thanks Martina) when I retired from teaching at Hendon in July 2006 with too much time on my hands. Later on inspiration came from the little Year 7 G and T s, Gifted and Talenteds (or Gin and Tonics as I called them) because they made me feel better.

References

'Jack and the Queen's Talk' a 'write pantomime' by Dennis E Bryant (support by Lynn Truss)

'Globish the World Over' by Jean Paul Nerriere

Globish – a simplified language constructed by Maduhar Gogate

'Globish How the English Language Became the World's Language' by Robert McCrum

The Itchy Coo Initiative: books for children in the Scots Language

The Rampant Scotland website

'A Scots Quair' a trilogy by Lewis Grassic Gibbon

…'Glaswegian Punjabi speakers with pink turbans'… might refer to Hardeep Singh Kohli, writer and radio and television presenter.

Balnahuig - Urquhart Primary School (now two bungalows)

Altnabervie – Milne's High School, Fochabers

Kipsigis Girls' School, Kenya

Tarantella a poem by Hilaire Belloc

Boots a poem by Rudyard Kipling

Lwitikila Girls' School, Zambia

The Black Hermit, a play by James Ngugi

Mpika Boys' School, Zambia

Kongi's Harvest, a play by Wole Soyinka

The Government Inspector, a play by Nikolai Gogol

The London Co-op School of English

LTC College of English and Secretarial Studies

Hendon School

Euro Disney

Le Journal de Zlata / Zlata's Diary by Zlata Filipovic

J K Rowling's *Harry Potter* Books

The Newspaper Education Trust (NET) Westferry, Docklands

Hendon, Whitefields and King Alfred's Schools, London

St Xavier's, Neptune and Shuvatara Schools, Kathmandu

From Goddess to Mortal by Rashmila Shakya, a former Kathmandu Kumari, as told to Scott Berry

Sons of Somerled music by Steve McDonald
Boom Boom Pow song by the Black Eyed Peas
The Greatest Love of All by Whitney Houston
Cha Cha Slide D J Casper

About the Author

Eliza Jane Goés (Grant) was born in Lower Speyside in Morayshire, Scotland where she grew up on a farm called Viewfield. She was educated at Urquhart Primary School, Milne's High School Fochabers, Aberdeen University and Aberdeen (Teaching) College of Education.

After teaching in Kenya and Zambia, she and her husband came to work in London. Since retiring after forty years of teaching, sixteen of those at Hendon School, she has been involved with many aspects of writing through various writing groups. She lives with her husband in North West London and their daughter and her husband live in Guildford.

The Not Quite English Teacher is her third novel and follows on from *Fusion* and *The Cosmopolites*. She also writes short stories, non-fiction including travel articles and poetry.

See **www.elizajanegoesahead.com** for more information.

Lightning Source UK Ltd.
Milton Keynes UK
UKOW042308160412

190820UK00001B/2/P